*Religious Drama 3*

# RELIGIOUS DRAMA 3

THE LAST WORD

THE HOUSE BY THE STABLE

GRAB AND GRACE

SANTA CLAUS

LET MAN LIVE

IT SHOULD HAPPEN TO A DOG

BILLY BUDD

THE GOSPEL WITCH

*Selected and Introduced*
*by* MARVIN HALVERSON

GLOUCESTER, MASS.

PETER SMITH

1972

All rights to these plays, including performance rig[ht]
protected by their individual copyright. On the tit[le]
of each play, it is indicated from whom permissio[n]
been and ought to be secured. Producers, amateur and pro
fessional, are expressly warned that performance rights
cover not only production but readings; that it is not per-
missible to mimeograph, and, in mimeograph form, to dis-
tribute any of this material; that permission is required to
perform even part of any of these plays; and that owners
of copyright, not producers, must decide when a "class-
room" or "studio" performance or reading is actually private. Lacking any better address, applicants for permission
may address copyright holders or their agents c/o Meridian
Books, 119 West 57 Street, New York 19, N. Y.

Reprinted, 1972, by Permisssion of
WORLD PUBLISHING
(Times Mirror)


ISBN: 0-8446-4012-3


AN ORIGINAL LIVING AGE BOOK (MERIDIAN)

Published by The World Publishing Company
2231 West 110th Street, Cleveland, Ohio 44102
First printing, October, 1959
Seventh printing, May, 1969
Library of Congress Catalog Card Number: 57-8864
Printed in the United States of America      7WP569

# Introduction by MARVIN HALVERSON

One of the significant developments in recent years has been the return of religion to the theater and the return of drama to the churches. While some have been astonished by the emergence of obviously religious themes in commercial theater and the sponsorship of good drama by the churches, the rapprochement is both understandable and perhaps inevitable. For drama is not only rooted in the mimetic impulses of man but derives fundamentally from man's religious apprehension of life as well. This is true whether it be a tragedy of the Greeks or of Shakespeare. It is equally true of that comedy which enables man to see himself in perspective, thus becoming a prelude to faith.

Historically and essentially the relationship between drama and religion is a close one. Among the Greeks, for instance, drama was an integral part of religious celebration for the entire community. Furthermore, it is commonly recognized that drama in the Christian era arose in association with the liturgy. While worship and drama were never equated in the Middle Ages, the Christian church through its worship—perhaps unconsciously more often than not—nourished drama because the Christian message with a beginning, a middle, and an end presents to the world the divine drama of redemption. Drama cannot be equated with corporate Christian worship and the worship of the Christian community cannot be regarded as drama. *But the bond is close.*

Even before the medieval miracle and mystery plays took form, corporate worship involved the community of the faithful, and the ceremonial participation of the peo-

ple in the liturgy partook of the dramatic. We have lost
this sense, for the most part, but there are occasional re-
minders of what once took place. For example, one of my
earliest recollections from a Minnesota childhood is that
of a Norwegian Lutheran congregation at worship in which
the celebrational and the mimetic first introduced me to
some of the elements of drama. The congregation wor-
shipped in an unpretentious frame building whose interior
was dominated by a pulpit at one side and an altar in a
small apse. Behind and above the altar was a poor copy,
by an itinerant artist, of a religious painting, surrounded
by baroque billowings of decoration in white and gold. I
remember the pastor standing in the pulpit, wearing a
black gown with a magnificent white ruff. (Thus a Rem-
brandt portrait of an old man brings me back to Minnesota
more than it takes me to Amsterdam.) And on Communion
Sundays the pastor stood before the altar as the male
members of the congregation, boys as well as grown men,
walked in solemn procession to the altar while a hymn
was sung, there to leave the offering with which the bread
and wine for the Lord's Supper were to be bought. Only
years later did I learn that this act which captured my
childhood imagination was a vestigial form of the offertory
procession in the early Christian church. While this act
was lost during the long centuries of decay in Christian
worship, it continued nonetheless in some of the obscure
corners of Europe. The practice was never completely lost
in Scotland where the "little entry" of the Bible at the beginning of worship and the "great entry" of the bread and
the wine at the Lord's Supper render Scottish Protes-
tantism remarkably close to the ancient and continuous
practices of Eastern Orthodoxy. It was this kind of celebrational life in the church which nourished the mystery and
mystery plays during the Middle Ages. And the liturgical
movement in our own day, whether it be in Roman Catholic or Protestant Christianity, seeks a renewal of worship

in which the people are enabled to act, as it were, before the world and before God. As this occurs I believe an even more rapid return of drama to the church will be fostered and drama will then be seen not as didactic but as ceremonial and celebrational.

Kierkegaard, in his *Purity of Heart,* deals with the relationship between the act of worship and the art of the theater in a way that illumines both drama and worship. To his way of thinking there are three roles in the theater: the prompter, the actor, and the audience. The prompter, Kierkegaard says, remains hidden as he whispers the lines for the actor; the actor appropriates the lines and becomes the embodiment of the role he is playing as he strides on the stage before the audience; the audience of theater-goers observes the actor and assesses the wholeness of being he manifests and the singleness with which he embodies the role. The temptation in religion, says Kierkegaard, is to transpose this pattern into the worship of the church. When this is done we conceive of God as the prompter, the minister as the actor, and the congregation as the audience. To so interpret worship is to misunderstand it altogether. For, says Kierkegaard, the minister is the prompter; each member of the congregation is the actor; and God is the one who fills the role of the audience, watching the way in which each one acts out his role on the stage which is eternity. Here one finds the fusion of the objective and the subjective. And while Kierkegaard's interpretation does not encompass all the dimensions of drama and worship, it nevertheless enables a rewarding perspective on both.

It is widely held that our drama is rooted in the drama of the Middle Ages, deriving on the one hand from the mystery or miracle plays, which arose in connection with the liturgy, and on the other hand, from the morality plays, which constituted a later medieval development. Of the two forms it is undoubtedly the morality play that has exercised the greater influence on Western theater. Certainly it is the morality play form to which most of the plays in this anthology are related. Yet they are modern plays, products of the twentieth century, and therefore representative of the contemporary mood and the idiom of theater today.

The medieval morality play as well as the mystery or miracle play arose out of a vastly different mode of thinking and realm of experience. They took form out of a community of faith possessing a common language of symbols. This was true of all forms of medieval drama. The miracle and mystery plays generally dealt with familiar lives of saints and with the Biblical story from creation to judgment. They were community festivals which retold the story of God's work among men and recounted the Biblical events year after year. In addition to their ritual character they were remarkable teaching devices, particularly because they were not intended primarily as such.

The morality play, in contrast, was a late medieval form of drama purposely aimed at instruction and moral teaching based upon dogma. It represented a new development that is considered by some historians of drama as a bridge to modern secular theater. However accurate this evaluation may be, the connection at first appears remote. For the characters in a medieval morality play are not fully developed in the manner that modern theater dictates. Neither were the characters Biblical figures or saints of Christian history as in the mystery and miracle plays. Instead they were abstractions such as Virtue, Vice, and Good Deeds. Nonetheless, through its theme and by its nature the morality tended to evoke the lonely debate of existential decision.

A comparison of *Everyman,* the best known of the medieval morality plays, with the two works by Charles Williams in this volume, for example, discloses the continuing influence of the medieval morality play, but also reveals the vast differences in the cultural ethos that informs them and the religious assumptions that undergird them. Charles Williams, for instance, has taken the form of the medieval morality play, baptized it in Reformation Christianity and brought it up to date. In contrast to the somewhat static nature of *Everyman*, for instance, *The House by the Stable* and *Grab and Grace* are lively plays indeed, for they take into account the vast changes in drama between the Middle Ages on the one hand and the theater of the twentieth century on the other hand. They are contemporary in feeling while ancient in form.

The medieval morality was concerned with instruction, with examination of conscience, and with moral influence. Much of the theater on Broadway which is reputed to be religious bears close resemblance to the medieval morality. Fundamentally both expressions deal with life on a horizontal level. Their assumptions are the morality of calculation. Honesty is the best policy. Vice is a trap. Sin, which is equated with sins, gets one nowhere. The path of easy virtue is a slippery road that leads downward. And most of the plays written for our churches and our Sunday schools represent but an extreme form of this understanding of life.

Certainly this is true as well of *Everyman*. The widespread assumption that it is the exemplary religious drama suggests that even more than its art is the persuasiveness of its religious assumptions. Its appeal is found, I believe, primarily in its religious message rather than its art—in its implication that man is the master of his fate. This is the premise of *Everyman* even though the characters are abstractions who are not involved in real-life situations. But the struggle within the soul of Everyman is in terms that all can experience. In this approach to morality God calls upon Death to approach Everyman:

> Go thou to Everyman
> And shew him, in my name,

> A pilgrimage he must take,
> Which in no wise may escape;
> And that he bring with him a sure reckoning
> Without delay or any tarrying.

Death responds:

> Lord, I will in the world go run over all,
> And cruelly outsearch both great and small.
> Every man will I beset that liveth beastly
> Out of God's laws and dreadeth not folly.
> He that loveth riches I will strike with my dart,
> His sight to blind, and from Heaven to depart—
> Except that alms be his good friend—
> In Hell for to dwell, world without end.

Death then moves to the stage of the world, and seeing Everyman with a company of men and women breaking into a dance, calls to him:

> Everyman stand still! Whither art thou going
> Thus gaily? Hast thou thy Maker forgot?

Everyman asks:

> What desireth God of me?

And Death replies:

> That shall I shew thee.
> A reckoning he will needs have
> Without any longer respite.

During the long pilgrimage that Everyman then begins, all those on whom he counted for help in reaching heaven fail him: Fellowship, Kindred, Goods, and all worldly things forsake him; only Good Deeds consents to follow over the passage of the grave. And the play concludes with the moral stated by the Doctor of the Church:

> This moral men may have in mind.
> Ye hearers, take it of worth, old and young,
> And forsake pride, for he deceiveth you in the end;

> And remember *Beauty, Five Wits, Strength* and *Discretion.*
> They all at last do *Everyman* forsake,
> Save his *Good Deeds* there doth he take.
> But beware and they shall be small,
> Before God he hath no help at all . . .
> And he that hath his account whole and sound,
> High in Heaven shall he be crowned.

The medieval morality play is based on the belief that man justifies himself before God by his good deeds. Man proves himself worthy of God's acceptance by the multitude of his good works. Thus *Everyman* sets forth the medieval notion that man, assisted by the various instrumentalities of the church, saves himself. It is a perennially appealing religious approach that has had great attraction to recent autonomous man. However, the experience of twentieth-century man does not substantiate such a view, for he has found the sign NO EXIT posted at the dead-end road of autonomy.

Thus the difference between the modern plays included in this volume and the medieval morality is not explained merely by the changes of fashion and the passage of time. These plays symbolize not only the changes in drama during the intervening centuries but they also embody a contemporary way of understanding life and a different comprehension of Christianity. Therefore one might properly assert that there are two types of moralities: a morality of works and a morality of grace. The one is medieval and Catholic. The other is contemporary and Protestant.

Some of the plays in this volume reflect a morality of grace and others are contemporary in their awareness of the absence of grace which points to the need of, the hope for, and the possibility of grace. Ours is a world that does not readily experience the reality of resurrection. The modern consciousness is one of estrangement and alienation, of guilt and judgment. Yet insofar as the dramatic

literature of our time poses questions of ultimate significance and remains open to the *possibility* of an answer,
it is not only expressive of our time but constitutes drama
of religious power. Thus several works in this collection
deal with man's loss of meaning and his search for self-
identity. Others deal with the problem of the individual
confronted by the justice of society, which is reminiscent
of the best justice in terms of which Jesus was judged.
And other plays deal with the issues of man's life in terms
of a morality grounded in grace.

This is especially true of *The House by the Stable* and
*Grab and Grace*. They are dramatic vehicles of the Biblical and Reformation understanding that man is saved by
grace; what man cannot do for himself God has already
done for him. Charles Williams wrote these plays out of
the knowledge that we live in a redeemed world. We have
but to recognize and accept what by God's action we already are, and we shall be what we are in the loving
favor and power of God. To live in terms of this understanding of life will not rob drama of its fundamental
basis: the continuing struggle between good and evil and
the determination of each; the battle for self-realization;
the fatal flaw in man, for the Greek tragedian and the
dramatist of the Christian era as well—man's *hubris*—his
pride. Drama is only heightened and deepened as we
perceive that man is a *homo viator*, as Luther described
him, and the human pilgrimage with its conflicts, its de-
feats and its joys, participates in the cosmic struggle of
God and his purpose of love for his creation against the
powers of evil in the world. But it bears within it the
promise of triumph because the ultimate victory has already been won in the Christ.

The reformation of the church recovered the Biblical
message that whatever goodness or righteousness man possesses is a gift. It made possible, in fact it made inevitable,
a morality of grace. In this religious understanding of life

the command "Be ye holy even as I am holy" is not abrogated. The moral demand is not obliterated but the demand is now seen in the light of God's action. As Truman Douglass has put it, "a Christian is not a good man but a forgiven man."

"To lead the Christian life is always difficult," says Pride to Man in *Grab and Grace*. "How we have to work. . . . Do you pray much?" When Man responds, "a good deal," Gabriel shakes his head and Man asks, "Gabriel, what do you mean?" "Sir," says Gabriel, "only that you have been constantly helped. This boy Grace does most of the work."

And to have conceived Grace as a boy, nimble and unpredictable as an elf, must have been a gift of grace to Charles Williams. For such a grace cannot be confined to the reach of man's own efforts or to the instrumentalities and channels of any church. Grace is at work in the world in places that are not ecclesiastical and ways that do not appear religious. Thus one can find grace at work in each of the plays in this collection although many of them are not couched in traditional religious language. They do not attempt to give answers or proclaim a universal ideal. Rather they assume that man's relationship to God is one of direct confrontation and that the action of drama is continued in the lonely debate of the human soul. A religious renewal in our world associated with a rebirth of the liturgy may prepare the way for new forms of religious drama which are celebrational and proclamatory. But until such a time the drama appropriate to our religious situation is that which is symbolized and represented in this collection.

# Contents

# THE LAST WORD

*Or, What to Say About It*

## JAMES BROUGHTON

# Editor's Preface: THE LAST WORD

The judgment that provoked examination of life and conscience in the medieval morality was the Last Judgment. Although the likelihood of this event largely has vanished from the mind of modern man, the new threats of annihilation through the achievements of science have become a symbol of a divine judgment on man's pretension. *The Last Word* deals with the remaining minutes before extermination by bombs when a husband and wife confront the end of their existence and thus begin for the first time in their lives to confront each other as persons. Despite the seriousness of the theme this short play is filled with humor. It is not an arbitrary device on the part of James Broughton, the author, but rather suggests that for modern man the eschatological is grasped through the comic. The litanies in the play invoking the gods and heroes of our day reveal more sharply and poignantly than do sermons or theological essays how contemporary man has invested new symbols with religious meaning as the old symbols of Christianity have been emptied of their power.

James Broughton is a San Francisco poet whose work in experimental cinema has won prizes in festivals at Cannes and Venice. *The Last Word* was presented together with three other verse plays by James Broughton under the title *Burning Questions* in San Francisco in April 1958.

# CHARACTERS

MR. RUSTY AUGENBLICK
MRS. DUSTY AUGENBLICK

SCENE: *A bar. Evening.*

DUSTY: What are you thinking?
RUSTY: I'm going through old thoughts.
DUSTY: Why don't you say something?
RUSTY: I don't want to think about it.
DUSTY: This is the Last Chance Bar
　　at the end of No-Passing Zone.
　　We ought to think of something to say.
RUSTY: What can *you* think of?
DUSTY: They say the world will end tonight.
RUSTY: They say, they say! They're always saying.
DUSTY: Can't you think of anything to say?
　　In the beginning there was some sort of word.
RUSTY: I can think of nothing . . .
　　In fact, I am thinking of nothing.
DUSTY: Tonight, tonight! That's what they say!
RUSTY: The world ends some night for all of us.
　　How many nights already have we been through it?
DUSTY: They've gotten the Word.
　　Explosions begin in half an hour.
　　It's in the papers. It's in the cards.
　　The rapid transit has already ceased.
　　That's the latest Word.
RUSTY: What Word? Whose Word?
DUSTY: How should one look? What should one wear?
RUSTY: Is it the Last Word? Or the First Commandment?
　　Is it the Second Coming? Or the Third Degree?
DUSTY: I do hope it won't be messy.
RUSTY: I hope it's a damn good show.
DUET (song):
　　They say the world will end it all.

**21**

> They say the world will end us all
> > and leave us in the soup.
> It may be cold tomorrow
> but we'll have a fire tonight.
> We may be smoke tomorrow
> but we'll have a bang tonight.
> They say the world will end it all.
> They say the world will end us all
> > in one swell foop.

*Pause.*

DUSTY: I forgot to collect the laundry.
I forgot to put out the garbage.

RUSTY: Forced to vacate! Everything must go!
Out of respect for the memory of
the about to be deceased
this place of business is closed for inventory.

DUSTY: Elsie Wallingford was planning to get married again.

RUSTY: Joe Jumper just got a new job with the telephone company.

DUSTY: Aunt Clara was expecting us for Easter.

RUSTY: Why did I never take that trip to Siam?
(*Sings.*)
Temple bells bing! . . . Gongs go bong!
There she'll be waiting for me,
Under the sighing Siamese moon . . .
(*sighs*)

DUSTY: You cannot go away.

RUSTY: Very well, very well.

DUSTY: You cannot go away.

RUSTY: Goodbye.

*Pause.*

DUSTY: Why can't we think of anything to say?

RUSTY: Several stars in close proximity
appear to embrace a single system,
but wider stretch the spaces to shoot between.

Tolerance is only that narrow space
between the moving body and the outer wall.
DUSTY: What is the matter with everybody?
RUSTY: They have followed the blind leader
to the very end of the game.
What can we do now about our history,
both private and political?
DUSTY: It's all so terribly unfair.
Why do we have to have war—or peace?
RUSTY: Are there enough phoenixes handy at the airport
to accommodate all the weeping and the vexed?
DUSTY: O Hercules! O Mrs. Roosevelt! Save us!
RUSTY: Quick, General, quick! Will there be time?
DUSTY: Wait, Madame Butterfly! Wait!
RUSTY: Noah! Noah! Where is our home?
*Pause.*
DUSTY: Shall I go and start packing?
They say the world will end tonight.
RUSTY: You cannot go away.
DUSTY: Very well, very well.
RUSTY: You cannot go away.
DUSTY: Goodbye.
*Pause.*
Have we anything to declare?
RUSTY: I've a cloudy soul and a rainy brain,
a muddy heart, and no very eager vigor.
O the rage of being becalmed!
No more trepidations of tomorrow.
No more appeals to the unforgiving fathers.
What will you say with your last gasp?
DUSTY: I don't want to think about it.
Think of all that's been said, all that's been heard . . .
RUSTY: In one ear and out the other.
DUSTY: I remember . . . I remember everything.
RUSTY: I remember the professor told me:
Always remember who you are.

But now I can't remember who to remember.
DUSTY: You're Rusty Augenblick,
the man in the unpressed suit.
RUSTY: With a sour stomach and a balding head.
With a second-hand sports car, and a hospital plan.
DUSTY: I remember what the mirror said,
I remember the hat I wore.
RUSTY: You're Dusty Millstone,
the apple-cheeked girl on the airedale farm.
No. You're my Mrs. Augenblick—
who loves to display her charga-plate.
DUSTY: I remember the minister saying:
You're the handsomest couple I have ever wed.
RUSTY: I remember the doctor saying:
With a heart like yours you will live to be 80.
DUSTY: I remember the ashes on my father's cigar.
I remember my brother's very first shave.
RUSTY: I remember in the cathedral once—
I thought I saw the Holy Ghost
flapping up under the roof
like a trapped bird trying to get out.
DUSTY: I remember the fortuneteller's promise.
RUSTY: I remember the world I was going to win . . . .
DUSTY: O remember, remember . . .
RUSTY: Remember, O man, that thou art dust! . . .
DUSTY: What a terrible thing to say!
*Pause.*
RUSTY: Bing! Bong! There she'll be waiting for me,
Under the sighing Siamese moon . . .
DUSTY: O once my lover, my once darling hubby,
I never knew when it really ended.
You never said a word. It simply ended.
RUSTY: Did we ever say anything worth remembering?
DUSTY: Did I ever express what I really felt?
RUSTY: Did I ever say what I really thought?

DUSTY: What were all the things we never said to each other?

RUSTY: I don't want to think about it.

DUSTY (*recitative*):

No matter how many dresses I buy,
no matter how many diets I try,
no matter how often I change my hair,
no matter how often I say a prayer . . .
O once my lover, where did you fly?

RUSTY: Man, this colloid, this angleworm . . . !

DUSTY (*song*):

O aluminum love, my plastic dove,
come coo in the wood with me!
Come coo, coo coo coo,
come coo in an old-fashioned tree!

RUSTY: Cock-a-diddle-dow, too-what, too-who.

DUSTY (*sighs*):

There's a short circuit in the electric blanket.

RUSTY: There's a split in the joint account.

DUSTY: Think of Mrs. Winterberg. She had a full life.

RUSTY: Think of Mr. Innerburn. He died young.

DUSTY: I wanted four children and a hawthorn tree.

RUSTY: They say the world will end tonight.

DUSTY: Did we ever get together? Beget together?

And where have we got to now?

RUSTY (*song*):

The time has come to go with time.
Time to part, time to depart.
Time for being far apart.
   Good night, my dear, good night.
We've come to the end of our rope together.
End of the rope at the end of the road.
Time to be hung on the farewell tree.
   Good night, my dear, good night.

DUSTY: O Time Time, stay away!

Time Time, come to me!
Stop Stop! Hurry hurry up!
Please come back again.
RUSTY: We have reached the unfinished parallel track
where a deeper tunnel begins
and a bridge hasn't yet been built.
Good night, my Dusty, good night.
DUSTY: O aluminum love, my plastic dove,
come back to the wood with me!
RUSTY: Perhaps I could tell you (or try to)
how little, how much it has meant,
what I know (or think I know)
and describe what I am (or I think so).
And if I could go where I'd like to go,
start anew, and experiment,
what I would want to make and do
and what I would be (or try to).
DUSTY: Possibly the best is yet to be.
Cheer up, cheerio, cheri beri bim!
Three cheers for every possibility.
RUSTY: When the night numbers stick on their agèd rounds
and the morning never rises again,
how will we act at the last-minute ditch?
And what will we have to say?
Standing or falling, kneeling or running,
will you be tongue-tied at the final moment?
DUSTY: I'll be glad when the agony's over.
RUSTY: Would anybody like to make a speech?
Would somebody like to ask a question?
Will nobody say, It's all been peachy,
they'd like to live it all over again . . . ?
DUSTY: Sit down. There's no one here. We're all alone.
RUSTY: Why don't we make a wild commotion?
Scream bloody murder, wake the dead!
Even if we don't have a thing to say

we can go down screaming,
screaming down!

DUSTY: Shut up! Shut up! You give me the willywams.

RUSTY: Open your heart! Speak! Speak!

DUSTY: What? What shall I say?

RUSTY: Is there nothing? Nothing?

DUSTY: Hush . . . ! Listen . . . !

*Pause.*

RUSTY: 10, 9, 8, 7, 6, 5, 4, 3, 2, 1 . . .

*Distant explosion*

DUSTY: Bingo!

RUSTY: Bongo!

*Lights dim.*

DUSTY: It's cold in here.

RUSTY: United Nations, have mercy upon us!

DUSTY: Elizabeth Arden, deliver us!

RUSTY: General Motors, have mercy upon us!

DUSTY: Sigmund Freud, deliver us!

RUSTY: Batten Barton Durstine and Osborn, have mercy
upon us!

DUSTY: In the name of Mutual Life and Cold Storage.

RUSTY: Amen.

*Silence.*

DUSTY: There's no answer.

RUSTY: (*song*):
Papa's in the deep freeze
turned all blue.
Papa's in the deep freeze
good as new.
Kelvinator liquidator
Out goes You!

DUSTY: Can't you think of something better to say?

RUSTY: I miss my mother.

DUSTY: I loved my teddy bear!

RUSTY: I want to hang on to my Shriner's cap.

DUSTY: My silver spoon is only slightly bent
   and it's been in the family a very long time.
RUSTY: All of my life I've had sinus trouble.
DUSTY: I never could pass any kind of test.
RUSTY: I still have my diplomas.
DUSTY: I never lost my freckles.
RUSTY: My birthmark . . .
DUSTY:    My scrapbook . . .
RUSTY:          And the ache in my bones.

# THE HOUSE BY THE STABLE

*and*

# GRAB AND GRACE

*Two Plays*

## CHARLES WILLIAMS

# Editor's Preface: THE HOUSE BY THE STABLE and GRAB AND GRACE

*The House by the Stable* and *Grab and Grace* have been mentioned in the introduction. Nonetheless, it is appropriate and necessary to make further comment on them. Since his death several years ago, Charles Williams, who was an editor of Oxford University Press, has come to be recognized as a man of rare religious sensibility and a writer of diverse talents. His history of the Christian movement, *The Descent of the Dove,* is becoming a classic and his metaphysical mystery tales are novels of exciting adventure and profound religious insight. His gifts as a playwright are not slight, as these examples of his work indicate. However, the terseness of his style and the compactness of his symbolism require close attention. For example, "since the great earthquake and the talking flame" is Williams's way of referring to the Resurrection and Pentecost. Nonetheless, the strict attention required is accompanied by the fun of his rollicking banter and wit. While the plays can be performed independently of each other, fundamentally they belong together. *The House by the Stable* deals with the general condition of man and the need for an incarnation of God's love and purpose for Man. The second play, *Grab and Grace,* portrays Man in the light of the new event—the Christ. Although the movement of these plays is set within the framework of the cosmic drama of God's action, Man is central to the plot. Except for Joseph and Mary, who appear briefly, the characters are abstractions in the manner of a medieval morality. Yet they overcome the limitations of abstractions to a remarkable degree and appear lively and contemporary as they confront the reader and the viewer.

# THE HOUSE BY THE STABLE

*A Christmas Play*

# CHARACTERS

MAN
PRIDE
HELL
GABRIEL
JOSEPH
MARY

*The Scene is in* MAN's *house on the one side and in its stable on the other.*

*Enter* MAN *and* PRIDE.

PRIDE: What, are you not tired? will you still walk?
   will you still talk of me and of us and of you?
MAN: I desire nothing better now, and nothing new.*
   It was a high and happy day when we met.
   Will you never forget it? and love me always?
PRIDE:                                       Yes:
   I will love you always.
MAN:                 So I believe indeed,
   and feed on the thought—to be everlastingly loved.
   Tell me, how did this surprise come true?
PRIDE: It is no surprise—if you think what you are.
   Indeed, it were stranger if I adored you less.
   You are Man, the lord of this great house Earth,
   or (as its name is called in my country) Sin;
   you are its god and mine; since you first smiled
   and stretched your hand to me and brought me in,
   since our tenderness began, I have loved you, Man,
   and will—do not doubt; kiss me again.
MAN: You are my worshipful sweet Pride; will you be
   so arrogant always to others and humble to me?
   Will you always make me believe in myself? I am Man,
   but before you came, Pride, I was half-afraid
   that someone or something had been before me, and
     made
   me and my house, and could ruin or cast aside.
   But when I look in your dove's eyes, Pride,
   and see myself there, I know I am quite alone
   in my greatness, and all that I have is quite my own.

* These first three lines may be omitted when a curtain is
available.

PRIDE: So this wonderful house where moon and sun
    run with lights, and all kinds of creatures crawl
    to be your servants, and your only business is to take
    delight in your own might—it is yours and mine,
    a shrine for your godhead, and for me because I am
      yours.
MAN: Thus endures my love for my own Pride.
    To thrust you out were to doubt myself; that
    is a bygone folly now—I will do so no more.
PRIDE: No; do not: be content to love me.
    See, to teach you (let me pretend awhile
    that I can add something to your style—I
    who am also and only your creature) I have brought
      here
    my brother, born of one nature with me, my twin,
    or a moment younger: let me call him in,
    and he shall tell you more of what I have planned.
        *Enter* HELL.
MAN: Are you my Pride's brother? give me your hand.
    We must be friends; tell me, what is your name?
HELL: I am called Hell.
MAN:               And where, Hell, do you live?
HELL: Why, as to that, it is not easy to give
    a clear definition of the place; it is not far
    as your journeys go, and no bar to finding,
    but the minding of the way is best found by going,
    and that (of all means) best at my sister's showing.
MAN: We will go there some time.
PRIDE:            O soon, sweet Man, soon—
    for, I must tell you, I have begged of my brother a
      boon,
    first because you are my sweetheart, and next
    because the laws you have made everywhere mean
    you should have all the best. This is a brave
    house you live in—and let me call it Sin,
    because my tongue trips if I name it Earth—

but my brother in his country has a house braver still
and has promised it to us, of his own kind will.

MAN: Aye, has he? that is noble, and yet he knows
perhaps I would take it from him, would he not,
and I saw it one day and chose to have it for mine.

PRIDE: O love, how I love to hear you talk so!
but for my sake do not be harsh to my brother;
for your Pride's sake, smile at her brother Hell,
and treat him well.

MAN:                    Why, that I will do.
How now, Hell, shall I have a house from you?
Tell me of it.

HELL:              It is strong and very old,
but (by a burning I have made there) never cold,
and dry—the only damp would be your tears
if Man could ever weep. The air provokes
hunger often—you are so sharp-set
you could almost eat yourself. The view is wide—
heavenly, as men say in your tongue, to the other side
of the sky at least, so far it seems away,
and whatever is there will never interfere;
that is quite certain. Because my sister desires
I will give you this house if you choose.

MAN:                              And because my thews
are strong enough to take it too perhaps?

HELL: That also, no doubt.

MAN:                        Well, let that be.
You are a good fellow, Hell; you shall live there
whenever you like, even if you give it to me.
The three of us could be royal in such a house.
We will have a drink on it first.
*He goes to fetch wine.*

HELL (*to* PRIDE): Have you seen the jewel yet?

PRIDE (*to* HELL):                              No chance;
I think he has forgotten where it is himself.

HELL (*to* PRIDE): What have you been doing all this
   while?

PRIDE (*to* HELL):                       Hush!
   I have a trick now; play to my lead.

MAN (*pouring out the wine*): This is good wine; I have
      had it in store
   more than I could guess; it improves with every flask.
   None could ask better. I must have tended the vines
   when I was young; there are no vines now
   or few: I have sometimes thought—were it not for my
      smile
   over it—the land would be more sterile than it was.
   Here; drink. You must need that.

PRIDE (*to* MAN):                       Sweet,
   for Pride's sake throw him something in return,
   some trifle; I would not have my lord
   seem under an obligation even to Hell
   my brother—though indeed I meant well enough
   in persuading him.

MAN:                       You are always right; no kindness
   but I am always just to pay it back.
   Now, brother, you must take something—yes,
   no words; I say you must. What will you have?
   Pride, what shall I give him?

PRIDE:                       If you would be
   kind, play a game of dice—the best of three:
   it would please him; he loves a gamble.

MAN:                       Dice? good.
   What shall we play for?

PRIDE:                       Something quite small,
   or even nothing at all; the game is the thing.

MAN: No; something I will chance in return for a house.
   What?

      *He drinks.*

PRIDE: A handful of dust of your own—Earth;
   or—if you want, as becomes you, to risk more—

say that old jewel your servant talks
often of—more often than becomes him.
Soul, he calls it, I think.

MAN:                          Soul? yes;
truly he does talk thus; but if
ever such a thing was, it has been tossed
one day away in a corner of the house and lost.
Besides, I have heard him sing sometimes of a bird
that sat in the leaves of paradise and sang,
and in his song he calls that bird Soul.
I do not know; my paradise is I,
and any soul that sings in me I will try
on the dice any time.

> *He drinks.*

                          Look at me, Pride; you will be
always faithful, will you not?

PRIDE:                          Always, by my will.

MAN: I would kill you else.

PRIDE:                          I am not easy to kill
by any who have loved me. Sweet, we forget my brother.
Come, let us risk this lost jewel your soul
on the dice, let Hell have his chance of finding.

> *Enter* GABRIEL.

GABRIEL: Sir, by permission; there are poor people outside
seeking shelter.

PRIDE:            Insolence!

MAN:                          Who?

GABRIEL:                          One
from these parts, a youngish working man,
and has his heart's love with him, his wife,
a fair-faced girl, and (I think) near her time.
It is a harsh night; if I may suggest
she needs immediate rest—a room, and a bed.

PRIDE: Man, this servant of yours clacks his tongue
more freely than mine should do; must you keep
rooms where any riff-raff tramps may sleep—

and have supper too, I suppose? you, sir,
I am speaking to you.

GABRIEL: And supper, madam, you suppose.

HELL: Hey, you, speak well to your lord's guest,
my sister, or. . . .

GABRIEL (*angelically*): Or . . . ?

MAN: Rest quiet, Hell:
I have had this fellow for servant a long time,
ever since before I came hither, wherever
I was before I came hither; he suits.
He is neat and quick and keeps out of the way,
and looks after my accounts—at least someone does,
and it isn't I; let him alone.

   *He drinks.*

GABRIEL: Will you choose, sir, to speak to them yourself?

MAN: Why . . . it were wrong to turn a mother away
and pity to turn a woman, on a hard night,
in a plight of that kind; but tramps in my rooms . . .
   yet
one should be tender when one is comfortable, sweet,
tender to the poor, yes?

PRIDE: I confess, dear Man,
I cannot see why; one cannot do what one would—
no, not you even, my bountiful god—
and (as things go) they are only encouraged to expect
more than anyone can do. My darling, have a care.

MAN: Well, there is that . . .

GABRIEL: I think, sir,
you should see them now.

MAN: Do you? Well . . . well,
just for a moment then; let them come in.
You are always ready to beguile me. And as for you,
Hell and my sweet Pride, be merry the while.

   GABRIEL *goes out.* MAN *drinks.*

HELL (*to* PRIDE): Surely that is Gabriel, that old gossip of
heaven?

PRIDE (*to* HELL): He? I cannot tell; angels and I
never met much, not for me to recognize.

HELL (*to* PRIDE): Your dove's eyes are not so sharp as
mine.
I have peered more deeps than you; besides, sleep
takes you sometimes; it never takes me,
and after a while he who wakes for ever
finds the tingling and aching make sight the sharper
in the land where the heart-breaking troubles the light.
I am sure it is Gabriel; wait; show no sign—
only be ready to whisper Man a little
and keep your eye on the door.

PRIDE (*to* HELL): Why, what can he do?

HELL (*to* PRIDE): I do not know; nothing, I hope; if Man
chooses to play, it is his affair and mine.
But keep close; we may win the jewel yet,
and Man get clear with us to my nice house.
        *He sniggers.*

PRIDE: Come, if you will see them, let us drink first!

MAN: Gabriel might have brought me more wine first.
The curst fellow! he must be taught his job,
and not to rob me of time for wandering tramps.
Well, I have promised this time. Here, now
let us drink to our union—

HELL:                          Eternal, eternal!

        GABRIEL *brings in* JOSEPH *and* MARY.

GABRIEL: Here, sir, they are.

MAN:                          What do you want?

JOSEPH: Sir, shelter for one night, by your permission.
Our mule has gone lame; the dark overtook us
and all but shook our hearts with perils of the road.
My wife is in no condition to go on.
To-morrow we will be gone.

MAN:                          Poor wretch!
She needs a fetch of care.

PRIDE:                          Beware, sweet.

It is easier to let them in than to get them out.
You are too kind. Besides, if you have a mind
to go on this journey with our brother Hell,
you do not want strangers to rack your house
when your back is turned: anyone as great as you
must be true to his glory.

MAN:                      She is a poor lass.

PRIDE: That is why; if she were of our class—
  not yours; you are non-pareil—but my brother's and
      mine . . .
  but do as you think best!

MAN:                  For a night's rest . . .

PRIDE: To have people like these in the house—imagine!
  But you, I know, are their master—and mine.
  I am only thinking of your glory.

MAN:                  Well, yes;
  I see that . . . Gabriel!

GABRIEL:           Sir!

MAN:             Think:
  is there no shed near where these could be stored
  for a night in reasonable comfort? I can't afford
  to have them inside; my Pride will not stomach it,
  and yet I am loth to push them both outside
  till their plight is a little better.

GABRIEL:           The stable, sir:
  it is empty since you chose to dispose of your stud.

MAN: Good: give them a shake-down of straw there:
  (*Half-aside to* GABRIEL) and hark! if you care to hand
    them a hunch of bread
  I shall look the other way.
    *He drinks.*

GABRIEL:          Sir, it is God's bread.
  I will do as you say.

MAN:         O God, God!
  Why must you always bring your fairy-tales in?

Did God build this great house Sin?
Did God send this pleasant leman Pride?
What has God ever done for Man?

GABRIEL: He gave that jewel your soul.

MAN:                                        O soul!
This is your old clack, Gabriel. In the whole
of my vast property I never found it anywhere—
with flesh, fish, or fowl. It must needs be some old
hidaway rubbish. And what is God doing,
if God is, being bounteous to me?
For anything I can see, I had neither God
nor father on earth: I was always just Man
since the world began. You tire me; go,
get them away.

GABRIEL:                Sir, just as you say.

JOSEPH: Sir, a blessing on you for this grace!
Thank him, Mary.

MARY:                        Sir, God will bless you;
nor will my Son, when he comes, forget
what you gave nor with what spirit. If
he can be ever of use to you, I vow
now, in his name, he will be well content to be.

MAN: You are heartily welcome. Gabriel, have them away.
        GABRIEL *takes them across to the stable.*
There, they are gone: now we can drink again.
Pour it out, Hell. Pride, give me your hand;
am I not a grand fellow?

PRIDE:                                Sir, just as you say!
Nay, I love you, dear Man, for being so fine,
so full of your own importance. Do you not find
me more to your mind than a girl like that?
        *While they dally,* GABRIEL *covers the Nativity, and
        the three sing the Magnificat, which* PRIDE *inter-
        rupts at the following points.*

MARY: My soul doth magnify the Lord, and my spirit hath

rejoiced in God my Saviour, for he hath regarded the low estate of his handmaiden: for, behold, from henceforth all generations shall call me blessed.

PRIDE: Henceforth, we shall be the only blessed ones on earth; and no generations of anything except our joy.

MARY: For he that is mighty hath done to me great things; and holy is his name. And his mercy is on them that fear him from generation to generation. He hath showed strength with his arm; . . .

PRIDE: Be my arm of strength, Man.

MARY: . . . he hath scattered the proud in the imagination of their hearts.

PRIDE: Imagine me in your heart.

MARY: He hath put down the mighty from their seats, and exalted them of low degree.

PRIDE: Be mighty on me; exalt me to your great degree.

MARY: He hath filled the hungry with good things; and the rich he hath sent empty away.

PRIDE: O rich, rich!—bear off, my dear;
no, my brother's here. Tower—will you?—
over me in your power? O but fling him too
your glory's world's wealth! let all my house
go down before your head's crown of splendour.
Tender us all our desires out of your greatness:
to him his gambling moment, his catch of chance;
then snatch me to yourself for ever.
Then, at the gate of your house, when we go
I will kiss you so . . . do you know? wait, my sweet!
Hell, have you the dice?

MAN:                                   I have dice here.
I used them often enough when I played with my friends, but since I met you I have forgotten my friends. Love of you tends to that.

HELL:                          Do we play for a stake?
I do not mind; the game is enough.

PRIDE:                                       Yes:

but a stake, all the same, makes the game more amusing.
And, brother, you forget—you play for that jewel
called soul.

MAN:          Why, it does not exist, or if,
you will never find it.

PRIDE:             It will do; it is in my mind
that to play for the chance to find it is well enough.
What do you say, Hell?

HELL:              Aye; if I have his will
to lay hold of it, if I can, by my own skill—
nothing unfair, no force; but if it is found,
I take it in free exchange for the house and ground.

MAN: You shall, brother, for your sister's sake and yours.

HELL: However precious?

MAN:             Though it were worth my all.
    *He drinks.*
I am no miser; I was always open-handed—
was I not, Pride my lass? give me a kiss
and I shall win the game and my soul as well.
Two out of three; throw.
    *They play.*

HELL:          Five.

MAN:          Six. Ha,
that is my gain. Kiss me again, Pride.

PRIDE (*to* HELL): Quick now, while he is blind with me.
    *While they kiss* HELL *changes the dice.*

MAN: Well tossed, Hell; you have a knack, but my luck
is in now, and I back my luck to win.
    *He drinks.*

GABRIEL: Man, where are you?

MAN:           Who was that called?

PRIDE: No one.

HELL:      The wind.

MAN:          It was a voice of some kind.
    *He looks out.*
The rain is over; the stars are out; one

over the stable is more sun than star.

PRIDE: How slow you are! Man, your Pride is waiting.

MAN (*he is now rather drunk*): Waiting, is she? let her
    wait then.

Why, you hussy, you are a part of me.

I am not to be called in as if I were Gabriel

to be scolded at pleasure.

PRIDE:                    No; it was but that leisure

of ours, in Hell's house, I was wanting . . . but so,

just as you say.

MAN:          Ha, yes: again.

To it again.

    *He throws.*

        Five.

    HELL *throws.*

HELL:          Six.

MAN: What tricks . . . ? let me see. Six: it is—you have
    won.

    *He roars with laughter.*

Ho, this is a fine thing we have done—

drawn the game.

HELL:          No; one throw more.

MAN: More? how many times have we thrown?

HELL:                    Twice.

Hurry!

MAN:          What, hurry? what do you mean?

you are as saucy as this quean herself.

HELL: Throw; I am impatient for you to go.

MAN: Do you hear that, Pride? he wants us to go.

He wants to hunt for my soul.

    *He roars again with laughter.*

PRIDE:          No.

I do not think he will long hunt for that.

MAN: Well, kiss me—a kiss hearty and strong,

better than before; give me the winning throw.

    *She leans over and kisses him lazily.*

JOSEPH: Man, Man, where are you?

MAN:                     Aye! . . . here.
Who wants Man?

PRIDE *and* HELL:     No one; no one; throw.

MAN: Someone wanted; someone called; who?

PRIDE (*seizing his hand*): Throw—with me, thus; and I
with you.

MAN: Let me go. I am Man; I will not be forced.
I will have you horsed on your brother's back, my girl,
and take such a cudgel to you as will crack
some of those pretty bones.

PRIDE (*to* HELL):         Throw first,
and he afterwards; or at the very worst
we will persuade him he threw and lost the game.

HELL (*throwing*): Six.

MARY:              Man, where are you?

MAN:                   That was the girl;
that was the pretty wife—hey, now
I am coming, Man is coming.

PRIDE *and* HELL (*seizing him*): No; throw.

MAN: What is this? what is happening? How
do I hear a voice I have not chosen to hear
outside my house? Who made my house?
There was no one, was there?

PRIDE:                 No.

HELL:                 No.

MAN:                  Then how
do I hear the voice of something outside me?
Or is one of you playing a trick on me? Pride,
if I thought . . . I am caught . . . my mind is twined
in a voice . . .
it isn't yours . . . whose is it? Ho, you,
Gabriel!

HELL:     No; leave Gabriel alone.

PRIDE: Sweet, sweet Man, leave Gabriel alone.

MAN: No; Gabriel is my fellow; he will help.

He was here before I came hither; he suits.
He will tell me the voices. Gabriel, Gabriel, I say!
GABRIEL (*coming across in his magnificence*): Here!
Sir, God made me and bade me wait
on this moment in your life: what do you need?
MAN: You are a good fellow: come here: listen.
My brother Hell and my leman Pride mean
to have me finish . . . that was not it neither;
there was something else . . . the girl, Gabriel, the
girl.
I heard her call out: where is she?
Is she in danger?
GABRIEL:             No; she is quite safe.
This is the game, sir, is it?
        *He picks up one of the dice and looks at it.*
PRIDE (*to* HELL): Fool, you have tried too many ways to
get him.
HELL (*to* PRIDE): Damn him, who would have thought
grace was so near
as to hear that small squeak of a drunken voice?
MAN (*sleepily*): The game, yes—but I don't know where
we were.
Throw for me . . . the girl is safe, is she?
and her baby . . . hadn't she got a baby?
GABRIEL:                           She has.
Now.
MAN: Yes . . . to be sure. . . . Pride . . . Pride,
where are you?
        *He dozes off.*
PRIDE:           Here, darling, here.
GABRIEL (*catching her by the hair and pulling her back*):
Peace:
let the poor fellow sleep a little; you
would never be caught by anything as natural as drink.
HELL: Let her go. What are you doing there with my dice?

GABRIEL (*tossing the dice in the air and catching it*): Dice
—ha! So: that is better.
It seems now to have only one six:
and now we can play the last throw again.

HELL (*whining*): I won't! I tell you I won't! I won't play.

PRIDE (*snarling*): Don't you, Hell: the nasty-minded scut,
pretending we cheated.

> GABRIEL *takes each of them by an ear, and knocks
> their heads lightly together.*

PRIDE:          Oo! don't—you hurt!

> *She drops to the floor, moaning and rubbing her
> head.*

GABRIEL: You wanted the game; you shall win or lose on
the game
by the luck of the game, but all luck is good.
Toil and spoil as you will, still in the end
the flick of every chance must fall right.
Throw.

HELL:    I don't . . .

GABRIEL (*terribly*): Throw.

> HELL *throws.*

Five

> GABRIEL *throws.*

Speak—

what is it?

HELL (*cowering*): Six.

GABRIEL.        You have had a long run,
you and all your tricks, but to-morrow's sun
rises on a world where untruth is always untrue.
That is simple enough but too difficult for you.
Get to your house and the burning you made—and not
even
that is your own; the fire is borrowed from heaven.

> HELL *goes.*

And as for you, sister, you poor cheap

cowardly shrew; you . . .

*With an awful angelic effort he restrains himself.*

I will teach you one lesson; kneel up; say after me:

*She obeys. He puts on his glory.*

Glory to God in the highest, and on earth peace:
goodwill to men.

PRIDE *repeats the words, snivelling.*

And now go.

*She begins to get up.*

No; on your knees: go.

*She shuffles away.*

MAN [*waking*]. I dreamt my Pride had gone.

*He stares round.*

Where is she? what has been happening? call her, you,
Gabriel.

GABRIEL: Sir, soon, if you tell me to.

They will wait, I know, by the gate you call Death,
which is the usual way to Hell's house.
you may catch them there or yourself call them back.
But there is a thing to do before you go.

MAN: What? do you bully me? I want my Pride;
I want to be a god; she made a vow
never to leave me.

GABRIEL: Nor did she—to be just.
It was I—for this single night—made her go.

MAN: You are above yourself.

GABRIEL: Above or beside—
distinct enough at least to deal with Pride.
There is a thing that you must see to-night
of your own sight, without Pride's arms round you
or Hell's hand in yours. This one hour
out of all time is given you to see it yourself.
To-morrow things may change. The woman you saved
half by your will from a little chill in the night,
and from blistered feet, has a word to say. Come.

MAN: It seems I made her a poor offer, yet

she was better in the straw than in the street:
do you not think so? You look grander than you used.
GABRIEL: Sir, it is only that you give me more attention.
When Pride is about, no one can see straight.
You shall see more than I. Come when I call.
    *He goes to the stable.*
JOSEPH: Blessed one, what is your will now?
MARY: Dearest lord, to show Man my child;
lest in some testy humour the rumour should fade.
If he sees, his heart may radically move to love,
whatever he forgets, wherever he sets his eyes.
JOSEPH: He who with all this Earth offered us the straw?
MARY: Did we deserve, dearest, under the law,
this birth that I kiss? Nothing at all is given
till all is given, I know; that is heaven.
But then also it is heaven to know that all
is given at once in the smallest free gift—
even sometimes when only half-given. O my Son
reckons as no arithmetician has done;
he checks his amounts by the least and the greatest at
    once.
O my Own, there are no, no accounts like yours!
JOSEPH: Blessed is he in his sole free choice!
GABRIEL: Lady, Man is a little drunk, and a little
sleepy, with a little hankering after hell,
but yet also he has a faint hurt
at having offered as he did; if it pleased you now
to expose the Holy Thing—
MARY:               O let him come!
let him come quickly!
GABRIEL:          Man! Man!
    MAN *stumbles across.*
MAN: It is almost too bright here to see. Where
is the lady? I did give her a hunch of bread
and a place to lie; she might else have been dead.
JOSEPH: Do not talk nonsense.

GABRIEL:                              Do not talk at all.

MAN: No, but I am trying to understand: why
    should I who had one house, and another beyond
    promised, have been so fond as to offer straw
    in a stable? and yet . . .

GABRIEL:                              Do not trouble your brain;
    gain is as difficult to understand as grace.

JOSEPH: Do not talk, I say, lest the Divine One sleep.

MARY: Nay, let him talk as he will; he is mine; come,
    Man my friend; it is true that but for you
    I might have come to an end—here, at least.
          *She gives him her hand.*
    Look, my Son thanks you.

MAN:                              Was he born here?

MARY: This very night, in your stable; therefore, dear Man,
    you, if you choose, shall be his god-father.

MAN: What will you call him, lady?

MARY:                              Jesus, because
    he shall presently save his people from their sins—
    and Hell shall play no trick on them more.

MAN: I did not quite refuse you, did I? or did I?
    I cannot tell; Hell has made me stupid.
    Did I deny you all or did I not?
    Look now, he must have something to please him.
    The house is full of things, and none right.
    Stop; I remember something out of sight,
    out of thought, but always I have had round my neck.
          *He fumbles at his breast and pulls out a jewel.*
    There; it was once bright; it might serve.
    I do not know what it is at all.
    But if you should want a bed for the rest of the night,
    there is my room the best.

GABRIEL:                              But this is your soul
    I have searched for all this time!

MARY (*laughing up at him*): Great Hierarch, even
    the angels desire to understand these things,

and a mortal hand does more than the Domination.
Leave Man and my Son and me our mystery;
let us think our own way and not yours.
Look, I will breathe on it—so, and see
how it dances, and how my Beloved's glances follow.
Take it again, Man, a little while;
we will go up to your room.

    GABRIEL *and* JOSEPH *help her to rise.*

                        Now be the gloom
of earth split, and be this house blest
and no more professed by poor Pride to be Sin,
for the joys of love hereafter shall over-ride
boasting and bragging and the heavy lagging of Hell
after delight that outstrips him—step and sight.

    *She makes the sign of the Cross towards the house.*
Take us, O exchange of hearts! this we know—
substance is love, love substance. Let us go.

    *They go out.*

# GRAB AND GRACE

## *Or, It's the Second Step*

(Companion and sequel to
THE HOUSE BY THE STABLE)

# CHARACTERS

**PRIDE**
**HELL**
**GABRIEL**
**FAITH**
**MAN**
**GRACE**

*The scene as before. Enter* HELL *and* PRIDE, *bedraggled and tired;* HELL *carrying a large bundle*

PRIDE: No rest? no comfortable house?
   These lands are as empty of homes as our bag of food—
   yet I should know this place!
HELL:                          Why surely this—
   yes, look, in this crook of the hills,
   look, here is Man's house once more!
   After this hundred years we have been wandering
   through the malignant lands, to think we have come
   again to your old home. What think you, Pride?
   Might it not be possible to find a rest here?
PRIDE: Why, it would be worth while to try; I
   and you too were so beshouted and bevenomed
   by that slug-slimy Gabriel that we lost our heads
   and ran too soon. Man cannot have forgotten;
   few do; their faithfulness to me is astonishing.
   Shall we knock, do you think?
HELL:                          Prink yourself first.
PRIDE: This accurst mud!
HELL:                          That dress will not provoke him
   under your yoke again.
PRIDE:                          Look and see
   if we have anything better in our odds and ends.
      HELL *opens the bundle, and they poke about: frag-*
      *ments fall out.*
PRIDE: I cannot think why we carry all this.
   What is this red stuff?
HELL:                          A little of Abel's blood.
   A drop of that in a drink gives a man heartburn.
PRIDE:                                        And this?
HELL: Take care; a bit of Adam's tooth

that he broke on the first fruit out of Paradise.
He has had neuralgia in his jaws ever since.

PRIDE: And this—thistledown?

HELL:                      The kiss of Judas.

PRIDE:                                  Judas?

HELL: You were sick of malignant plague when it happened—
but the child whom Man sheltered when we had gone
grew, and grew spoiled, and Judas, one of his friends,
encouraged Man to kill him in a sudden brawl.
There is no time now to tell you all.

PRIDE:                             All
meaning that when Man had got rid of me
things did not go so well as Gabriel thought?
You fool, Hell, why did you not tell me
all this sooner?

HELL:                 I had forgotten; my fits
make me dull. We are not what we were;
neither you nor I have ever been the same
since the great earthquake and the talking flame.

PRIDE:                                Hell,
did we not hear that Man had a changed heart?
I am sure that some antipodean rumour
reached us of his altered humour; that he likes now
prayer and servile monochromatic designs.
Draggled decency might better suit us?

HELL: I will say, looking at our bag, it would be easier.
May not you be converted as well as he?
Try that style: (*He grabbles about*) look, what of this?
    *He holds up a dirty rough cloak.*
How of this for a man's earthenware embrace
and a chaste kiss? (*She puts it on*) Your very face looks
holy.

PRIDE: What is it?

HELL:                Devil knows; the original figleaves, I
should think.

You will need a belt. (*He holds one up*) Jezebel's?

PRIDE: My dear, too bright.
What's that?

HELL. The cord with which Judas hanged himself,
afterwards used to tie Peter to his cross.

PRIDE: That is the very thing; give it here.
*She looks at herself.*
I don't know who Peter was, but if
he was crucified, it is something anyone might be proud
of.
Pride in a nutshell! (*She wriggles*) with the shell of
the nut inside.
Hist, someone is coming!

HELL (*throwing the things in the bag*): Is it Man?

PRIDE: No; it's a woman; what the devil—

HELL: Chut!
There's Gabriel! Out of sight till we find out more!
*They hide. Enter* FAITH, *meeting* GABRIEL. *She is
dressed as brightly and sophisticatedly as is possible.*

FAITH: Good-morning, Gabriel: where is my lord?

GABRIEL: Madam,
he was in the stables just now, but I think he has gone
back with Grace to the house.

FAITH: The stables?

GABRIEL: Yes.
He has not been there much since the Holy One died,
but this morning something stirred.

FAITH: A word in a song!
O to-day is such a morning as I love,
cloudy and cool; one feels rather than sees
the sun heavenly: he is distilled in the air,
and my heart filled with his future; in the dawn
I made a new song, and would fain sing it,
if Man my lord were free to hear.

GABRIEL: Madam,
could he do better than listen to Faith's songs?

FAITH: Well, to be frank, that depends; but thank you
　　for the kind thought. I will go and find him out.
　　O loveliness, to feel day in the dawn!
　　　　*Exit.*
PRIDE (*aside to* HELL): And will you tell me who Faith is,
　　and what
　　Faith, in that dress, is doing in Man's house,
　　and I in this—shroud?
HELL (*aside*):　　　　　Not so loud; hush!
GABRIEL (*looking round*): You need not trouble yourselves
　　to hush; your smell
　　would give you away; surely it is Hell and Pride?
　　The old obscene graveyard stink; I think
　　honest anger and brutal lust smell pure
　　beside you.
PRIDE:　　　　Stew-faced bully!
HELL:　　　　　　　　　Sister, be at ease.
　　Once he had power even over us for an hour,
　　but not twice thus, not twice.
　　Abuse you he may; he cannot turn you away.
　　He must let Man choose now for himself.
PRIDE: Are you sure you are right?
HELL:　　　　　　　　　Of course—
GABRIEL:　　　　　　　　Of course he is right.
　　I could be, were angels ever other than glad,
　　a little sad to see you with more tricks.
　　But now Man has friends if he will,
　　and if you can cheat him, why, you must.
　　I can do no more than tell him who you are.
PRIDE: I will tell him that myself.
GABRIEL:　　　　　　　So do.
　　You seem perhaps more true than most
　　sins to their nature—and so catch more.
　　Double temptation when a sin pretends to be truthful.
HELL: No, sir. We need not trouble you to announce us.

GABRIEL: No need; here is Man.

MAN *enters with* GRACE.

HELL:                                  Now!

PRIDE:                                          Get away!

Much better for me to be alone. Man!

MAN (*to* GRACE): We will build then; I have decided that.

The cottages are clammy; we need several more

and more to the mind of those likely to live there.

First, we must find an architect.

GRACE:                                          O sir,

I know a fine one, in design and execution

better than any; all the worlds praise

his work these many days.

MAN:                                          Who then is he?

GRACE: He is called the Spirit; those who know his degree

add a worshipful title and say the Holy Spirit:

that as you choose.

MAN:                              The Holy Spirit? good.

We will ask him to come while I am in the mood,

which passes so quickly and then all is so dull.

GRACE: Sir, purposes last.

MAN:                              Yes, but heavily.

Madam?

PRIDE:        Man!

MAN: Do I—ought I—to know . . . ? I have met few

of your veiled kind; yet—

PRIDE:                              Man!

MAN: By my soul, it is Pride.

PRIDE:                                          Yes. (*A pause*) Do you grieve?

Would you have me leave, without a word changed?

I will, if you say go.

MAN:                              No; stay.

Where have you been? I have not seen you since—

PRIDE: Since your servant told—yes; they *were* lies.

Though indeed I was foolish then, now more wise.

But to mistake folly for foul thought,
to drive me out while you slept! Have you sometimes
    kept
a thought of me?—no; that is folly again.
I am professed now to other vows,
as my dress shows. I have even changed my name
and am called Self-Respect.

MAN:                                 What, you are one
of Immanuel's people?

PRIDE (*drooping*):      He has a use for all.
        *She turns aside and gets near to* HELL; *then aside.*
What was her name? quick, the great sinner,
the woman.

HELL:        Mary Magdalene.

PRIDE (*returning*):                  Even Mary Magdalene—
and so for me, who did not (I may well say)
sin as much as she—and was she more beautiful?
Once, dear Man, you thought me well enough.

MAN: It is astonishing to see you; you have not changed.
The same lovely eyes under that hood.
It is good to see you once more, my own Pride;
no, I must call you my own Self-Respect.
It is what I will try to remember.
        GRACE *whistles.* PRIDE *and* MAN *turn away.* GRACE
        *and* GABRIEL *speak to* HELL.

GRACE: And here is poor old Hell!

HELL:                           Little tin trumpet,
how do you know me?

GABRIEL:            O we of heaven
know you all. This boy, whom we call Grace—
he is part of Faith's household, and she of Man's—
is older than you. Indeed, he does not look it,
but your travels in the malignant lands have aged you
more than our millennia.

GRACE:                  A thousand years
being as a day. Poor Hell, time to you

is a sorry plod-plod; even Man knows better,
but Hell of all pedestrians is the most tired.
And why are you here, little brother?
HELL: What is that to you?
May we not talk to Man without your leave?
GABRIEL: Unfortunately, yes.
GRACE: And is she doing it now!
PRIDE: And tell me, dear Man, how you are faring in
  Religion.
MAN: Well, I am trying to lead the Christian life.
It is not easy, is it, Gabriel?
GABRIEL: Sir,
I do not think you have found it too difficult.
PRIDE: To lead the Christian life is always difficult.
How we have to work! digging, building,
giving alms, prayer. Do you pray much?
MAN: A good deal. Gabriel, what do you mean?
GABRIEL: Sir, only that you have been constantly helped.
This boy Grace does most of the work.
MAN: I know Grace has been useful, but to say
he does most—I was up as early as he
and as bustling round my property.
PRIDE: That I am sure.
I know how dextrous and diligent you always are.
MAN: I will give praise where praise is due, but something
is due to me.
PRIDE: Much, indeed.
GABRIEL: Sir—
GRACE: Chut, Gabriel; you will never defeat her so.
Do not argue; make her come out with herself
quickly; believe me, it is your only way.
Call Faith; she is better than you at the game,
and can frame a neater trap, woman to woman.
  GABRIEL *goes out.*
PRIDE: It is no credit to any cause not to know
if one has kept its laws well. Flaws

will come, but when one has minded laws—why,
then a certain proper pride may grow.
I have taken Self-Respect for my new name
to adjust properly praise and blame, to keep
myself in mind as a true centre for myself.

MAN:                                                  True.
One has more belief, so, in what one can do.

PRIDE: That is it: no weakness, no false meekness.
This humility is too much praised.
One may look at oneself, I hope, without sin.
You, my Man, can keep your thought so poised
that any noised silliness does not hurt.
You are pious—good! but it is *you* who are pious.

MAN: I had not thought of that. Faith sings
only about Immanuel and what he does.
That brings a sense of vacancy sometimes.

PRIDE: Yes: one needs at first a kind of defence
against even heaven. Perfection comes slowly;
and we must not be too holy all at once.

> *Enter* FAITH *and* GABRIEL.

FAITH: Good-morning, my lord.

MAN:                                    Good-morning, Faith.

PRIDE (*to* MAN):                                          This
is another friend of yours?

MAN:                          Her name is Faith.
She was a friend of Immanuel, the child born
the night you went. . . . O well, Pride—
I beg your pardon; it is old habit in me—
we need not go into all that now.
There was a misunderstanding of what he meant
and a tussle—you, my dear, will understand
there was something to be said on my side;
but anyhow—it was all rather unfortunate—he died.
But he left with me these two friends,
she and the boy Grace. Let me introduce—

PRIDE: She will despise me, Man. I am poor

and of no account, but I have enough respect
for myself not to push in among the elect,
among—look at her clothes!—my ostensible betters.

MAN: Clothes—nonsense. You look very nice—
quiet and . . . becoming.

PRIDE:                     Man!

MAN:                            Well, I
have you in my mind as you were when . . . but come;
it suits you. You are my own Self-Respect,
and this is my own Faith; you must know each other.

>       GRACE *whistles.*

Faith, this is an old friend of mine,
called—do I say Sister?

PRIDE:                     Yes—I suppose,
Sister.

>       *She clings to his hand and looks deep into his eyes.*

MAN: . . . called . . . Sister Self-Respect.
And this, dear friend, is Faith.

PRIDE:                            Pleased to meet you.

FAITH (*coldly*): Good-morning.

PRIDE:                     Is it not a good morning?
(*To* MAN) This house was always good in the spring
days.

FAITH: You have known Man a long while?

PRIDE:                            Very long.
(*To* MAN) Of course, times change; I know now
you have other friends.

FAITH:             Yes.

MAN:                No.
You must not say so; at least, if I have,
I do not forget my old.

FAITH:             It seems not;
especially when they return in a neat religious
habit, and are prettily disposed to public prayer.

PRIDE: What do you mean—public?

FAITH:                     I do not mean

praying with others present, but rather that sedate
praying to oneself, with oneself too as listener;
a ubiquitous trinity of devotion the temple-Pharisee
practised long and successfully.

PRIDE:                                    At least I
earned my lodging here by a decent return—
by something other than songs; night was my time.

FAITH: Yes; *my* joys encourage sight,
accuracy, and reason.

PRIDE:                          My kisses were accurate:
Man enjoyed them and himself and me.
I did not confine myself to singing him songs.

MAN: O now, Self-Respect, they are beautiful songs.
Everyone to his own gift . . . indeed,
you always had beautiful shoulders.

PRIDE:                                        Have I not?
as beautiful bare as hers bundled on Sundays?
          GRACE *whistles.* HELL *creeps towards him.*
I am sorry, Man. I did not mean to snap.
I had better go.

MAN:                  O no, you must not go.
We shall all be great friends—I, Man,
and his Self-Respect and his Faith: why not?

FAITH: His Self-Respect and his Faith! No. Man,
you must make up your mind. There is a strong feud
renewed for centuries, from our very making, between
this lady and myself.

PRIDE:                      There is indeed—
between my pleasure and your procrastination,
you promising what you do not pay,
and I paying what I need not bother to promise.
          GRACE *whistles.*

HELL (*to* GRACE): Stop that noise!

GRACE:                                Noise yourself;
Adam called the birds on that note

while you were squeaking and squealing among the
   crocodiles.
O crocodiles' guiles and smiles and wiles,
when Hell styles himself a judge of music.
      HELL *threatens him.* GRACE *trips him.*
Heels up, gossamer!

MAN:                               Less noise over there!
   Grace, keep yourself quiet in your own place.
   Now, let us agree here to be friends.
   Love puts all ends at one, and spends
   much to do it: come, wine for a pledge.
   Gabriel!

GABRIEL: Sir, the ladies will never agree.
   If you wish to turn Faith out of doors . . .

MAN: What! my friend's friend! Immanuel's friend . . .
   why do you remind me? No; I promised; I am firm.

GABRIEL: Then send Pride away.

MAN:                               O now, Gabriel,
   I owe her, after all, a great deal,
   and she understands me, she soothes me.

PRIDE:                               I am not Pride.
   Indeed, Gabriel, I have forgotten all that.
   I am the old woman on the new way:
   look at me, a demure modest Self-Respect;
   nothing spectacular or dishonourable about *me*.
   Of course, I am not *blind;* I cannot help
   noticing where sinners thrive, or where they sin,
   or how parasites and amateur prostitutes are dressed.

FAITH: The professional always hates being outclassed—
   I agree there: for the word—let it stand.
   Our feud, on my side, is too deep
   to use abuse. I say I will not sit down
   nor eat nor drink nor sleep in the same house
   with—Self-Respect. I do not and will not know her.

PRIDE: And I— *I!*—used to be called Pride!

Is this your charity, you over-painted, over-powdered,
verminous haunch of a hag-bone! you snorting porcu-
pine,
pet of a fellow whose hands never kept his head!
Why, you dilly-down doveling, you mincing mosquito—
GRACE *whistles.* HELL *runs at him; they dodge out,*
*shouting, while* PRIDE *is screaming and* FAITH
*speaking.*

FAITH: I will not abuse you. I simply will not know you.

MAN (*shouting*): Silence! Gabriel, keep the house quiet!
See what Grace is doing and tell him not to.
And now, you two, am I to say nothing?
Am I not to have my own way?
You shall behave in this house, both of you,
as if I were someone.

PRIDE: O Man,
that is right! keep us in order; send us to prayer.
Rebuke us! Have I hurt you? O beat me
if I disturb you; I am only yours—
and of course God's; but I *am* wholly yours
in a new love, if you choose!

MAN: This fiddle-faddle!
Argument in, argument out. Man
will have his way sometimes; if I choose
you shall both stop with me, stop you shall.
I will tie you up, Pride!

PRIDE: Anything, anything!
GABRIEL *has been looking out.*

GABRIEL: Sir, look!

MAN: What is the matter now?
What are they doing there? who is the fellow?
Why, it is Hell! Was he here too?

GABRIEL: He is throttling Grace!

MAN: He is throwing him into the lake—
he will drown; it has no bottom. Hi!
Hell there, Hell, leave him alone!

Grace, we are coming!
> *He runs out.*

GABRIEL: Sir, Grace can swim;
indeed, there is very little Grace cannot do—
for example—get out of the bottomless pit.
Well, it is proper that Man should run fast
when heaven seems in danger; heaven has done
as much for him.
> *He goes leisurely out.*

FAITH: O sister, sister, now we may talk sense.
You must find it exhausting always to be
on guard, watching every word. Myself,
help though I have and celestial succour,
I am glad sometimes when my sister Hope
takes my place for a night; and I can speak
right and direct; the muscles in my face
are controlled naturally and not by sheer work
to please Man's variable moods. Poor Man,
he is a sweet darling, but O I wish
he had an adult intelligence.

PRIDE: You can drop this feud
when Man is not here!

FAITH: He is a born mimic,
and therefore I must refuse to have you here,
or you would catch him with one or the other ruse.
Alone, we may leave it to God.

PRIDE: Why are you so bent
to have him? he will never do *you* good.

FAITH: To obey Immanuel is in my blood; and he
chooses so. But how will Man serve *you?*

PRIDE: O yes; when we have him—as we shall;
you will call one day to an empty house;
anything else is not possible; well, then,
while your songs echo and re-echo, none
to mark them, except perhaps the sun in heaven,
think that Man is another vagrant I

and Hell shall sometimes meet where the sky
has no sun, in the clammy malignant lands
that Hell once made.

FAITH:                    And now finds
everywhere terribly following him; even here.
O I know well wherever you go,
he and you, you sooner or later feel
the air of the cold iceberg or hot oasis
breaking into the same clamminess, the same
disgusting invisible froth against the skin—
ugh! every wind, every rain-drop,
every grateful beam crawling and sticky.

> HELL *creeps in behind her, making signs to* PRIDE.

PRIDE (*getting nearer*): Yes; we shall have a companion
    then, to bear
the bag over there of the odds and ends
we stole out of his house; in a dim mist
he shall stumble after us, afraid to lose even us,
or sometimes be pricked by me or kicked by Hell
forward before us, among the shallow pools
or the miry grass under the malignant trees
where the baboons sit and scratch and yowl.
There with us tramping and trapesing for ever.

FAITH: Poor wretch! but you haven't . . .

> HELL *seizes her.* PRIDE *covers her mouth.*

HELL: I have thrown Grace into the lake; quick,
Shove this cloth in her mouth; tie it.
If we can hide her we may lure Man
out of his house into the malignant lands.
Keep him till the sun sets and leave me alone
to draw him down among the pits and pools.

PRIDE: Twist her arms behind her: use your fist.

> HELL *strikes at* FAITH; *she dodges; he hits* PRIDE.

Damn! O anyhow: be quick.

HELL: Give me that cord; they will be a few minutes.
Hang on to her waist while I tie her legs.

PRIDE (*panting*): She is so supple.

HELL: All right. Now—
in front then—pull! there. Where shall we put her?
behind that tree?

PRIDE: No; Hell, the bag!
the bag! throw our things behind the tree,
anyhow, in a heap, and then have her in.

HELL: Excellent! empty it. Now—over her head!

FAITH *digs him in the stomach.*

Ouch! Her hands are about as delicate as iron.
There . . . steady . . . *there.* That settles Faith.

PRIDE: She can have her feud all to herself there,
and fill her belly with her own gaudiness.

HELL: Here—
help tie it under her feet; so.
I hear them; quick; carry it over here.

*They carry the bag to the back.* MAN, GABRIEL,
*and* GRACE *come in.*

MAN: Hell, this is outrageous. He might have been
drowned.

O yes, I know he is a tiresome boy.
I am sure he provoked me often, his jokes
and his insolence, but to treat him so—

HELL: I would have seen to it he came to no hurt,
had you not been by: since you were—
But I was rash. I agree I did wrong.
I apologize—gentleman to gentleman. As for him—
here, lad, and another time watch your tongue.
Catch!

*He throws him something.*

GABRIEL: One of the thirty pieces, was it?
Grace will win them all back, one day,
and not by playing dice.

MAN: Well, now . . .
where is Faith?

PRIDE: Gone into the house.

She would not even take the air with me;
she preferred her own room to my company.
(*aside to* HELL) For the devil's sake give me a better
    belt;
I can't keep my things together.

HELL (*aside*):                Jezebel's?
It is all we have.

PRIDE (*aside*):      Any damn thing.
Your friends, dearest Man, are a little difficult.
Faith is rude to me and Grace to my brother—
not that I mind—and I (poor soul!) thought
just for once I would replace the cord
of my habit with a little brightness, my old lightness
of heart took me so to be with you.
     *She puts on the belt.*
Does it look silly?

MAN:              No, but more like you.

PRIDE: Of course, I do forgive your friend. You know
that is where Religion helps. One can forgive.
Is it not pleasant, dearest, to forgive others?
It is far sweeter than anger, more satisfying.
Lying in bed at night, I love to think
how many sinners poor little Self-Respect
has forgiven—even in a week or so. To be oneself
is always to find how much better than others
one surprisingly is. I take no credit,
of course, for that, though indeed, Man,
you loved me: did I seem—never mind.
You loved me.

MAN:         Yes.

PRIDE:           It was something of a joy.
Did you not feel yourself to be noble then?

MAN: Yes.

PRIDE:    O come for a little; come!
No, not in the house—out here,
away from all your people. Yes indeed,

I know we now are otherwise turned
and so will be; but an hour—come!
You shall be true to Faith and I to my vows;
only a little walk, a little murmur,
a reverie, a day-dream, a distant noon-glimpse
of our past joy, a thing forgotten but
for just this one companioned glance,
this twy-memoried gleam far below.
Come.

MAN:     I have never been able to forget you.

PRIDE:                        Come.

MAN: O how the blood runs quicker! O—
Pride, Faith's songs are very sweet
but strange, alien with that accent, sweet
terribly, but to be with you is to lose terror,
to lose the beauty that strips me of comfort. Pride,
that is a dull dark dress you are wearing;
your belt shows it up; it is not like you.

PRIDE: We will see if we can find something brighter,
more to my lord's liking; we might. Come.

      GRACE *has been poking up among* HELL's *properties.*
      *He plays a tune.*

Would you not like to see me? no, say,
there is no dress for Pride as beautiful as she,
as you used to. Only for a moment; only for joy
of the memory; then back to Immanuel and Faith.
Kiss me and say so. Kiss me.

MAN: Hark a minute. Who is that playing?
It is that strange distant song
which pricks a point of fire in each joint.
Grace, what have you there?

GRACE:                 This, my lord?
I found it hidden in a heap behind a tree,
It is one of the dulcimers Nebuchadnezzar's orchestra
played at the grand show of the Three-in-the-Fire,
who became, unexpectedly, Four.

MAN: How Four?
Is that the song's name?

GRACE: O my lord,
the tale is old: it was one of Immanuel's doings.
Faith afterwards made a good song
on the dance of the Four-in-the-Fire. Hear me play,
and see if your heart does not move to the steps of the
Fourth.
Sit, my lord; here is something to sit on.
*He begins to roll the bag out.*

PRIDE *and* HELL: Leave that alone!

PRIDE: Man, make your servants leave untouched
Our few poor belongings. It is my bag
and my brother's dulcimer.

GRACE: Nebuchadnezzar's dulcimer;
stolen like Abel's blood and Adam's tooth
and all the rest, from this very house.
I only recover it.

GABRIEL: Indeed, sir, you have
a right to your own antiques—to give to Hell
if you wish, but even Hell must not steal.
Your museum was unique, but that bag holds much.
Roll it nearer, Grace.

HELL: Leave it alone.
That dulcimer never came from the bag.

PRIDE: Yes; it is mine.

HELL: Yes; but not from the bag.
That is full.

GABRIEL: Ah but what fills it?
Tell me that, Hell. And look at it!
It is moving.

GRACE (*striking an attitude and sepulchrally*): And where
is Faith?

HELL: How do I know?

PRIDE: Back in the house.

MAN: Something is inside the bag.

PRIDE: Dear Man, only my own pet scorpions.
  I cannot bear to leave them behind; one day
  I will show them to you, but not just now.
MAN: Scorpions! no scorpion ever moved like that.
  What have you got there?
GRACE:                    Aha!
HELL:                         Man,
  We did not come here to be insulted.
        GRACE *whistles.*
GABRIEL: The bag, sir, is trying to attract your attention.
  I submit that the whole affair is so suspicious
  you have a right to open it.
HELL:                  No!
PRIDE:                      No!
        *The blade of a knife appears.*
GRACE: Ladies and gentlemen, observe the scorpion's sting.
  Little sister, your scorpions may stab you yet.
MAN: It is opening all of itself. Nothing like this
  has ever happened in my house before.
GRACE:                            My lord,
  nothing like my lady Faith and I
  ever happened in anyone's house before.
  Adored be the Omnipotence for ever and ever!
        FAITH's *head appears through the cut.* GABRIEL *and*
        GRACE *run to help her out.*
GRACE: Faith in a bag is Faith at her best!
GABRIEL:                          No;
  even Faith must flag when she is stifled,
  and Faith with vision is wiser than Faith without.
FAITH: Faith—and Faith may say so—is pretty well
    smothered.
  O this old smell of Man's horrors
  clings to the cloth, the beastly evidence
  of things unhoped and undesired,
  the present substance of things past and unseen.
  Pah!

*She stands up.*

MAN: Faith, who has done this? I vow
  I will now do justice. I keep promise—
  I? no; I do not see my way
  or what to say, but I swear the promise shall be kept
  that I made Immanuel when he leapt into heaven—
  mocking (O I know it! I know it!) my serious sin.
  Tell me, who has done this?

PRIDE:                         One
  who will finish her work!
      *She snatches a dagger from* HELL's *belt and leaps*
      *at* FAITH.

HELL:                    Fool, leave it alone!
  She is immortal like us! O imbecile!
      FAITH *catches* PRIDE *and bends her back, twisting*
      *the hand holding the knife.*

MAN: Drop that!
      *He makes a movement forward.*

FAITH:             Stop there, Man.
  She has challenged me alone and I alone
  will take the challenge. Since you will not choose
  by honour or love, will you take the mere fact?
  Will you believe in the power?
      HELL *moves;* MAN *seizes him.*

MAN:                   A little else!
  There shall be none beside to interfere;
  that at least I can do!

FAITH:            Blessed Man,
  I will swear at the Judgment that you helped me here.
  So, Pride, so.
      MAN *wrestles with* HELL.

PRIDE:         Ah, beast!
  Help me, Hell!

HELL:        Pride, help me!

GABRIEL:              Grace,
  would not your quick touch finish the trick?

GRACE: I have brought them to a clear field! now yield
the weaker! well I know who that will be.
O Man, well thrown! poor Hell!
>   MAN *throws* HELL *and puts his foot on him.*
MAN: Well sung, Grace! had you not found
and struck the dulcimer, I should have fallen to folly
deeper and darker, and my Faith died.
O the sight of the knife cured all.
Does she need help?
GABRIEL:                    Probably not. I have known
Faith live and thrive in odd places
by her own mere valour. Look now.
>   *In the final stress* PRIDE *breaks down; the dagger is*
>   *twisted from her, and she falls.*
GRACE: Well done, Faith! well done, Man! So.
>   *He picks up the dagger.*
I thought so; Cain's old obsidian knife!
What will you do with them now, my lord?
MAN:                                         I?
What have I to do with giving sentence?
>   *He moves away.* HELL *rises.*
It seems to me that when I say *I*
or when I think myself someone I am always wrong.
GABRIEL: Sir, you have known that all the time
if you let yourself think.
GRACE:                    O chut, chut!
Gabriel, you archangels are so stern—
let our sweet lord make his own discoveries:
do not be so severe on his human reason
you with your communicated heavenly intuitions!
GABRIEL: I too have—never mind. You are right, Grace.
This is not the place or the time for rebuke.
Sir, it is true that for ever in this house
you hold the high, the low, and the middle justice
over all things; yet, as Hell said,
they are immortals; they cannot be put to death.

I do not advise perpetual prison here,
not trusting Pride—nor, sir, to be frank,
thinking you would have much chance against her.
We have seen—

GRACE:                Gabriel! Come off your grand angelic
passion for instruction. This is Man's affair;
I would swear (if I could) he would do himself right,
and us.

GABRIEL: Very well. Sir, what will you do?

MAN: Do? it is they have done their last and worst.

        GRACE *whistles*. MAN *looks at him*.

GRACE (*hastily*): My lord, I am sorry; that was old habit.
When I am sceptical I always whistle,
and as for doing their *last*—forgive me; speak.

MAN: Let them go then to their own place.
    Up and out!

        PRIDE *rises; she and* HELL *look at each other; she*
        *screams*.

PRIDE:        O no, no!
    Man, I will repent, I will do better,
    I will be good one day—no, to-day.
    Do not send me out to the malignant lands;
    do not send me out with Hell! Save me!

GABRIEL: Sister, it was your choice.

PRIDE:                        No, never;
    not with him. O Man, Man—

GABRIEL: Man is not to be asked now; he judged.
    The execution is remitted to us. We
    are his household; we wear his livery; we do his will.
    The Mercy of God takes Man at his word
    and enforces it, by us who obey him on earth. Go.

PRIDE: Man, I loved you—

GABRIEL:                Loved! O little sister,
    if anything was wanting, that has finished all.
    Call Love in and Pride is lost.

HELL: Come, sister; the journey begins again.

PRIDE: No, no! (*She rushes from one to the other;* MAN
   *hides his face*) Save me! You have not gone,
   you have not walked with him among the pools,
   beyond the baboons and the crocodiles, beyond all
   but the quicksands that never quite swallow us, under
      a moon
   that never quite lights us, in the death that never quite
      dies,
   and *he*—
GABRIEL:     Is this Pride?
PRIDE:                     No, no.
   No Pride! O if you had carried that bag—
   the things we stole from you are beautiful beside
   the things he can fill it with.
FAITH:                        But what does he *do*?
PRIDE: Denatures.
GABRIEL:        Denatures!
FAITH:                   O horrible! O
   God, pitiful God, have mercy on all!
      *There is a pause.*
PRIDE: Yes. Hell. I am coming to you, Hell.
   *She stumbles towards him.*
HELL (*softly*): The bag, Pride; do not forget the bag.
   It will be filled soon down there,
   and now it is your turn to carry it—harlot!
PRIDE: Yes, Hell. (*She fetches it*) Here it is, Hell.
HELL: Come then. (*To the others*) We will be back
   presently.
      *They go out.*
GABRIEL: So. That is done. Now—
FAITH and GRACE: Sh-h!
GRACE: Gabriel, there must be many things in the house
   waiting for you. The silver needs polishing
   perhaps; or the accounts—think of the accounts!
GABRIEL: Grace, if you were not a Divine gift—
GRACE: Yes, but I am—

GABRIEL:                  You are. If you were not—

GRACE: I know; I know; you said so. The silver, Gabriel,
     the accounts! the dinner! We must dine, Gabriel!
     While Man is on earth, he must dine;
     and I do better myself on a certain nourishment.
     Remember Cana of Galilee!

GABRIEL:                Cana of Galilee!
     Really . . .

         *He goes out.*

FAITH:       It is the second step that counts.
     My lord, I can say nothing now to cheer
     a broken heart; only that mine too
     broke; we are not adult till then—O
     we are not even young; the second step,
     the perseverance into the province of death,
     is a hard thing; then there is no return.
     Most dear lord, if I could do you good,
     I would; as it is—

MAN:                O Faith, Faith, I loved her.

FAITH: Yes.

MAN:       I loved her; God knows how I loved her.

FAITH: Therefore God shall make all things well—
     O agony! O bounteous and fell judgment!— . . .
     When you want me, if you want me, I will come
     quicker than you can think. The Peace be with you,
     and Love which is all substance in all things made.

         *She goes out.*

MAN: A second step . . . a second step in love . . .
     What, O almighty Christ, what of the third?

# SANTA CLAUS

*A Morality*

## E. E. CUMMINGS

FOR FRITZ WITTELS

# Editor's Preface: SANTA CLAUS

Although the work of e. e. cummings (as he customarily writes his name) has seemed esoteric to many readers, since his first book, *The Enormous Room*, published in 1922, he has established his reputation as one of the most serious and competent American poets. He has explored a variety of literary forms which indicate the range of his sensibility and imagination. The son of a Cambridge minister, he has memorialized his father's life and work in a most penetrating interpretation which begins with the lines:

> my father moved through dooms of love
> through sames of am through haves of give. . . .

Whether it is his conscious intent or not, Cummings's prose as well as his poetry expresses the paradoxes of life and the fulfillments that are contrary to the ways of the world and the rational expectations of man. It is for this reason that his work possesses hidden resources and religious meanings. The same may be said of *Santa Claus*, a morality that deals with Santa Claus, who wants to give to a world that does not want to receive, and Death, who wishes to take and can find no one who is ready to give. While the play abounds in satire, it concludes on the note that it is love alone that abides and it is through love that one's self-identity is realized.

# CHARACTERS

DEATH
SANTA CLAUS
MOB
CHILD
WOMAN

DEATH, *strolling—he wears black tights on which the bones of his skeleton are vividly suggested by daubs of white paint, and his mask imitates crudely the face of a fleshless human skull. Enter, slowly and despondently, a prodigiously paunchy figure in faded red motheaten Santa Claus costume, with the familiar Santa Claus mask-face of a bewhiskered jolly old man.*

DEATH: Something wrong, brother?
SANTA CLAUS:                 Yes.
DEATH:                   Sick?
SANTA CLAUS:                       Sick at heart.
DEATH: What seems to be the trouble? Come—speak out.
SANTA CLAUS: I have so much to give; and nobody will take.
DEATH: My problem is also one of distribution, only it happens to be the other way round.
SANTA CLAUS: The other way round?
DEATH:                   Quite.
SANTA CLAUS:                 What do you mean?
DEATH:                         I mean
I have so much to take; and nobody will give.
SANTA CLAUS: Strange.
DEATH:         Strange, indeed. But this is even stranger: I'm certain I can help you.
SANTA CLAUS:               Very kind—
DEATH: Tut, tut; who helps another helps himself.
Now if I may be allowed to analyze your case—
SANTA CLAUS: Analyze?
DEATH:         Listen. You're trying to give people something —right?

SANTA CLAUS: Right.

DEATH: And people won't take it?

SANTA CLAUS: Right.

DEATH: Why not?

SANTA CLAUS: Why not, indeed; I wish I knew.

DEATH: Because, my poor misguided friend, they can't.

SANTA CLAUS: Can't?

DEATH: Cannot.

SANTA CLAUS: But surely nothing could be simpler
• than taking something which is freely offered?

DEATH: You're speaking of a true or actual world.
Imagine, if you can, a world so blurred
that its inhabitants are one another
—an idiotic monster of negation:
so timid, it would rather starve itself
eternally than run the risk of choking;
so greedy nothing satisfies its hunger
but always huger quantities of nothing—
a world so lazy that it cannot dream;
so blind, it worships its own ugliness:
a world so false, so trivial, so unso,
phantoms are solid by comparison.
But no—you can't imagine such a world.

SANTA CLAUS: Any more than such a world could imagine
me.

DEATH: Very good. Now as to this ungivable something
you're trying to give, this gift which nobody can take
—what, just exactly, is it?

SANTA CLAUS: I don't know.

DEATH: I do.

SANTA CLAUS: Do you?

DEATH: Yes. It is understanding.

SANTA CLAUS: Understanding?

DEATH: Yes.

SANTA CLAUS: Tell me, how do you know?

DEATH: You told me, when you answered "I don't know."

And when you said you had something to give, you told
    me;
for isn't understanding the only gift?
Well, there's precisely your predicament.
We are not living in an age of gifts:
this is an age of salesmanship, my friend;
and you are heavy with the only thing
which simply can't be sold.

SANTA CLAUS:                May I ask you a question?
DEATH: Go right ahead.
SANTA CLAUS:            What's the easiest thing to sell?
DEATH: Knowledge.
SANTA CLAUS:        Knowledge—without understanding?
DEATH: Correct.
SANTA CLAUS:    No.
DEATH:                Absolutely.
SANTA CLAUS:                    But that's absurd!
DEATH: Absurd—and also tragic; yet a fact.
    In this empty un-understanding world
    anyone can sell knowledge; everybody wants knowledge,
    and there's no price people won't pay to get it.
    —Become a Scientist and your fortune's made.
SANTA CLAUS: Scientist—?
DEATH:          Or, in plain English, a knowledge-salesman.
SANTA CLAUS: I have no knowledge . . . only under-
    standing—
DEATH: Forget your understanding for a while,
        (*he plucks off* SANTA CLAUS' *mask, revealing a
        young man's face*)
    and as for knowledge, why, don't let that worry you:
        (*he slips off his own mask, revealing a fleshless
        human skull, and crams the skull mask over the
        young face of* SANTA CLAUS)
    once people hear the magic name of "Science"
        (*slipping the* SANTA CLAUS *mask over his own skull
        face*)

you can sell people anything—except understanding.

SANTA CLAUS: Yes?

DEATH: Anything at all.

SANTA CLAUS: You mean, provided—

DEATH: Provided nothing!

SANTA CLAUS: You don't mean to tell me
I could sell people something which didn't exist?

DEATH: Why not? You don't suppose people exist, do you?

SANTA CLAUS: Don't people exist?

DEATH: People?—I'll say they don't!
I wish to heaven they did exist; in that case
I shouldn't be the skeleton I am.
No—in this "Science" game, this "knowledge" racket,
infinity's your limit; but remember:
the less something exists, the more people want it.

SANTA CLAUS: I can't seem to think of anything which
doesn't exist
—perhaps you could help me.

DEATH: How about a wheelmine?

SANTA CLAUS: A wheelmine?

DEATH: Surely a wheelmine doesn't exist
and never will, and never has existed.

SANTA CLAUS: A wheelmine . . . but that's perfectly fantastic!

DEATH: Why say "fantastic" when you mean "Scientific"?
—Well, I'll be strolling. So long, Mister Scientist!


SCENE TWO

(SANTA CLAUS, *masked as* DEATH, *haranguing a Mob*)


SANTA CLAUS: Hear ye! Hear ye! Hear ye! I am a Scientist!
And just to prove it, ladies and gentlemen,
I'll tell you anything you want to know.
—Go ahead: ask me something; anything.

VOICE: Mister.

SANTA CLAUS: Yes?

VOICE: How can I make a million dollars?

SANTA CLAUS: A million dollars—is that all you want?

VOICE: Well, I could use a couple, if you've got 'em.

SANTA CLAUS: Could you use ten or twelve?

VOICE: Ten or twelve million dollars? —O, boy!

SANTA CLAUS: You're kidding.

VOICE: Kidding! Why, you can't tell me anything I wouldn't do for ten or twelve million.

SANTA CLAUS: I'll bet you I can.

VOICE: O yeah? How much'll you bet?

SANTA CLAUS: I'll bet a dollar.

VOICE: You're on! What wouldn't I do?

SANTA CLAUS: You wouldn't spend five hundred measly dollars

for a share of preferred stock in a giltedged wheelmine.

VOICE: Wheelmine?

SANTA CLAUS: Don't tell me you never heard of a wheelmine!

VOICE: Well, maybe—

SANTA CLAUS: Maybe you don't even know what wheels are.

VOICE: Wheels?

SANTA CLAUS: They're the things that make the world go round.

VOICE: Sure, I know wheels—why, wheels are everywhere.

SANTA CLAUS: I'll say they are: including people's heads —now can you tell me what a mine is?

VOICE: A mine? Why, a mine is a hole in the ground.

SANTA CLAUS: Now can you tell me

what one and one make?
VOICE: One and one?
SANTA CLAUS: Yes.
VOICE: Two.
SANTA CLAUS: You're wonderful! My boy, with a brain like that
you ought to be President of the United States
—now listen carefully: one and one make two;
but what do wheel and mine make?
VOICE: They make wheelmine.
SANTA CLAUS: Congratulations! You know everything—
VOICE: But people don't dig wheels out of the ground.
SANTA CLAUS: I'll say people don't!
VOICE: Well, who does?
SANTA CLAUS: Can't you guess?
VOICE: Science?
SANTA CLAUS: By Jove, you're just another Einstein!
I certainly was a fool to bet with you
—here's your certificate of preferred stock.
VOICE: Here's your five hundred dollars—
SANTA CLAUS: Five hundred? Listen:
you may have been dealing with conmen all your life,
but I'm a Scientist: here's the dollar you won.
VOICE: Thanks, mister.
SANTA CLAUS: You're quite welcome. —Anybody else?
VOICES: Me! Me, too! Gimme!
SANTA CLAUS: —Just a moment. Friends,
it never shall be said that Science favored
or slighted anyone. Remember: Science
is no mere individual. Individuals
are, after all, nothing but human beings;
and human beings are corruptible:
for (as you doubtless know) to err is human.
Think—only think! for untold centuries
this earth was overrun by human beings!
Think: it was not so many years ago

that individuals could be found among us!
O those dark ages! What a darkness, friends!
But now that hideous darkness turns to light;
the flame of Science blazes far and wide:
Science, impartial and omnipotent,
before whose superhuman radiance
all dark prescientific instincts vanish.
Think—only think! at last the monster, man,
is freed from his obscene humanity!
—While men were merely men, and nothing more,
what was equality? A word. A dream.
Men never could be equal—why? Because
equality's the attribute of supermen
like you, and you, and you, and you. And therefore
(superladies and supergentlemen)
when the impartial ear of Science hears
your superhuman voices crying "gimme,"
Science responds in Its omnipotence
"let there be enough wheelmine stock for all."
VOICES: Adda baby! Long live Science! Hooray for wheelmines!


SCENE THREE

(DEATH, *masked as* SANTA CLAUS, *strolling: angry voices offstage*)

DEATH: I've got him now!
(*Enter* SANTA CLAUS, *masked as* DEATH, *running*)
—Hello there: what's your hurry?
SANTA CLAUS: Help—quick—for mercy's sake—they're
after me—
DEATH: After you?
SANTA CLAUS:     After me, yes! They're coming!

DEATH: Who's coming?

SANTA CLAUS: Everybody!

DEATH: Why?

SANTA CLAUS: It's the accident—

DEATH: Accident?

SANTA CLAUS: To the miners in the mine—

DEATH: Miners?

SANTA CLAUS: Wheelminers!

DEATH: Are you crazy?

SANTA CLAUS: I don't know—will you tell me something?

DEATH: Tell you what.

SANTA CLAUS: Does a wheelmine exist, or doesn't it?

DEATH: A wheelmine?

SANTA CLAUS: Yes.

DEATH: Don't be ridiculous.

SANTA CLAUS: You mean it doesn't exist?

DEATH: Exist? Of course not!

SANTA CLAUS: In other words, a wheelmine is nonexistent isn't it?

DEATH: Perfectly.

SANTA CLAUS: O, then tell me; tell me:
how can it maim, how can it mutilate;
how can it turn mere people into monsters:
answer me—how!

DEATH: My friend, you've forgotten something:
namely, that people, like wheelmines, don't exist
—two negatives, you know, make an affirmative.
Now if I may be allowed to analyze—

SANTA CLAUS: Do you want to die?

DEATH: I die? Ha-ha-ha-ha! How could Death die?

SANTA CLAUS: —Death?

DEATH: Didn't you know?

SANTA CLAUS: I'm going mad. You: tell me,
whatever you are, Death or the Devil, tell me:
how can I prove I'm not to blame for the damage
caused by an accident which never happened

to people who are nonexistent?

DEATH: You can't.

SANTA CLAUS: My God—but what am I going to do, then?

DEATH: Do?
why, my dear fellow, it looks to me as if
you'd have to prove you don't exist yourself.

SANTA CLAUS: But that's absurd!

DEATH: —And tragic; yet a fact.
So make it snappy, Mister Santa Claus!
(*Exit. From the opposite direction enter Mob,
furious: a little girl follows*)

VOICES: There he is! Grab him! Listen, Mister Science
—you're going to hang for this!

SANTA CLAUS: What do you mean?

A VOICE: You know what we mean!

SANTA CLAUS: Why, who do you think I am?

ANOTHER: Think? We don't think; we know! You're
Science!

SANTA CLAUS: Science?

ANOTHER: Science—the crook who sold us stock in a
wheelmine!

ANOTHER: Science—the beast who buries men alive!

SANTA CLAUS: —Stop!
Ladies and gentlemen, this is all a mistake:
I am not Science; wheelmines don't exist,
and as for burying people alive—that's nonsense.

VOICES: We say you're Science! Down with Science!

SANTA CLAUS: —Wait!
Ladies and gentlemen: if you all have been
deceived by some impostor—so have I.
If you all have been tricked and ruined—so have I.
And so has every man and woman, I say.
I say it, and you feel it in your hearts:
we are all of us no longer glad and whole,
we have all of us sold our spirits into death,
we are all of us the sick parts of a sick thing,

we have all of us lost our living honesty,
and so we are all of us not any more ourselves.
—Who can tell truth from falsehood any more?
I say it, and you feel it in your hearts:
No man or woman on this big small earth.
—How should our sages miss the mark of life,
and our most skillful players lose the game?
your hearts will tell you, as my heart has told me:
because all know, and no one understands.
—O, we are all so very full of knowing
that we are empty: empty of understanding;
but, by that emptiness, I swear to you
(and if I lie, ladies and gentlemen,
hang me a little higher than the sky)
all men and every woman may be wrong;
but nobody who lives can fool a child.
—Now I'll abide the verdict of that little girl
over there, with the yellow hair and the blue eyes.
I'll simply ask her who I am; and whoever
she says I am, I am: is that fair enough?

VOICES: Okay! Sure! Why not? Fine! A swell idea!
The kid will tell him who he is, all right!
Everybody knows!

SANTA CLAUS:     —Silence! (*To* CHILD) Don't be afraid:
who am I?

CHILD:     You are Santa Claus.

VOICES:                . . . Santa Claus?

CHORUS: Ha-ha-ha-ha—there ain't no Santa Claus!

SANTA CLAUS: Then, ladies and gentlemen, I don't exist.
And since I don't exist, I am not guilty.
And since I am not guilty, I am innocent.
—Goodbye! And, next time, look before you leap.
     (*Exit. Mob disintegrates slowly, muttering*)

SCENE FOUR

(SANTA CLAUS, *masked as* DEATH, *strolling*)

SANTA CLAUS: That was a beautiful child . . . If only I
    were sure—
        (*Enter* DEATH, *masked as* SANTA CLAUS)
    Hello there!
DEATH:        O—hello. You're looking better.
SANTA CLAUS: Better? Why not?
DEATH:                  I take it, my advice
    proved efficacious?
SANTA CLAUS:        Death, you've saved my life!
DEATH: You don't say so.
SANTA CLAUS:        Absolutely!
DEATH:               Well, my friend,
    I'm going to ask you to do me a favor now.
SANTA CLAUS: Go right ahead!
DEATH:              I've got a heavy date
    with a swell jane up the street a little way,
    but something tells me she prefers plump fellows.
    Will you give me your fat and take my skeleton?
SANTA CLAUS: With all the pleasure in the world, old-timer;
    and I'll throw in a wheelmine, just for luck!
DEATH: No wheelmines, thank you.
        (*They undress*)
SANTA CLAUS:        That was a beautiful child.
DEATH: —Child?
SANTA CLAUS:    I was . . .
DEATH:           Thinking of the old days, eh?
    Well, children are your specialty.
SANTA CLAUS:        I love them.
  I have always loved them, and I shall love them always.

(*They exchange costumes, and dress as each other*)

DEATH: De gustibus non disputandum est;
or, in good American: I prefer women.

SANTA CLAUS: Have you ever loved a woman?

DEATH: Pardon me,
did you say "loved"?

SANTA CLAUS: I said "loved."

DEATH: No. Have you?

SANTA CLAUS: Once.

DEATH: Well, everybody makes mistakes
—I'll see you later. So long, Mister Death!

(*Exit* DEATH *as* SANTA CLAUS, *paunchily swaggering.
From the opposite direction enter, on tiptoe,* CHILD)

CHILD: Hello.

SANTA CLAUS: —Well, hello!

CHILD: You remember me?

SANTA CLAUS: Of course I do.

CHILD: You're different, aren't you.

SANTA CLAUS: Yes;
I am.

CHILD: Much thinner.

SANTA CLAUS: Do you like me this way?

CHILD: I guess . . . I like you any way—if you're you.

SANTA CLAUS: I guess that makes me very happy.

CHILD: But I guess . . .

SANTA CLAUS: What do you guess?

CHILD: You could be happier,
couldn't you?

SANTA CLAUS: Perhaps I could.

CHILD: —Because you're looking
for somebody?

SANTA CLAUS: I am.

CHILD: And I'm looking for somebody, too.

SANTA CLAUS: Somebody very beautiful?

CHILD: O, yes;
she's very beautiful. And very sad.

SANTA CLAUS: Very beautiful and very sad.
Tell me: is she sad because she lost you?
CHILD: Because we lost each other—and somebody else.
　　(*Confused voices, far offstage*)
Goodbye—
SANTA CLAUS: Why are you going?
CHILD: 　　　　　　　　　　Don't be afraid:
we'll find her.
SANTA CLAUS: 　I should never be afraid
of anything in the sky and on the earth
and anywhere and everywhere and nowhere,
if I were only sure of one thing.
CHILD: 　　　　　　　　　　What.
SANTA CLAUS: Who was that somebody else?
CHILD: 　　　　　　　　　　　That somebody
we lost?
SANTA CLAUS: Yes.
CHILD: 　　　　Can't you guess who?
SANTA CLAUS: 　　　　　　　　Can I?
CHILD: 　　　　　　　　　　　　You.
　　(*She dances away*)


SCENE FIVE

　(*Enter* WOMAN, *weeping*)

WOMAN: Knowledge has taken love out of the world
and all the world is empty empty empty:
men are not men any more in all the world
for a man who cannot love is not a man,
and only a woman in love can be a woman;
and, from their love alone, joy is born—joy!
Knowledge has taken love out of the world
and all the world is joyless joyless joyless.

Come, death! for I have lost my joy and I
have lost my love and I have lost myself.

(*Enter* SANTA CLAUS, *as* DEATH)

You have wanted me. Now take me.

SANTA CLAUS: Now and forever.

WOMAN: How fortunate is dying, since I seem
to hear his voice again.

VOICES (*offstage*): Dead! Dead!

WOMAN: Could the world be emptier?

(*Tumult offstage. She cringes*)

SANTA CLAUS: Don't be afraid.

WOMAN: O voice of him I loved more than my life,
protect me from that deathless lifelessness—.

(*Enter Mob in procession, reeling and capering:
the last Mobsters carry a pole, from which dangles
the capering and reeling corpse of* DEATH *disguised
as* SANTA CLAUS)

CHORUS: Dead. Dead. Dead. Dead. Dead.

VOICES: Hooray! Dead; yes, dead: dead. Hooray!
Science is dead! Dead. Science is dead!

VOICE: He'll never sell another wheelmine—never!

VOICES: Dead! Hooray! Dead! Hooray! Dead!

VOICE: The filthy lousy stinking son of a bitch.

CHORUS: Hooray hooray hooray hooray hooray!

A VOICE: He fooled us once, and once was once too much!

ANOTHER: He never fooled us, pal: it was the kid.

(WOMAN *starts*)

ANOTHER: Yeah, but the second time—boy, was that good!

ANOTHER: I'll say it was!

ANOTHER: Did you see the look she gave him?

ANOTHER: Did you hear her say *"that* isn't Santa Claus"?

(WOMAN *turns: sees the dangling effigy—recoils
from the real* SANTA CLAUS)

CHORUS: Ha-ha-ha-ha—there ain't no Santa Claus!

(*Exit Mob, reeling and capering, booing whistling
screeching*)

WOMAN: Yes, the world could be emptier.

SANTA CLAUS:                                   Now and—

WOMAN:                                                        Never.

I had remembered love—but who am I?

Thanks, Death, for making love remember me.

> (*Enter dancing Child: sees Woman, and rushes to her arms*)

WOMAN: Joy—yes! My (yes; O, yes) my life my love
my soul myself . . . —Not yours, Death!

SANTA CLAUS (*unmasking*):                    No.

WOMAN (*kneeling to* SANTA CLAUS):                    Ours.

# LET MAN LIVE

*A Play in One Act*

Pär Lagerkvist

# Editor's Preface: LET MAN LIVE

*Let Man Live* (*Låt Människan Leva*), as the title implies, is an affirmation of man not only against the enormous crimes of this century but also the long story of man's inhumanity to man. This has been one of the major themes of Pär Lagerkvist, the Swedish author and Nobel Prize winner. Although he made few accommodations to public taste over the years, his integrity as a human being and an artist has won him renown. This particular work itself does not fit into the accepted pattern of dramatic conflict and dialogue. In an effort to characterize this work some have called it a "stage oratorium" and others a "morality play." The theme, which is deceptive in its simplicity, attempts to demonstrate that man should not judge and that when he attempts to do so he brings about evil by distorting the processes of truth and justice. Fourteen characters from Christ and Socrates down through Giordano Bruno and Jeanne d'Arc to a World War II underground figure from Norway and an American Negro emerge before a backdrop of darkness on a bare stage and relate the circumstances of their martyrdom. The struggle is an internal one rather than a struggle between persons, the characters being stripped of externals so that the innermost self may be seen.

# CHARACTERS

RICHARD
JOE
COMTESSE DE LA ROCHE-MONTFAUCON
A SERF
A WITCH
GIORDANO BRUNO
THE INCA CHIEF
JEANNE D'ARC
PAOLO MALATESTA
FRANCESCA DA RIMINI
A CHRISTIAN MARTYR
JESUS
JUDAS ISCARIOT
SOCRATES

CHORUS OF VOICES (*out of the darkness on the stage*): Who is the accused? Who is the accuser? Who is the judge? (*The stage is lit. All the characters stand drawn up in a semi-circle. Behind them it is dark.*)

ALL: We are the accused! We are the accusers! We are the accused! We are the accusers! Who is the judge?

A SERF (*in ragged smock and patched trousers steps out of the semi-circle. Goes downstage center*): I am François, hanged because I stole a shoulder of mutton. (*Bows. Goes back to his place.*)

COMTESSE DE LA ROCHE-MONTFAUCON (*steps forward in the same way*): Comtesse de la Roche-Montfaucon, guillotined by the mob on the fourth of October, 1793— *Ces sales cochons!* (*Returns to her place*)

GIORDANO BRUNO (*comes forward*): Giordano Bruno. To the stake for the Truth. (*Returns*)

THE WITCH (*comes forward*): Buried alive on All Saints Day, 1634. For me the day of resurrection will never come. (*Returns*)

(PAOLO *and* FRANCESCA, *always side by side holding hands, come forward to the middle of the stage*)

PAOLO (*bows with his hand to his heart*): Paolo.

FRANCESCA (*in a similar manner*): Francesca.

PAOLO (*after they have again clasped hands*): Killed because we loved each other.

(*They return to their place*)

RICHARD (*comes forward*): Richard, aged seventeen, executed because we had a radio transmitter. (*Returns*)

JOE (*comes forward*): Joe Brown, lynched in Columbia, South Carolina, in the spring of 1922. (*Returns*)

THE MARTYR (*comes forward*): Torn to pieces by wild

103

beasts because I believed in God's loving son, the Saviour of the World. (*Returns*)

THE INCA CHIEF (*comes forward; kneels and bows his head*): Beheaded together with our whole people, by unknown white men. Their god was mightier than ours. (*Rises. Returns*)

JUDAS (*comes forward*): I am Judas Iscariot, who hanged himself. (*Returns*)

JEANNE D'ARC (*comes forward*): Jeanne d'Arc of Domremy. Died for France. (*Returns*)

SOCRATES (*comes forward*): Socrates the Athenian, who drained the cup of poison. (*Returns to his place in the semi-circle*)

ALL: We accuse! We accuse! We accuse!

JESUS (*steps out of the semi-circle, goes down to the center of the stage*): I am Jesus, who was crucified. I accuse no one. (*Bows and returns to his place*)

JUDAS (*comes forward again*): Neither do I, for, as I said, I hanged myself. Of course I didn't intend to do that. What I meant to do was to have fun with the money. Thirty pieces of silver is not so bad. You can get a lot for that. Good food and good wine, as much as you can drink. And a girl to play around with afterwards—there are lots of fine girls in Jerusalem. I figured on letting myself go for once—Good Lord, a man is only human! But just for one evening! After that I was going to use the money quite differently. I was going to get hold of a stock of first-quality cloth, that I knew I could get for from twenty to twenty-five denarii—it was smuggled, see? Then I would go and offer it in the fine houses at a little less than the usual price. In that way I'd get still more money. And then I'd open a little shop where I'd sell anything that people thought they wanted, any rubbish whatever. And when I'd made enough money out of my little shop, I'd begin to operate on the exchange. That's where you can rake in the big money as easily as you like. And that way I'd get rich and have a fur overcoat and a car, and a house on the most expensive street, and a pretty wife and a pretty mistress, and so on, and there I'd be, with everything really first-class and genteel and comfortable. That's the way I had it figured out. That's what I pictured to myself. Good Lord, a man is only human, you know.

I didn't know that the man I sold was the Son of God. I didn't understand that till afterwards. And then it was too late. They had already taken him prisoner. I saw how they dragged him away, bound and manhandled— yes, I stood inside a doorway so that, thank God, he didn't see me. I was confused—a proper hangover— and I felt disgusted with myself. And when I thought over what I had done, well, I simply went out and hanged myself.

As far as that goes the money was already spent, so that in any event there would never have been a shop or anything else. Otherwise, perhaps, I might not have hanged myself, I can't tell. (*He takes his place again*)

GIORDANO BRUNO (*comes forward*): I am Giordano Bruno, martyr in the cause of science. Although things went so badly for me, my faith is unshaken and I am full of confidence where science is concerned. Science is destined to lead man along the right road, I'm convinced of that. It will abolish all prejudice and error and make the nations happy on earth. It will be a blessing for all humanity and will transform everything. Alas, I was not allowed to live in a time when this could happen. Had I been born several centuries later, I am certain that no heretic's pyre would have been built to suppress the truth. When I stood amid the faggots and the flames began to lick my body, I looked into the future, and it was light; you seemed to look into another world. That is where I would like to live, I whispered to myself, it would be good to be there. And then the smoke choked me. And after that I was never able to find out what happened. (*He returns to his place*)

RICHARD (*comes forward*): We put together a transmitter from a generator-tube and two amplifiers. We also had condensers, how we got them doesn't matter. And the antennas and all the lines and so on. It was a hell of a job; we spent several weeks on it and had a lot of fun. I've always been crazy about radio and all that sort of thing, and so were Helge and Ivar. We worked in our carpenter shop, we had turned it into a complete plant. And at last we had it assembled and could begin to broadcast. And then we went to Anton, who we knew must be one of the leaders of the underground, and told him all about it, and said we wanted to do our bit, and that was why we had made the set, and that it had a capacity of almost thirty watts. So they came and looked at it and found it was O.K. Then we began sending secret messages and reports that they brought us at night, and it was terribly exciting and we were highly praised for our work. But at last of course we were tracked down, for the general location from which the messages were sent was obvious, and they came along with their detectors, and the first thing we knew there they were. I was alone in the workshop when they came, I sometimes stayed there even when we were not sending because I liked to be there, and there was always something to putter about with. But Helge and Ivar were at school, and they never found out that they had been with me. That meant only one was caught. But of course they knew I couldn't have done the whole thing alone, so they worked on me a good deal. And then I was shot one Monday morning together with five others I didn't know.

What I am sorry about is that I'll never be able to meet Else again. She was the nicest and smartest girl I'd ever met, in fact there never was such a perfect peach. We'd been going together for a whole year when this happened and every evening we went out walking and visited a restaurant or dance hall or some place or other. And that evening I was caught I was going to meet her and I'm sure she walked up and down in the park waiting for me; I kept thinking of that all the time in my cell.

Now I'll never be able to go with any girl again. And I'll never be able to live either, for you can't say you've lived when you're only seventeen years old. And I'm sorry about that. Yes, I am. (*Steps back toward his place—but turns and comes forward again*) If they had let me live I should have become a radio-technician. (*Resumes his place among the rest*)

JOE (*comes forward*): I am Joe—I had a saxophone. I took an extra job in the evenings washing dishes at the Embassy to save up for it; I had to give my pay from the factory to my mother at home. I thought I'd go crazy the day I was able to buy it; it was so beautiful and shining, with its silver valves and bell-piece plated with gold on the inside, and it cost $210. But I never learned to play much on it, for when I went home that night from the Embassy they began to shout "Grab him!" "Grab him!"—I had taken the short cut through the park as usual, and it was only a few days after I had bought the saxophone. They shouted—there was a woman and a few other people shouting—and I couldn't understand what they were shouting about, only that it was something about "the nigger," and I began to run, I ran as fast as I could, I got crazy with fear and I just ran, and then they began to run after me, and they were all shouting, and over by the exit some others came up from the street and headed me off, rushed me and knocked me over—and kicked me—and . . .

(*He puts his hand over his eyes for a moment*)

I've never had any white girl. I've never wanted one.

I don't like them at all. I've not even danced with them; I don't like dancing with them. They don't really dance, not properly. Although they wanted me sometimes when they were drunk I never wanted them. They smell so strange, I think. I don't like them at all.

I'm very fond of dancing, it's more fun than anything I know. But I always danced with the colored girls and they are the only ones I like. They dance the way you ought to dance and with them everything is all right.

Now I'll never dance again. And I'll never learn to play my saxophone properly, though I know that I could have learned and it cost $210. Perhaps I might have got into a jazz band just as I dreamed of, it would have been wonderful to join a band and keep on playing all the time.

Now I'll never be able to play or dance any more. And never see any girls again. Neither Lizzie nor Peggy nor Bess, never any of them again. And I'll never get to walk on a street again, down Fourth Street or any other. It's so sad never to live any more. Never to laugh or be happy. And never to sit in the window and practise in the evenings when the work in the factory is over. I would have liked that so much. And it could so easily have been. And so many other things could have happened to me. So many, many things that I dreamed about.

I am Joe; I had a saxophone.

(*Bows and returns to his place*)

THE MARTYR (*comes forward*): While we sat and waited in the dungeon under the gallery, Marcus Flavius the Lydian said: "Let us not be downcast. Let us remind ourselves that this world is not good, but a difficult and evil place in which to live. Why then should we be distressed at leaving it? The earthly life is our prison, and should we not rejoice at escaping from it?" And everyone agreed with him. And Drusus, the son of

Silas, started a hymn—Our Redeemer Liveth—and we all sang it with him. And so we quieted our anguish. And the boxing-match went on outside and we could hear the shouts and yells from the galleries. But when the noise stopped we knew that the match was over and that our time would soon come. Then we took leave of one another and slowly pressed one another's hands. And when the warder came to fetch us we fell upon our knees and prayed: "God, our Father, into Thy hands we commit our souls." And then we arose and went out into the arena.

*(Returns to his place in the semi-circle.*

*An early Christian hymn is played. After a time it gradually changes into a modern blues melody.* JOE *and* RICHARD *leave their places and begin, each by himself, to dance to it with arms outstretched as if each were holding a woman partner. When the dance has gone on a time, the music suddenly stops. They then stop dancing but each stands for a moment or two with outstretched arms in the same pose. Then they let their arms sink. They go back to their places.*

*A chorus of birds is heard.*

PAOLO *and* FRANCESCA *begin to walk around on the stage, close together.)*

FRANCESCA: What a beautiful evening. The whole garden is filled with the perfume of roses and the nightingale is singing in the myrtle-hedge. About what, do you suppose?

PAOLO: About our love. How could he sing of anything else? About how we love each other.

FRANCESCA: Yes, how we love each other. (*They stand and listen*)

PAOLO: Is this a moment, a fragment of time, something just now? No, dearest, that can't be. Time doesn't exist, nothing exists except love.

FRANCESCA: No, nothing except love . . . (*They walk on. She stops and looks down.*) How quietly the river flows! It scarcely seems to move.

PAOLO: Why do you wonder at that? The trees are not moving either. Everything is still because we love each other. The very stream of time . . .

FRANCESCA: I shall pick rose-leaves and strew them over the water to see if the stream is moving.

PAOLO: Dearest, don't. Don't break the spell that holds us bound.

FRANCESCA: Why are you afraid of that? Why are you afraid of anything? You ought not to be. What do you think we have to fear? (*Stoops and breaks off a rose, pulls it apart and strews the petals over the water*) Look, they are moving. They are gliding away.

PAOLO: Now time has come back. Now the seconds are flying, the minutes, the hours. Now we shall soon die.

FRANCESCA: Don't call it dying. Take my hand, dearest, and let us follow the stream. (*They go together along the stream, then back to their places among the others*)

JEANNE D'ARC (*comes forward*): I too have loved greatly, but I loved a country. I never experienced any other love. Now I feel perhaps it is rather sad to think about that. For after all I was an ordinary mortal girl and could have wished to live like the others. That is what I'd have liked if it had been possible. I might have married one of the boys in Domremy, one I liked very much, and lived happily as a farmer's wife on some farm there. But the voices had something else in mind. And then it had to be that way. I do not regret it, please don't believe that I do. But you mustn't think either that it is so pleasant to give up everything that ordinary people are able to enjoy. My only joy was to sacrifice myself for my country, and that was a painful joy.

And I was never able to find out if it did any good

But I hope it did. I hope that France was saved and that afterwards she was a happy country. (*She returns*)

COMTESSE DE LA ROCHE-MONTFAUCON (*comes forward*): I don't care a rap for what you call "the people," in whose name it pleased you to accuse me. I don't even know what they are. I've heard there's supposed to be something of that kind, but I've had no reason to come into any close contact with them. So it's quite possible that in my ignorance I've managed to offend them. In that case I have no regrets. I prefer not to have had anything to do with the mob. That is my defense—if I need any.

Have I anything further to plead? Nothing whatever! Will you permit the "citizeness" to retire again to your dirty jail?—Accept my thanks, gentlemen. (*Returns*)

THE SERF (*comes forward, fingering his cap*): Yes, yes, I really did it. Yes, I really took it. You see when I went into the larder there were so many shoulders of mutton hanging up and I thought if I take one it will never be noticed, it can't matter much, can it, with all these here? I hadn't thought of taking a shoulder, I was sent there for something quite different, it was to get salt, but I thought the shoulder would come in handy, for at home we were badly off for food and my wife was whining all the time for something to give the children—no, no, I'm not defending myself, I don't do that, I just want to say I took it—yes, yes, I *stole* it, certainly I *stole* it, and I knew quite well that was a bad sin against both God and man. And especially against Herr Guibert, the bailiff, and against Herr Raurent, the tenant—yes, against His Grace, too, of course, yes, certainly, but I didn't think of that, because I have never seen him. Yes, certainly, it was wrong, very wrong —I understand that now. God forgive me my sin. (*He stands listening and nods as if in agreement*) Yes— Yes— That's right— That's right— (*Shudders as if someone had given him a blow. Goes back to his place in the semi-circle.*)

THE WITCH (*comes forward and falls down on her knees*): I will confess! I will confess! I want to unburden my heart and confess everything. I have associated with devils all my life; even in my childhood I had been with them, they came to me in the night, I dared not go to sleep because I knew they would be coming. And I have had intercourse with Satan himself; many a time he came to me, and he is hairy like a goat and smells like a goat. I never wanted to do it, but I had to do it all the same; he decides and I have to do what he says, or else I never get any peace. He is my Lord and I must cleave to him, he is the only one who bothers about me. I have prayed to God in heaven, but He doesn't take the least notice of me, but Satan helps me, and he is like our goat, the one we had when I was a little girl and I was so fond of. But I never got any pleasure out of it, never the least pleasure out of it. I only did it so I could get some peace. That's how it is, that's how it is. Now I've confessed everything. And now you can do what you want to me. I can never be punished enough. And nothing can be so hard as living.

SOCRATES (*comes forward. He sees her lying there wringing her hands*): Are you a barbarian? (*When she does not answer*): Why are you wringing your hands? Because you are going to die?

THE WITCH (*listens to something in front of her, does not hear him*): Yes, yes, I want to die— Yes, bury me deep in the earth where I belong. Bury me deep in the earth, so that at last I can find peace. (*Rises and goes away— out into the darkness*)

SOCRATES: She seems to have been condemned for something just as I was. But she must have belonged to a people unknown to me.

As for myself, I received my sentence several days

ago. And now all I await is its execution. Men have judged me. And so the judgment is quite imperfect. Men themselves are imperfect, so it is not surprising if their judgments are imperfect too. I do not mean by this that it is harsh or cruel. Certainly not, I mean quite the contrary. They certainly meant to make it cruel, but their lack of foresight, as usual, led them completely astray. For look here, when they desire now to punish me severely, really severely, they take possession only of my body, which, as everyone can see, is quite worthless, extraordinarily defective. But my soul, that they permit to go free, they don't bother about it. Isn't that ridiculous? And my thoughts, the really criminal thing, the thing that they are punishing me for, those they just let go, they can travel anywhere at all, they simply don't bother to execute them. Ridiculous, isn't it? Surely they're just a lot of jokers!

Quite seriously, the fact is I have been haled before the wrong court. I have been condemned by men and by the laws of men—but I am subject to those of the gods. To divine law. I have nothing to do with their legal administration, I do not fall under this jurisdiction. And when they deal out my punishment which they think is so severe, it really means that they deliver me into the hands of the real law, that I am summoned before the court to which I am truly subject. Through the very punishment itself I am delivered to a higher court which is going to declare that their judgment was invalid. And is going to set me free. *Free.* Just as my judges themselves are free. I've already been summoned to appear before them and my soul already belongs to them. I already stand under divine protection.

Therefore it is only right that my accusers, men, have this morning unlocked my fetters, that they have sent their servant, the prison warder, to me in order to release me from them by his announcement: Today you die. Now I no longer have any power over you; now you are no longer mine.

A quite significant custom, is it not? A custom that must interest the thinker, the philosopher, because of its implications.

But why is the ship from Delos delayed? (*He looks for a moment out into the darkness*)

You see, among us it is ordained that no man may be deprived of his life while the ship of Apollo is on its way bearing the garlanded ones. As long as the vessel bearing the seven youths and the seven maidens who are dedicated to him, to the god of light, is on its way to and from Delos, whither they are sent to be bearers of his sacrifices. This is for us a holy time, a most holy time. But when they return from there, from their service in the temple of light, then once more life may be sacrificed, then once more blood may be shed, and the poisoned cup may be handed to me.

Yes, that may well seem to be a strange institution, it certainly may. But once for all it is so ordered, and is there really any reason to be surprised at it? You know what men are like. You know them, don't you? After all, you yourselves are men.

Yes, as I said, blood may be shed once more, guilty blood and innocent. Then everything goes back to daily routine, and nothing can be done about it. The holy time is at an end.

So I am wondering at the delay, why the ship does not anchor and the young people remove their garlands. (*Goes back to his place*)

CHORUS (*of them all*): We accuse! We accuse! We accuse!

JESUS (*comes forward*): You have so many accusations to lodge. You turn toward your judges and your destiny, and you are surely justified.

But I, whom shall I accuse? I cannot accuse you, can

I? No, for of course I had to be sacrificed, because that was precisely what was intended, and if you had not crucified me what would have become of my life—of its significance? And I cannot accuse God, for of course He meant well when He sent me to you; He hoped that my coming would help you. If it has not helped, neither He nor I is responsible. We have both done our best.

The question is whether *you* too have done your best. Well, what do you think yourselves? That is not easy to answer; indeed it is a hard question. It is not quite certain that you will have to answer "No" to it. It is quite true that you have behaved dreadfully. It is quite true that you have been guilty of the most terrible acts. But what chances had you to avoid that, how could you fulfill your high destiny and be quite different? One must know that before one can rightly judge your actions. Nor must one forget how much you have done that was good and beautiful, how much that shows you to be not entirely evil but makes up to some extent for your evil deeds. I don't want to be unjust. I shall try to do you justice. I recognize your difficulties and I know that it is not easy to be a man. One cannot say that it is an enviable lot.

My Father is full of reproaches against you; He judges you much more severely. For He has never lived among you. Then it may seem to you that He is not qualified to understand you. That one who has never himself experienced your lot cannot sit in judgment upon you. That He is altogether too unfamiliar with your difficulties and far too remote. Yes, He is. He is, in one way, a stranger in His own life, in the life He has created. And you are right in saying that He is very remote. He is far, far away. He lives in an entirely different world, you might say in an altogether different universe from the one you call yours. Unfortunately, that must be. He is a very lonely man. And He is an old man, too, who is beginning to get weary and dejected and who often feels bitter when He thinks back on his work and how much of it did not succeed, how much of it did not turn out as He had wished. I sometimes try to console Him and to encourage Him, but it is not easy when one has so little real reason for rejoicing, so few facts to point to. What He asks for is not words pulsing with hope, but realities. Therefore let me beg you not to be so evil and cruel but instead to try as far as possible to show the good side that I know you also possess. That would make it easier for me when I face my Father. And it would help me if you did not begin to despair. I do not want to do that, for then what would happen? I too must not cease to hope, however difficult it may be to hope. I am the light that was come to the world; I must bear that in mind. (*Returns to his place*)

THE INCA CHIEF (*comes forward; kneels*): Their god was stronger than ours. I only learned his name. They called him Christ. For his sake we had to die. (*Bows his head. Rises and goes—out into the darkness.*)

THE SERF (*right up by the footlights*): I'm not going to drop my charges just because Jesus does. I have the right to accuse, and I'm going to do it. I accuse you because of what you have done to me. You people, yes, you. Isn't it you who have oppressed me and squeezed me dry, let me wear myself to the bone for you—so that you could take life easy? For centuries I have slaved for you, starved for you and fared ill. And simply because I took that shoulder of mutton, you send me to the gallows. Is it so strange for a man to take a shoulder of mutton when his children are starving? Wouldn't you perhaps do the same? Thief! Are *you* the right people to say that? You who live only by stealing, by grabbing everything for yourselves. Who live by other men's misfortunes, by their being in hell! Who handle them as beasts, nay, worse than beasts, for you think they are of no value. How about your own value, then? Now I have to go to the gallows for your sake! So that you are sure to eat your fill, so that, for God's sake, no one shall dare to touch your food, but you shall always have a lot more than you can eat. Because I took one of all your shoulders of mutton. "Shame upon you!" I say before I go. (*Leaves stage*)

THE COMTESSE DE LA ROCHE-MONTFAUCON (*comes forward to the footlights; yells and roars can be heard*): Here I am standing in the cart that rattles through the streets on the way to the guillotine. I don't sit as the others do! *I am standing!* So that you can see me better, you curs! Now I have got to know you. Now I have got to know the people in whose name thousands have been sent to death, in whose name rivers of blood are flowing. You are a pack of curs. Curs! I despise you. I despise you still more now that I have got to know you. And I gladly leave a world that is ruled by the mob, by people like you. Gladly, do you hear me? Don't think I'm afraid. We've never been afraid of ourselves! And we are not degenerate! Come with me to the scaffold and you shall see how a noblewoman dies. (*Exit*)

JEANNE D'ARC (*comes forward to the footlights. A sound as if faggots were being thrown onto a pyre*): Now they are preparing my pyre, I can hear. Now I must soon mount it. I am called and I go. I never had any choice, and so in a way it was not so hard. But I blame all of you for my death. (*She goes out into the darkness*)

THE MARTYR (*comes forward to the footlights; kneels*): Heavenly Father, into Thy hands I commend my spirit. (*Remains there for a while. Then rises and goes out.*)

JESUS (*comes forward to the footlights. Several hammer blows are heard*): Now they are nailing my cross together. I can hear it. So I must go now.

You have not done right in this. But in spite of everything I shall not condemn you. You have crucified so
many. I do not condemn you especially because you do
it to me. And the meaning of my death is that it should
serve a greater purpose than the others'. I hope this
will be so. But only time will make that clear.

And even if I too die in vain I shall never cease to
love you. So great is my love for you.

Farewell. Farewell. Farewell one and all of you.
(*Exit*)

> (RICHARD *and* JOE *come forward to the footlights
> hand in hand*)

RICHARD: We say goodbye now and go out into the darkness. (*They bow and go*)

JUDAS (*comes to the footlights with a length of rope in his
hand*): Here is the rope with which I intend to go and
hang myself. I didn't believe my life would end this
way. But it's a strange thing—I have no desire to live
any longer. I saw Him go by—and I realized at once
that I no longer wished to live.

Was He the Son of God? Yes, He probably was, but
I am not quite certain even of that. But, what I am
certain of is that I betrayed Him. And that it was on
my account that He was bound and beaten. And so I
wish to live no longer.

It wasn't really true what I said about probably not
hanging myself if the money hadn't come to an end.
It wasn't really true. A man isn't quite so bad as people
say or even as he believes himself. I did something that
was not right. There was something that I betrayed. I
don't quite know what it was. But there *was* something
—and so I don't wish to live any longer.

I too say farewell, although probably no one cares.
(*Exit*)

SOCRATES (*comes forward to the footlights. One hears flapping sails being lowered. He stands and listens. Then*):

I regret, my friends, that we cannot finish this conversation which, even if in a merely cursory manner, touched a theme that must have a certain interest for every man. I must go now, for the hours sacred to the god of light are over, and the poison that men offer each other to drink is standing in a cup that is intended for me. Do not think that I have any objection to draining it. Not at all. I am an old man and life has no longer any charm for me. The only thing that still tempts me is the search for truth, the exchange of thoughts that can lead to an increased knowledge of truth. I am a so-called philosopher, as you perhaps know, and am very fond of fruitful conversation. But every exchange of thoughts must come to an end, and every chain of thought has one link at which the seeker after truth must break off and admit that as far as he is concerned the chain does not have any more links. As circumstances have now ordained that I cannot stay any longer, I beg you to forgive me for leaving you although we have not reached any clear ideas about the matter we have been concerned with. It is, however, with the hope that we have discussed these issues to the best of our ability that I break off and go to deliver this worthless body to decay and my soul to the gods. (*Exit*)

GIORDANO BRUNO (*comes forward to the footlights*): Now I stand in the fire and look into the future. I see that it is bright, that there is an entirely different world. Yes, an entirely different world.—What a wonderful sight! You cannot see it, but I, I here on the fire, I see it. That it is filled with light.—There I would like to live.—There I would like to live.—(*Stands for a moment and looks forward in ecstasy. Exit*)

(PAOLO *and* FRANCESCA *come in side by side*)

FRANCESCA: How lovely it is to walk along the river! How lovely it is to be alive!

PAOLO: Yes, nothing is so lovely as to live. (*They walk on.*

*He stops and clutches his heart.*) Did you feel the dagger go through your heart, dearest?

FRANCESCA: Yes, and did you, through yours?

PAOLO: Yes. But how is it that we do not fall to the ground?

FRANCESCA: Fall to the ground? Why should we? Do you think death has such power? How could it? It is life that is mighty and not death. It is life that is great and infinite—although men do their best to deny it.

PAOLO: Yes, that is true. It is life that is great and infinite. Come, dearest, let us live! Live forever! (*The stars of heaven light up. It seems as if they walk out into their midst.*) Let us go through the starry portals.

FRANCESCA: Through arches of Milky Ways.

PAOLO: Let everything be endless.

FRANCESCA: Everything *is* endless.

PAOLO: Let man rejoice without end.

FRANCESCA: Let man live.

PAOLO: Without end.

FRANCESCA: Let man live.

PAOLO: Let man live.

FRANCESCA: Let man live.


**CURTAIN**

# IT SHOULD HAPPEN TO A DOG

*A Play in One Act*

Wolf Mankowitz

# Editor's Preface: IT SHOULD HAPPEN TO A DOG

*It Should Happen to a Dog,* says the author, "is a serio-comic strip, which, those who know the story of Jonah will see, is faithful to the original." Written by the well-known English novelist Wolf Mankowitz, this play tells the story of Jonah's attempt to escape God's voice, which directs him to a vacation he does not want. Its effectiveness derives from the humor that resides in the story itself, man's ineffectiveness in fleeing from the presence of God. Furthermore, Jonah is not depicted as a prophet whose stylized postures and phases are transparently pious. Rather he is seen as a traveling salesman who has his eye out for a sharp bargain but also takes pride in satisfied customers along the eastern Mediterranean seaboard. This play belongs to a growing body of dramatic literature deriving from Biblical stories, eschatological in theme, existential in demand, and comic in development.

# CHARACTERS


JONAH
A MAN

JONAH: Please, please, what do you want from my life? He won't leave me alone. All these years I've been running—a traveller—Jonah, the traveller, representing Top Hat; Braces For The Trousers; Fair Lady Fancy Buttons; Hold Tight Hair Grips—only good brands in the suitcase. Ask them in Tarshish, ask them in Aleppo, in Carthage even; they all know Jonah ben Amittai, regular call once a month for more than thirty years. I don't complain, only I'm tired of running, that's all. Now at last I'm tired. I get this good pitch here—at last—so I shouldn't have to run with a suitcase any more. And still he nags me. All right. I heard. I'm going. What happens to me shouldn't happen to a dog.

(A MAN *stands in his way*.)

MAN: It's a nice pitch you got here.

JONAH: It's nice.

MAN: So what are you looking so down in the mouth for?

JONAH: What's the use of talking? It has to happen to me.

MAN: What happens?

JONAH: This dream.

MAN: Dream?

JONAH: I tell you, this is a most terrible dream. The voice comes like the voice of a bird. In the middle hours of the night it comes chirping, chirping, "The end of the world is at hand. The end of the world is at hand."

MAN: Could be right. It wouldn't be the first time.

JONAH: So all right then, let it be the end of the world. Is it my business? Am I to blame?

MAN: And this is *all* the voice says?

JONAH (*lying*): Certainly that's all. Isn't it enough? What else should it say?

125

MAN: Nothing. Only if that is all the voice says you got nothing to worry about. Look—if it *is* the end of the world, what can you do? On the other hand—if it isn't— you got nothing to worry about. I'll take a quarter ounce Archangel Gabriel tobacco.

JONAH: (*handing him a small packet of tobacco*). That's a good brand. I opened up the Tarshish territory for Archangel Gabriel.

MAN: I never smoke nothing else. (*Starts to go out.*)

JONAH: Ay, ay.

MAN: Oh. (*Giving coin.*) Chirp, chirp? Chirp, chirp, heh, heh. (*As he goes.*)

JONAH: I hate birds. You know what it says? "Arise, Jonah, arise. Go to Nineveh, that great city, and cry against it." I ask you. Why pick on me? Why sort me out? Chirp, chirp. It's in my head the whole time. Once I could sleep fifteen hours—like a short course of death. No more. I don't sleep that good no more. I hate birds. (*To God.*) All right, I'm going—to the docks—for a ship— I'm going. (*He walks into the next area and set-up.*)

SCENE II

*The same man as before, as a sailor, is untying a rope from a capstan as* JONAH *enters.*

JONAH (*to God*): Certainly I'm on my way. By ship. You expect me to fly? If you are so clever and in such a hurry, make me sprout a couple of wings so I'll take off. It's quicker by air. But so far is only invented the ship. (*To the* SAILOR.) Which way you going, shipmate?

SAILOR: Tarshish.

JONAH: You don't say. I got a lot of friends there. It's a

beautiful place. In Tarshish they got more people over a hundred years old than anywhere else.

SAILOR: Who wants to live so long?

JONAH: In some circumstances, chirp, chirp, who gets a chance to live so long? Tarshish, eh? (*Aside.*) It seems silly, if I'm going all this way to Nineveh (where I am certainly eventually going) why don't I break my journey and look up a few old friends in Tarshish. Why not? (*To the* SAILOR.) It's a crime? You can take passengers?

SAILOR: First class or tourist?

JONAH: In the old days when I was travelling for myself, nothing but first class for J. B. Amittai. But in these circumstances, one tourist.

SAILOR: Single or return?

JONAH: What's the matter with you? Return, of course. I got a wonderful little business waiting for me when I come back.

SAILOR (*shouts*): One more tourist coming up. Tarshish return.

JONAH (*aside, as he begins to board ship*): I'll spend a couple of days there to build my strength up and then I'll give such a shout against Nineveh. After all, it's a tough territory, and what difference can a couple of days make? Thank you. (*Sits.*) Oh, it's a beautiful day for sailing. Any more for the Skylark?

BLACKOUT

SCENE III

JONAH *asleep on some bales of goods. The* SAILOR *wakes him.*

JONAH: Chirp, chirp. The end of the world is at hand. (*He wakes up.*)

SAILOR: If it isn't troubling you.

JONAH: The weather's come over black all of a sudden.

SAILOR: In all my years I never knew a storm this time of the year.

JONAH: Are we far from Tarshish?

SAILOR: Are you barmy? We been stuck out here the past five hours, and all the wind does is try to blow us back. In all my years I never see anything like it.

JONAH: Very interesting phenomena. Like St. Ermin's fire; caused by electricity in the atmosphere, you understand? And take the sea serpent, for example.

SAILOR: I will.

JONAH: The sea serpent is really a very big eel. Science proves it.

SAILOR: I don't take any chances. After I tried every trick I know, I pray. (*He prays for a few moments. Then he looks at* JONAH.) You too, guv'ner.

JONAH: I already said my prayers today. To duplicate is just silly. When it comes to the evening I'll say my evening prayers.

SAILOR: Don't take no chances. Pray now.

JONAH: It should happen to a dog what happens to me. Listen, God. Stop messing me about. Didn't I give you my word of honour I will go to Nineveh? Ask anybody anywhere in these territories. Jonah's word is his bond. (*A gale begins to blow.*) Do me a favour just this once. I will catch the first boat from Tarshish to Nineveh. The very first boat. (*The gale blows stronger.*)

SAILOR: Did you make a sacrifice yet? We got all the passengers making sacrifices to all the different gods. That way we must hit the right god sooner or later and he'll stop the storm. Guv'ner, did you make a sacrifice yet?

JONAH: Here. I sacrifice this beautiful meat pie. I only ate a small portion of it.

SAILOR: Right. Throw it overboard with an appropriate prayer.

JONAH: Here, God. And remember I'm catching the first boat from Tarshish. All right? (*He throws the pie overboard. The pie is thrown straight back, and* JONAH *catches it. The* SAILOR *looks at him significantly, then calls out.*)

SAILOR: Aye, aye. This is it folks.

JONAH: It's a perfectly natural phenomena.

SAILOR: This man is the trouble-maker.

JONAH: It's got a perfectly natural explanation.

SAILOR: His sacrifice was definitely refused. He's the one. Overboard with him—overboard. (*He advances on* JONAH.)

JONAH: You can't do this to me. I am on very important business. I can drown in there. What happens to me should happen to a dog. (*He backs away from the influence of the* SAILOR *till he falls overboard and the gale stops and the sun comes out.*)

SAILOR: I never did like the look of that fella. To me, he always looked a trouble-maker. Uh? What? (*He follows the progress of* JONAH *in the water.*) You could live a thousand years, you wouldn't see a man swallowed by a whale. But who would believe such a story.

BLACKOUT

SCENE IV

JONAH *gropes in the dark, then strikes a match.*

JONAH: Faugh—it smells like Billingsgate in here. All right. Now what am I supposed to do. Now I can't go to

Nineveh. All I wanted to do was to go to Nineveh and cry against it, and look at me. Maybe I'm dead. I must be dead. Who would have thought that being dead was a black-out in a fish shop? Maybe *this is* the end of the world. But if it isn't, if, for example, don't laugh, I happen to have been swallowed by a whale, tee-hee, I categorically put it on record that if I could go to Nineveh at this moment I would definitely and unconditionally go to Nineveh at this moment (*A crash of thunder; lightning.* JONAH *executes a double somersault into the light. Looks round, amazed.*) Honestly, God, sometimes I can't make you out. You've got such a mysterious way of carrying on. (*He stretches himself.*) So where's Tarshish? Tarshish. (*Disgusted.*) If I'm not dead and if I'm not mistaken and if my memory serves me right that great city in the distance is—*Nineveh.* It should happen to a dog. (*Exit, towards Nineveh.*)

SCENE V

KING (*enters, sits, sorts papers, looks up*). Jonah B. Amittai.
JONAH: Yes, Your Majesty.
KING: You are up on a charge of vagrancy.
JONAH: Uh?
KING: Vagrancy.
JONAH: Oh.
KING: Also it seems you have been talking a lot of seditious nonsense about the end of the world is at hand. Also— what's this? Also you keep saying "chirp, chirp." This official work is beginning to get me down. All night long I get the most terrible dreams. Mmm—what have you got to say for yourself?
JONAH: Just a minute. (*He mounts the throne and sings.*) The Lord saith: Cry out against Nineveh, that great

city, for their wickedness is come up before me. Stop.
Yet forty days and Nineveh shall be overthrown. Stop.
The end of the world is at hand. Stop. Repent lest ye
perish. End of message. And that, Your Majesty, in
short, is what I am instructed to tell you. (*Sits.*) Personally it makes no difference to me. I should be just as
pleased for Nineveh not to be destroyed. For my part it
can go on being as wicked as you like, though, if you
was to ask my opinion, as a business man of some experience, I'll tell you straight out that honesty is always
the best policy. A satisfied client is better than Government consuls. Especially as, I am instructed to tell you,
the Government is not going to last too long, anyway.

KING: What's the source of your information?

JONAH: A little bird tells me every night.

KING (*alarmed*): A bird?

JONAH: A little bird. Chirp, chirp. It makes just like that.

KING: What colour the feathers?

JONAH: The feathers! One wing is blue, the other wing
white, the breast red, the tail purple, but the funny thing
is, this bird has one brown eye and . . .

KING: . . . and the other a blue!

JONAH: You are familiar with it?

KING: I have been getting the same dream.

JONAH: Oh. So *your* little bird tells *me* one hundred times
nightly to come to Nineveh and inform *you* that in
forty days from now *you* are completely in liquidation.
And that's what *I'm* telling *you*? It's a madhouse here!

KING (*stands up and tears his robe*): Let neither man nor
beast, herd nor flock, taste anything. Let them not eat
food nor drink water; but let man and beast be covered
with sack-cloth and cry mightily unto God. Yea, let
them turn every one from his evil way, and from the
violence that is in their hands. Let them turn from the
violence that is in their hands for the sake of the smallest
bird, for the bird also is God. (*To* JONAH.) Who can

tell if God will turn and repent, and turn away from his fierce anger, that we perish not?

JONAH: Who can tell? But if you ask my opinion, I don't think so. Otherwise he doesn't go to all this trouble. No, king, this is the end. Still, you can always try. There's no charge for trying.

(*Exeunt.*)

SCENE VI

JONAH *is sitting on a rock in the scorching sun. In the background a celebratory fair-ground noise, like a Bank Holiday Monday.*

JONAH: It should happen to a dog, what happens to me. Here after all this the King himself takes my personal word that in forty days it is the end of the world; and what happens? The forty-first day is proclaimed a national holiday. Government stock rises, and I am the biggest bloody fool in the Middle East. I am a laughing stock, that's all, a laughing stock. I don't move. I'm going to sit here until I get a sunstroke. You can do what you like with Nineveh, Miniver, Shminever. I'm finished. "Yet forty days and Nineveh shall be overthrown." (*Laughter off and voices singing: "Jonah, Jonah—He pulled a boner."*) Listen to 'em. Laugh your heads off! Three-four hours I won't hear you any more. And I won't hear that damned bird either no more. I hate birds. (*A shadow is thrown over* JONAH.) What's this? By my life. A tree! (*A palm tree has sprung up from nowhere. He reaches down a coconut.*) What do you know? Coconuts as well with a patent zipper. You just pull it open and drink the milk. Ice cold. Delicious. And what's this. The *Tarshish Gazette.* Well, this is certainly a novelty. (*Reads.*) Aha. I see that Mrs.

Zinkin has been presented with her third daughter. That's bad. Young Fyvel is opening a café espresso bar on the High Street. That's a good position. He should do well. It's just like a summer holiday here now, and believe me, I earned a vacation. This is certainly a wonderful place you made here, Lord. I got to hand it to you. For land development you're the tops.

(*Standing beside him is the* MAN *dressed as an angel.* JONAH *sees him and looks away, back to his paper.*)

ANGEL: A beautiful day.

JONAH: Yes, it's certainly marvellous weather we're having.

ANGEL: That's a remarkable palm tree. (*He reaches out for a coconut.*) This I never saw before.

JONAH: It's got a zipper.

ANGEL: What will he think of next, eh?

(*He offers the coconut to the irritable* JONAH.)

JONAH (*throwing down the newspaper*): All right. Cut out the performance. You are an angel, right?

ANGEL: I must give you credit, Jonah. You're certainly quick off the mark.

JONAH: But an angel?

ANGEL: Archangel.

JONAH: Oh—so now what do I have to do? Go back to Nineveh? Tell the King the Lord has changed his mind again? He is going to give him ten more days and then bring the world to an end? He made a laughing stock of me.

ANGEL: What can you do?

JONAH: Admitted. But at the same time this is a terrible way to treat someone who goes through all the trouble I go through. For what—only He knows. And He won't tell. (*Turns, bangs into tree.*) Feh! Fancy trees yet!

ANGEL (*wheedling*): That's certainly a *wonderful* tree. Help yourself.

JONAH: Perhaps just another coconut. These coconuts are

delicious. (*As he turns the tree withers, collapsing into dust; that is, the coatstand is removed.*) What a terrible thing to happen. Such a wonderful tree. With such trees mankind could live in plenty for ever. A quick death from some palm tree disease, I suppose?

ANGEL: It's a small worm crawls through the arterial system of the tree, cuts off the life from the heart. And boom.

JONAH: A quick death to that worm.

ANGEL: Ah. You notice something. How annoyed you are with this worm which after all only killed a tree, which after all didn't cause you an hour's work. After all, you don't hear God complain; He made the tree to come up in a night. He can make it go down the night after.

JONAH: It cranks me such a beautiful tree should die like that, apart from now I am in the sun again and can catch a sunstroke any minute. Pity about the tree. Hey-hey. This is some kind of parable, ain't it? You are trying to teach me something, isn't it?

ANGEL: That's my boy. By this little experiment He is saying, if you feel sorry for the tree, which after all didn't cost you anything, why shouldn't He feel sorry for Nineveh, that great city, in which there are one hundred and twenty thousand human beings on whom after all He has taken a great deal of trouble even if they still don't know what time it is, or their left hand from their right hand. Also much cattle.

JONAH: You got a point there, there was never any harm in those cattle. But if you don't mind a question . . .

ANGEL: Any help I can give you.

JONAH: If God knew right from the start exactly what He is going to do about everything—right?

ANGEL: That's right.

JONAH: Then He knows He isn't going to destroy Nineveh. Right?

ANGEL: Right!

JONAH: Then what does He want of my life? What's the point of all this expensive business with whales and palm trees and so on?

ANGEL: You mankind, you can't see no further than your nose.

JONAH: So what's the answer?

ANGEL: You see—(*Long pause.*) frankly, I don't know.

JONAH: It should happen to a dog.

ANGEL: Me too. After all, it's no joke following you or any other prophet I happen to get assigned to around the whole time. You think it's such a wonderful thing to be an angel and do a few conjuring tricks? It *should* happen to a dog.

JONAH: On the other hand, come to think of it, whose dogs are we?

ANGEL: We are the dogs of God.

JONAH: So . . .

ANGEL: Nu?

JONAH: Whatever happens to a dog . . .

ANGEL: . . . must happen to us, eh? (*He chuckles with admiration.*)

JONAH: Can you give me a lift back home?

ANGEL: It's a pleasure. (JONAH *jumps on* ANGEL's *back.*)

JONAH: On the way we could call in at Tarshish. I got a lot of friends there.

ANGEL: That's a good idea. So have I. (*As they go out.*) Did you hear that young Fyvel opened a café espresso bar on the High Street?

JONAH: I read it in the paper. He's a clever boy.

**CURTAIN**

# AUTHOR'S NOTE

*It Should Happen to a Dog* is a serio-comic strip, which, those who know the story of Jonah will see, is faithful to the original. If the characters speak as people we know personally, it is because there is no other way for us to know characters. If Jonah is somewhat familiar in his manner of address to the Almighty—it is because one may assume that a greater intimacy exists between Prophets and their source of instruction than does for the rest of us.

In the staging of *It Should Happen to a Dog*, a coatstand is required from which the rope of the ship is hung, and upon which any practical props may also hang. The coatstand becomes the tree in the last scene, and should be placed behind Jonah's back in full view of the audience by the Angel or by a property man who may be written in at the director's discretion. A thunder-sheet will be found useful. The characters should be dressed in an anachronistic selection of garments suggestive of our own time and of biblical times, and the piece should be played at a fast tempo.

As to the message of the story—"Why should I not spare Nineveh?" This is, one hopes, how God feels about Man— unlike Man who is less tolerant of himself.

# BILLY BUDD

*A Play in Three Acts*
*Based on a Novel by Herman Melville*

## LOUIS O. COXE & ROBERT CHAPMAN

# Editor's Preface: BILLY BUDD

Repossessed after decades of public indifference and critical neglect, Herman Melville is now recognized as one of the major figures in American and English literature and one of the giants of the nineteenth century. The play *Billy Budd* is a dramatic adaptation by Louis O. Coxe and Robert Chapman of the novel bearing the same title written by Melville in 1891, near the end of his life. Melville's work belongs to that strain in American literature which runs counter to the dominant theme of nineteenth-century optimism. For Melville was preoccupied with the fact and the mystery of evil. As a residual Calvinist he inherited the awareness of man's sinfulness, but he did not know the experience of being one of the Elect. Nonetheless, his pessimism was conjoined with the romantic vitality of his age in such a way that makes his work appealing on many levels. *Moby Dick* is considered, apart from its other meanings, to be Melville's fictional exploration of the problem of evil, and *Billy Budd* an answer to the mystery of iniquity. *Billy Budd* is an exciting sea tale of a handsome sailor who was impressed into service on a warship filled with the possibility of mutiny. The action involves the conflict between the personifications of evil and good, Claggart and Billy Budd. The adapters of the story have worked remarkably well with difficult material, for the novel contains little dialogue and sparse dramatic action. Instead the reader is invited, for instance, to speculate on the content and quality of the final encounter between Billy Budd and Captain Vere, in which we glimpse the redemptive role of the innocent man put to death. Captain

Vere is caught in the necessity of enforcing a justice he realizes does not fulfill justice in the situation. Thus Billy's acceptance of necessity becomes the channel for a grace that transcends the evil. Because it has so many veins of meaning and because of its redemptive note, *Billy Budd* is regarded by many as a major expression in literature of Christian faith.

The play *Billy Budd* was first produced under the title *Uniform of Flesh* by the Invitational Series of the Experimental Theater under the sponsorship of the American National Theatre and Academy at the Lenox Hill Playhouse on January 29, 1949. In its present form it opened at the Biltmore Theatre in New York on February 10, 1951.

# CHARACTERS

EDWARD FAIRFAX VERE, *Captain, Royal Navy*
PHILIP MICHAEL SEYMOUR, *First Officer*
JOHN RATCLIFFE, *First Lieutenant*
BORDMAN WYATT, *Sailing Master*
GARDINER, *a Midshipman*
REA, *a Midshipman*
SURGEON
JOHN CLAGGART, *Master-at-Arms*
SQUEAK, *Master-at-Arms' man*
THE DANSKER, *Mainmast man*
JENKINS, *Captain of the Maintop*
PAYNE, *Maintopman*
KINCAID, *Maintopman*
O'DANIEL, *Maintopman*
BUTLER, *Maintopman*
TALBOT, *Mizzentopman*
JACKSON, *Maintopman*
BILLY BUDD, *Foretopman*
HALLAM, *a Marine*
MESSBOY
STOLL, *Helmsman*
DUNCAN, *Mate of the Main Deck*
BYREN, *Relief Helmsman*
DRUMMER
OTHER SAILORS, *crew of the* INDOMITABLE

The entire action takes place aboard *H.M.S. Indomitable* at sea, August, 1798, the year following the Naval mutinies at Spithead and the Nore.

# ACT ONE

SCENE: *Although outside it is a fine morning in early August, the between-decks compartment of the crew's quarters assigned to the maintopmen is dark and shadowy except for the light spilling down the companionway from above and, through the open gun-ports, the flicker of sunlight reflected on the water. The smoking-lamp burns feebly over a wooden mess table and two benches lowered for use.*

JENKINS *sits at the table mending a piece of clothing. In the shadow the* DANSKER *sits motionless on a low sea chest, smoking a pipe. Neither man speaks for a long minute.*

*Then* JACKSON *appears on deck at the top of the companionway and lurches down into the compartment. He is doubled up in pain.*

CLAGGART (*off*): You there! Jackson!

JACKSON: Oh Christ, he's followed me!

JENKINS: Who?

JACKSON: Master-at-Arms. He'll send me aloft again sure, and I can't hang on . . .

JENKINS: What the devil's wrong with you, jack? Here, sit down.

CLAGGART (*entering down the companionway*): Why have you come down off the mainmast, Jackson? Your watch over?

JACKSON: Sick, Mister Claggart, I'm bloody sick, so I'm shaking up there on the yard till I near fell off.

JENKINS: Grab an arm, mate, I'll take you along to sick-bay.

CLAGGART: Stand away from him, Jenkins. (*To* JACKSON) Just where does this sickness strike you, in the guts, or limbs? Or in the head? Does it exist at all?

JENKINS: You can see he's sick as a puking cat, plain as your stick.

CLAGGART: The role of Good Samaritan hardly fits you, Jenkins. (*To* JACKSON) Now up, man. Turn topside.

JACKSON: I can't, I can't, I'm deathly sick, God help me, sir!

CLAGGART: That's hard. But this ship needs all hands. We're undermanned. The aches and pains of landsmen have their cures, but ours have none. You'll have to get aloft. Now move!

JACKSON: I ain't bluffing, sir, swear I'm not! Please, Mister Claggart . . . I got Cooper's leave, he says all right, I can come down.

CLAGGART: You have not got my leave. Cooper is captain of the maintop and ought to know better. Four men to every spar, and no replacements. Now up. Back where you belong.

JACKSON (*starts up the ladder*): God, sir, I can't, I can't stand it! It'll be my death, sure!

CLAGGART: No more talk, man! Up you get! Start! (JACKSON *goes painfully up the ladder and out of sight on deck.* CLAGGART *starts out after him*)

JENKINS (*mutters*): God damn your bloody heart!

CLAGGART: Did you say something, Jenkins? (JENKINS *does not answer.* CLAGGART *goes out, calling after* JACKSON) Now Jackson, get along. Up! Up!

JENKINS: I'll stick him one day before long! I will, if I hang for it.

(*Laughter and talk in the next compartment followed by entrance of* BUTLER, TALBOT *and* KINCAID)

BUTLER: Messboy!

TALBOT: Haul in the slops!

KINCAID: Suppose we'll get the new man? The jack they 'pressed this morning off that merchantman? I see 'em come along side just now.

TALBOT: I pity that poor bastard, so I do. I hear they get good pay on merchant ships. Eat good, too, and them treated like the Goddamn Prince of Wales. (MESSBOY *enters with an iron pot of food and spits on the deck*) Spit in it, damn you. Can't taste no worse.

MESSBOY: Ain't nobody making you eat it, mate. You can wash your feet in it if you like. (O'DANIEL *and* PAYNE *enter*)

TALBOT: What's eating you, Jenkins? Ain't you going to join the banquet?

JENKINS: By God, I seen a thing just now I won't stand for! I'm sitting here off watch, and I seen it all. That black-snake Claggart kicked Jackson back aloft, and him sick as a pinkass baby in a cradle, as any fool could see.

PAYNE: He's the Master-at-Arms, ain't he?

JENKINS: Cooper sent him down. Who's captain of the starboard watch, him or Claggart? Cooper could have found him a relief. Plain murder, by God!

TALBOT: You think Claggart can get away with what he does without Captain Starry Vere knows what's going on? Him and that red snapper Seymour, and them other bloody officers!

JENKINS: Jackson'll fall. By God, no man can hang to a spar sick like that. He'll fall sure.

O'DANIEL: Tush, man, nobody falls in His Majesty's Navy. We lose our footing. 'Tis flying we do, to be sure.

TALBOT: I tell you it's Vere that's the cause of it! Our glorious fine Captain Vere, with a league of braid around his arm and a ramrod up his bum.

O'DANIEL: Vere, is it. As captains go, mate, let me tell you, he's an angel with a harp alongside of the skipper on the *Royal George*. Every day that one flogged a dozen

men. Picked 'em by lottery, by God. Never took the
gratings down till they was rusty with blood. Ho! This
Vere's saint in heaven after him.

JENKINS: Ram the *Royal George* and everybody in her!
Claggart's the man we want, and the sooner the better,
say I!

O'DANIEL: Ah, we'd had him puking his blood at Spithead,
the devil rot his wick.

BUTLER: You was there, O'Daniel? At Spithead?

O'DANIEL: Aye. I was. Wherever you do find Englishmen
doing a smart thing, you'll find an Irishman is at the
bottom of it. Oho, fine it was, every day of it, with the
officers quaking in their cabins, spitting green, and the
whole English government wetting their breeches from
the fear of us! Ah, lovely it was, lovely!

TALBOT: Belay your Irish noise, you fat-mouthed mackerel-
snatcher. I'll tell you this, we need men on here is not
afraid to use their knives if it come to that. And you can
be bloody sure it will come to that, mind my word,
Mickey Cork.

JENKINS: What did you ever use your knife for, Talbot,
but to scratch your lice? Ah, you're a dancing daredevil,
you are for sure.

TALBOT: I'll be happy to show you, if you like.

JENKINS: Trouble will be hunting you out, mate, if you're
not careful.

TALBOT: Trouble! You whoreson cockney cullion! There's
not a man aboard don't know you for a coward, you
whining bitch-boy!

JENKINS: Get out.

TALBOT: Damn your seed, I'm not afraid of you, or your
sniveling hangbys, either!

JENKINS: Move! Get out of it, or by God I'll run my knife
to the hilts in you!

TALBOT: You son of a whore! Pigsticker!

(*They attack one another with drawn knives,* JEN-

KINS *reaching suddenly across the table to seize* TALBOT. *Silently they thrash around the compartment upsetting benches and food while the others look on unmoved*)

O'DANIEL: Ah, I do love to see two Englishmen fighting each other. It's fonder they are of killing themselves than fighting their proper foes. (*laughs hoarsely*)

PAYNE: Tomorrow's rum on Jenkins. Any bets?

KINCAID: He never lost one yet.

(JENKINS *throws* TALBOT *on the deck and holds the knife at his throat for a moment before letting him up, first taking his knife. He holds out his hand*)

JENKINS: I'm leading seaman in this compartment, mind that. (TALBOT *hits* JENKINS' *hand and goes off angrily*)

KINCAID: You're captain, that's all right by me.

O'DANIEL: Eyes in the boat, lads. Here comes *pfft*-face.

(SQUEAK, BILLY *and* GARDINER *appear on deck and start down the companionway*)

GARDINER: Hang it, step lively, boy! Your ship is . . . Doff your hat to officers when they speak to you! By God, I'll teach you to touch your hat to a midshipman's coat, if it's only stuck on a broomstick to dry!

BILLY: Aye, sir. (*The men react to* GARDINER *with yawns and gestures behind his back*)

GARDINER: Very well. Your ship is H.M.S. *Indomitable* now, and we sail her tautly, and we tolerate no nonsense. Is that clear?

BILLY: Aye, sir.

GARDINER (*to* SQUEAK): See this new man is assigned to a watch, and get him squared away. (*To* BILLY) You're green, of course, I can see that. But I expect we'll ripen you. (*He trips going up the ladder and* SQUEAK *tries to help him*) Carry on. (GARDINER *exits*)

SQUEAK: My name's Squeak. I'm the Master-at-Arms' man. Have you met the Master-at-Arms yet, Mister Claggart?

(BILLY *shakes his head*) Oh you'll like him. He's a nice fellow. (O'DANIEL *chokes on his pipe smoke and the other men react similarly*) Stow your gear along in there. This here's the larboard section of the maintop. Captain of the watch is Jenkins. Him, there. Report to him. (*He pats* BILLY *on the chest and grins before starting up the ladder*)

JENKINS: What's a green hand dumped in here for?

SQUEAK: Complaining, Jenkins?

JENKINS: I'm asking. What's wrong with that?

SQUEAK: Mister Claggart wants him here, that's why. Maybe he wants for Billy Boy to set you pigs an example. Refer any more complaints to the Master-at-Arms! (*exits.* BILLY *grins at the men, who return his look*)

BILLY: My name is Budd. Billy, if you like.

KINCAID: I'm Kincaid. This is where you swing your hammock. That's O'Daniel, this here's Payne, and Butler. This is Jenkins, captain of the watch, and that old jack's called the Dansker. Don't know why, unless maybe he's Danish. You ever had a real name, Dansker?

DANSKER: Not for many years.

BUTLER: You'd be the new impressed man?

BILLY: Aye, so I am. I just came off the *Rights of Man* this morning.

DANSKER: Forget about the Rights of Man now, lad.

JENKINS: How long you been going to sea, baby?

BILLY: About ten years, but in the merchant service.

O'DANIEL: Merchant service! Whissht! (*laughs hoarsely*)

BILLY: I know I'm new at Navy work, and probably there'll be some things I'll need help w.th.

JENKINS: No doubt, little boy.

BILLY: I'll learn fast, never fear. But she's a big old girl, this ship. I never was in a ship-of-the-line before. I'd have got lost trying to find the mess by myself. Maybe fallen in the magazine!

O'DANIEL: Ah, you get used to it. She's big, is this tub, but she's not so big you can get lost in her.

PAYNE: Sometimes I wish to God you could. Maybe we could lose O'Daniel. (BILLY *laughs and the others join*)

BILLY: You're Irish, aren't you? I like the Irish. There was an Irishman on the *Rights of Man*, with big red whiskers . . . when I came away, he gave me a silver knife. This is it.

O'DANIEL: It's a beauty. Mind you keep an eye on it.

BUTLER: What's the matter, boy?

BILLY: I was just thinking, maybe I won't ever see my friends again.

O'DANIEL: If they was Irish, don't you worry at all. The Irish is liable to turn up almost anywheres, excepting England and the fires of hell, which is much the same.

PAYNE: Danny, if it wasn't for the harps, the devil wouldn't have nothing to do. What was potato-eaters doing on a merchant ship?

BILLY: Just sailors, like me. Most of us had no other home, even the skipper. He was a kind old bloke. Looked fierce, but he always had a kind word. Used to keep a bird in a cage in his cabin. The skipper let me feed the bird sometimes. Worms right out of the ship's biscuit. That was mostly all the meat we got.

O'DANIEL: The bargemen is in Navy biscuit would eat the bird.

KINCAID: Sit down here, Bill. Maggots or not, this is what we get. You hungry?

BILLY: I'm always hungry.

KINCAID: Try your first sample of His Majesty's bounty. We don't know what it is, but we been eating it for a long time.

BUTLER: Here, eat mine. Tastes like its been eat before, anyhow.

JENKINS: Give him more lobscouse, Butler. We got to keep the roses in his cheeks, ain't we, boy?

BILLY (*laughing*): I could eat anything right now. Even this.

O'DANIEL: Help you to forget about home and mother, lad.

JENKINS: Tell us about home and mother, Baby Budd.

BILLY: There's not much to tell. I've got no home, and never had a family to remember.

JENKINS: Ain't that too bad.

BILLY: Oh, I'd feel a lot worse if I'd been 'pressed with a wife and children.

KINCAID: That's the truth.

O'DANIEL: We're all patriotic volunteers.

KINCAID: Guano! Wait till my hitch is up, you won't see no more of me.

BUTLER: Three weeks drunk in Portsmouth, then back in the ruddy fleet.

DANSKER: Men like us got no other home.

O'DANIEL: No other home, is it? Ah 'tis so thick the sweet thoughts is in here, I can scarce breathe.

PAYNE: Then you can strangle or get out.

JENKINS: Aye, get along, you lousy harp, give us some fresh air.

O'DANIEL: If you begged me to stay itself, I'd be off to where there's smarter lads. Boy, let you pay no heed to these white mice, mind what I say. And be hanged, the lot of yous! (*He starts up the ladder*)

KINCAID: You'll catch it, Danny, if Captain holds an inspection.

O'DANIEL (*returning*): Ah whissht, I was forgetting that. And I do think that me figure shows up better here below than it does in the broad daylight.

BILLY: Inspection today?

PAYNE: Ah the Old Man crawls over the ship from arse-hole to appetite any time he ain't got nothing else to do. You never know when till you see him.

KINCAID: What the devil he wants to inspect this hooker for, I can't figure. He's seen it before.

BUTLER: He ain't seen Billy.

BILLY: What's the Captain like? On the *Rights of Man,* the captain . . .

JENKINS: You going to jaw some more about that rocking horse? I suppose *you* was at Spithead, too?

BILLY: Spithead? Where is that?

JENKINS: A little party the Navy had a year ago. A mutiny, Baby, a mutiny. Know what that is?

BILLY: Why did they mutiny?

O'DANIEL: Arra, it's easy to see you're new to the Navy.

JENKINS: Jimmy-Legs is ten good goddam reasons for it, himself.

BILLY: Who's Jimmy-Legs?

KINCAID: Master-at-Arms. We call him Jimmy-Legs.

BUTLER: Watch out for that one, Billy.

PAYNE: He's the devil himself between decks.

O'DANIEL: What d'you expect, the saints of heaven? Not in an English tub.

BILLY: Why don't you like the Master-at-Arms?

JENKINS: You'll find out soon enough, Baby.

BUTLER: Watch him, boy. Jenkins can tell you. He's had a time or two with Claggart.

JENKINS: Aye, and I'll have another one day before too long.

BUTLER: Sure, Jenkins. You look after Bill.

JENKINS: How old are you, kid? Sixteen?

BILLY: I don't know, maybe . . . twenty.

JENKINS: He don't even know how old he is! My guess is, too young to know what his parts are for.

O'DANIEL: Is it anybody is that young?

KINCAID: Stow it, Jenkins. Come on, don't pay no attention to him. He's feeling ugly today.

JENKINS: Well now, ain't you getting holier than a bloody bishop. Let him talk for himself, if he don't like it.

KINCAID: Stow it, I say. You got no reason to crawl over Bill. Let him be.

BILLY: That's all right, Tom. I don't mind a joke. Black's the white of me eye, mates! (*All laugh except* JENKINS)

JENKINS: Mama taught you pretty manners, huh? Oh! Ain't got no mama, you say? Well now, think what that makes you! (*laughs*)

BILLY: Tell me what you mean, Mister Jenkins.

PAYNE: What's gnawing your arse, Jenkins? Can't you see the boy's trying to be friendly?

JENKINS: You forgetting who's leading seaman here? Come on, Baby, talk back, why don't you? Scared?

BILLY: N-no. Why do you think I'd be scared, M-M-Mister Jenkins?

JENKINS: He stammers! What do you know! The little bastard's so scared he's stammering.

BILLY: Don't call me that again.

JENKINS: Sounds good, ha? Sounds fine. I like the way it rolls out your mouth. Bastard Baby Budd . . .

(BILLY *strikes him.* JENKINS *staggers and falls, pulls a knife and gets up, lunging at* BILLY. PAYNE, BUTLER *and* KINCAID *get up and stand close to* BILLY, *silently protecting him*)

JENKINS: Get away, God damn you! He's got to find out who gives orders here.

KINCAID: Not his time, Jenkins. Lay off.

O'DANIEL: Belay it. You're wearing me out, the pair of yous.

BUTLER: Put away the knife. (JENKINS *sees their determination and relaxes a little, uncertain what to do*)

BILLY: Will you shake hands? Or would you rather fight?

JENKINS: You little bas . . . (*lunges forward.* BILLY *catches his arm and bends it, holding* JENKINS *cursing and powerless*)

BILLY: That's enough, mate. Pipe down and let us be.

O'DANIEL: Good lad! Save the great strength is in you, Jenkins, for fighting the devil is after your soul.

JENKINS: All right, all right. You can let me go now.

O'DANIEL: Leave him go, lad. I won't hurt him at all.

BILLY: You're like Red Whiskers on the *Rights*, he liked to fight too. (*freeing him*) Will you shake hands, mate?

JENKINS (*momentarily uncertain what to do*): Shake hands, is it? . . . Well, you beat me fair. You got guts, which is more than I give you credit for. (*They shake hands*)

KINCAID: You're a hell of a peacemaker, Bill.

PAYNE: That's the only time I ever hear Jenkins eating his own words.

O'DANIEL: Ah, that's a terrible diet, would make any man puke.

JENKINS: Don't you be getting any wrong ideas. I'm still a match for you!

KINCAID: Better belay your mess gear, Bill.

JENKINS: Where you come from, Baby?

PAYNE: Stow it! Jimmy-Legs! (BILLY *goes on talking as* CLAGGART *enters*)

BILLY: I don't know, I guess from Portsmouth. I never lived ashore, that I can remember. Where do you come from? (*drops a pot on deck.* CLAGGART *stands over him*)

CLAGGART: Handsomely done, young fellow, handsomely done. And handsome is as handsome did it, too. You can wipe that up, Jenkins. (*To* BILLY) What is your name?

BILLY: Budd, sir. William Budd, ship *Rights of Man*.

CLAGGART: Your ship is *H.M.S. Indomitable* now.

BILLY: Aye, sir.

CLAGGART: You look sturdy. What was your station aboard the merchantman?

BILLY: M-m-mizzentopman, sir.

CLAGGART: You like that station?

BILLY: Aye, sir, well enough.

CLAGGART: How long have you been at sea?

BILLY: Ten years, sir, near as I can tell.

CLAGGART: Education?

BILLY: None, sir.

CLAGGART: So. You come aboard with nothing but your face to recommend you. Well, while beauty is always welcome, that alone may not avail us much against the French. There are other requirements in the service.

BILLY: I'll learn quickly, sir.

CLAGGART: The sea's a taskmaster, young fellow. It salts the sweetness out of boyish faces. You cannot tell what motion lies asleep in that flat water. Down where the manta drifts, and the shark and ray, storms wait for a wind while all the surface dazzles.

BILLY: I am a seaman, sir. I love the sea. I've hardly lived ashore.

CLAGGART: Then let the wind and sea have license to plunder at their will. As of today, a new maintopman swings between sky and water. (*He turns toward the ladder and notices the mess on deck*) I thought I asked you to wipe that up, Jenkins.

JENKINS: That's the messboy's job.

CLAGGART: Clean up, Jenkins. (*JENKINS hesitates*) That is an order. Turn to.

BILLY: I'll give you a hand, Jenkins. Come on.

CLAGGART: Ah, there. See how helpful Billy is. Why can't you take a leaf from this innocent young David's book, Jenkins? (*turns away. JENKINS accidentally brushes against him and receives a savage cut from CLAGGART's rattan across his face*) Watch what you're doing, man!

JENKINS: I swear . . . !

CLAGGART: Yes, what is it that you swear? Well, speak. Nothing at all to say? Then hear me: I have my methods with unruly tempers.

> (*On deck there is a loud crescendo scream and a crash. Running footsteps, shouts, voice calling for the SURGEON. The men surge toward the ladder*)

CLAGGART: Stand fast! (*SQUEAK enters down the hatchway, whispers to CLAGGART*) All right, I know. (*SQUEAK comes down into the compartment and runs off*)

JENKINS: It's Jackson! I knew it, by God, I told you so!
(*Men turn to stare at* CLAGGART *as several sailors
enter down the companionway, bearing the body of*
JACKSON, *inert and shattered. They carry him
through the compartment and off to sick-bay*)

SURGEON (*as he moves through the compartment*): Clear
the way, you men. Take him into the sick-bay, through
here. Carry him gently. Easy, now. Easy. (*exit*)

JENKINS (*pointing to* CLAGGART): He sent him back aloft.
Killed him, he did!

O'DANIEL: Might as well have knifed him.

CLAGGART: Stand fast. Stop where you are. Your man
Jackson is looked after.

O'DANIEL (*in a low voice*): Then he's a dead man surely.

CLAGGART: Who spoke?

JENKINS: We'll have a showdown now! After him, mates!
Cut into him!

(*The men move toward* CLAGGART *in a rush, drawing knives and cursing him, as* CAPTAIN VERE *appears in the companion hatchway*)

VERE: Stand fast! Hold where you are. Master-at-Arms,
what is the matter here? (*The men stop in their tracks
and stare at* VERE, *who comes part way down the ladder*)

CLAGGART: These dogs are out of temper, sir.

VERE (*to men*): You will come to attention when I address
you! Let me remind you that this ship is at war. This
is a wartime cruise, and this vessel sails under the Articles of War. Volunteer or 'pressed man, veteran seaman or recruit, you are no longer citizens, but sailors:
a crew that I shall work into a weapon. One lawless act,
one spurt of rebel temper from any man in this ship,
high or low, I will pay out in coin you know of. You
have but two duties: to fight and to obey, and I will
bend each contumacious spirit, each stiff-necked prideful
soul of you, or crush the spirit in you if I must. Abide

by the Articles of War and my commands, or they will cut you down. Now: choose. (*The men are silent*) Very well. Master-at-Arms, this accident on deck, the sailor fallen from the yardarm. Do you know how it occurred?

CLAGGART: I do not, sir.

VERE: You are his messmates. Does any man of you know how this occurred? (*To Butler*) You?

BUTLER: No, sir.

VERE: Jenkins, do you?

JENKINS (*hesitates a moment.* CLAGGART *moves slightly, tapping his hand with the rattan*): No, sir.

VERE (*notices the cut on* JENKINS' *face*): What's this, what's this? Speak up, man. I want no random bloodshed aboard this ship.

JENKINS: I . . . fell, Captain. Fell, and . . . and cut my cheek.

VERE: I see. You fell. Master-at-Arms, you will excuse this man from duty till the Surgeon tends him.

CLAGGART: Aye, aye, sir.

VERE: We must not wound ourselves, draining the blood from enterprise that takes a whole man. (*He turns to go up the ladder and sees* BILLY) Well. This is a new face. Who are you, boy?

CLAGGART: Maintopman 'pressed from the *Rights of Man* this morning, sir. William Budd.

VERE: Let him speak for himself. (BILLY *tries to speak but can only stammer incoherently*) That's all right, boy, take your time. No need to be nervous.

BILLY: I saw a man go aloft, sir, as I came on board just a while ago. He looked sick, sir, he did. This officer was there, too, he can tell you. (*To* CLAGGART) Don't you remember, sir?

VERE: Did you send a sick man aloft, Master-at-Arms?

CLAGGART: I did not, sir.

VERE: Very well. (*to* BILLY) Well, Budd, I hope you take to Navy life and duty without too much regret. We go to fight the French and shall need wits and hearts about us equal to the task.

BILLY: I'll do my best, sir.

VERE: I'm sure you will. We are all here to do our several duties, and though they may seem petty from one aspect, still they must all be done. The Admiral himself looks small and idle to the man like you who can see him from the maintop, threading his pattern on the quarterdeck. The Navy's only life. (SURGEON *enters*)

SURGEON: Captain—Jackson, the man who fell just now—he's dead, sir.

VERE (*after a pause*): Carry on, Master-at-Arms. (*He goes out up the companionway.* SURGEON *exits*)

CLAGGART: You've made a good impression on the Captain, Billy Budd. You have a pleasant way with you. If you wish to make a good impression on me, you will need to curb your tongue. Jenkins, I thought you were ordered to sick-bay. Jump to it. And I suggest you change that shirt. See how fouled it is with a peculiar stain. Why can't you keep clean like Billy here? (*He strikes* JENKINS *viciously on the arm with his rattan, smiles at him, and exits up the ladder*)

JENKINS: God damn his flaming soul! I can't stand it no more!

BILLY: I don't see what you can do, mate. He didn't mean it when he hurt you then.

JENKINS: Listen, boy, I know Jimmy-Legs. He lives on hurting people. Stay away from him, and keep your mouth shut, if you don't want trouble.

O'DANIEL: Did you hear the lad speak up to the skipper?

PAYNE: Aye, you watch your tongue, Bill. Claggart will be after you for talking up like that.

KINCAID: He's a cool one, Billy is. None of us got the nerve.

BUTLER: It's nerve gets a man in trouble in this tub.

DANSKER: Jimmy-Legs is down on you already, Billy.

BILLY: Down on me? Why he's friendly to me.

JENKINS: Claggart don't make no friends.

O'DANIEL: You seen Jackson when they brought him below. That's how friendly he gets. (*Bosun's pipe off*)

DUNCAN (*off*): Relieve the watch!

KINCAID: First watch on the *Indomitable*, Bill. Better lay up to the mainmast and report. (*exit*)

BUTLER: Don't slip off the yardarm.

PAYNE: Watch your step.

BILLY: Not me. You watch for me. Got to find the mainmast, and I'm in a hurry.

O'DANIEL: You'll never find your way in this old tub. I'll come along and show you. If anybody comes calling for O'Daniel while I'm out, take the message.

PAYNE: O'Daniel couldn't find his breeches if they wasn't buttoned on. You come with me. (BILLY *and* PAYNE *go off*)

JENKINS: Poor bastard. I pity him, I do.

BUTLER: He's dead, ain't he? Better off than us.

JENKINS: Not Jackson. I mean the baby here. Billy.

BUTLER: We could have fared worse for a messmate.

JENKINS: Aye. He can take care of himself. Heave up the table.

### End of Scene One

**SCENE TWO**

SCENE: *In the early evening of the same day, the off-duty sections of the crew are mustered aft on the maindeck for* JACKSON's *funeral. Above them* CAPTAIN VERE *stands uncovered at the forward break of the quarterdeck, reading the Committal Prayer. The westward sky is bright yellow and red, but fades into darkness as the scene progresses.*

*The men are uncovered and stand at attention.*

VERE: Unto Almighty God we commend the soul of our brother departed and we commit his body to the deep, in sure and certain hope of the resurrection unto Eternal Life, through our Lord Jesus Christ, at whose coming in glorious majesty to judge the world, the sea shall give up her dead, and the corruptible bodies of those who sleep in Him shall be changed and made like unto His glorious body according to the mighty working whereby He is able to subdue all things unto Himself. Amen.

MEN: Amen.

> (*Short drum-roll followed by a muffled splash as* JACKSON's *body slips over the side. Then the bosun's pipe. Officers cover and march off*)

CLAGGART: Ship's company: Cover! Petty officers, dismiss your divisions.

VOICE (*off*): Carpenters and gunners: Dismiss!

VOICE (*off*): Afterguardsmen: Dismiss!

VOICE (*off*): Fore, main, and mizzentopmen: Dismiss!

> (*The men break formation and go off, excepting* BUTLER, JENKINS, PAYNE, KINCAID *and* BILLY, *who gather near the ratlines, at the rail*)

BUTLER: I suppose in this clear water you could see him go down for quite a way.

BILLY: We're moving slow in this calm.

JENKINS: There'll be wind enough before dawn.

BUTLER: And that's the end of Enoch Jackson. Over the side he goes, and his mates forget him.

JENKINS: Whatever's happened to Jackson, he ain't worried none. He's got a hundred fathoms over him to keep him warm and cosy.

BILLY: I'd rather be buried at sea than on the beach, when I come to die. Will you stand by the plank, Tom, so I'll

shake a friendly hand before I sink? Oh! But it's dead I'll
be then, come to think! (*all laugh*)

PAYNE: Don't you worry none. By that time, you won't
give a sailmaker's damn.

KINCAID: It's only living makes sense to me, anyhow.

BILLY: Aye, I like to live. Even when it seems bad, there's
a lot that's good in it.

JENKINS: Maybe for you, Bill. You wouldn't know trouble
if it come up and spit in your eye.

BILLY: Don't you try now, mate! You might miss, and I got
a clean jumper on!

PAYNE: That's the way to be, if you ask me. There's always trouble, if you know where to look for it.

BUTLER: You don't have to see nothing if you close your
eyes.

KINCAID: When I close my eyes I sleep sound as a drunk
marine.

BILLY: Aye, after I roll in my hammock, it's one, two,
three, and I'm deep down under.

JENKINS: Well it's down under for me right now. Let's lay
below.

KINCAID: Aye, we'll be on watch before long. Coming,
Bill?

BILLY: I think I'll stay and watch the water for a while. I
like to watch the sea at night.

JENKINS: Aye. It's deep and silent, and it can drown a man
before he knows it.

BILLY: Sleep sound, mates. (*All but* JENKINS *go down the
companion hatchway*)

JENKINS: Billy: stay clear of Jimmy-Legs.

>(JENKINS *exits down the hatchway.* BILLY *is left
alone staring over the side until* CLAGGART *enters.
He does not see* BILLY, *but stops near the quarterdeck ladder and gazes fixedly seaward*)

BILLY: Good evening, sir.

CLAGGART (*startled, then subtly sarcastic*): Good evening.

BILLY: Will it be all right if I stay topside a bit to watch the water?

CLAGGART: I suppose the Handsome Sailor may do many things forbidden to his messmates.

BILLY: Yes, sir. The sea's calm tonight, isn't it? Calm and peaceful.

CLAGGART: The sea's deceitful, boy: calm above, and underneath, a world of gliding monsters preying on their fellows. Murderers, all of them. Only the sharpest teeth survive.

BILLY: I'd like to know about such things, as you do, sir.

CLAGGART: You're an ingenuous sailor, Billy Budd. Is there, behind that youthful face, the wisdom pretty virtue has need of? Even the gods must know their rivals, boy; and Christ had first to recognize the ills before he cured 'em.

BILLY: What, sir?

CLAGGART: Never mind. But tell me this: how have you stomach to stand here and talk to me? Are you so innocent and ignorant of what I am? You know my reputation. Jenkins and the rest are witnesses, and certainly you've heard them talking to me. Half of them would knife me in the back some night and do it gladly; Jenkins is thinking of it. Doubtless he'll try one day. How do you dare, then? Have you not intelligence enough to be afraid of me? To hate me as all the others do?

BILLY: Why should I be afraid of you, sir? You speak to me friendly when we meet. I know some of the men . . . are fearful of you, sir, but I can't believe they're right about it.

CLAGGART: You're a fool, fellow. In time, you'll learn to fear me like the rest. Young you are, and scarcely used to the fit of your man's flesh.

BILLY: I know they're wrong, sir. You aren't like they say. Nobody could be so.

CLAGGART: So . . . ? So what, boy? Vicious, did you mean to say, or brutal? But they aren't wrong, and you would see it, but for those blue eyes that light so kindly on your fellow men.

BILLY: Oh, I've got no education, I know that. There must be a lot of things a man misses when he's ignorant. But learning's hard. Must be sort of lonely, too.

CLAGGART: What are you prating of, half-man, half-child? Your messmates crowd around, admire your yellow hair and your blue eyes, do tricks and favors for you out of love, and you talk about loneliness!

BILLY: I just noticed the way you were looking off to leeward as I came up, sir. Kind of sad, you were looking.

CLAGGART: Not sadness, boy. Another feeling, more like . . . pleasure. That's it. I can feel it now, looking at you. A certain . . . pleasure.

BILLY (flattered): Thank you, sir.

CLAGGART (annoyed at BILLY's incomprehension): Pah.

BILLY: Just talking with you, sir, I can tell they're wrong about you. They're ignorant, like me.

CLAGGART: Compliment for compliment, eh, boy? Have you no heart for terror, fellow? you've seen this stick in use. Have you not got sense and spleen and liver to be scared, even to be cowardly?

BILLY: No, sir, I guess not. I like talking to you, sir. But please, sir, tell me something.

CLAGGART: I wonder if I can. Well, ask it.

BILLY: Why do you want us to believe you're cruel, and not really like everybody else?

CLAGGART: I think you are the only child alive who wouldn't understand if I explained; or else you'd not believe it.

BILLY: Oh, I'd believe you, sir. There's much I could learn from you: I never knew a man like you before.

CLAGGART (slowly): Do you—like me, Billy Budd?

BILLY: You've always been most pleasant with me, sir.

CLAGGART: Have I?

BILLY: Yes, sir. In the mess, the day I came aboard? And almost every day you have a pleasant word.

CLAGGART: And what I have said tonight, are these pleasant words?

BILLY: Yes, sir. I was wondering . . . could I talk to you between watches, when you've nothing else to do?

CLAGGART: You're a plausible boy, Billy. Aye, the nights are long, and talking serves to pass them.

BILLY: Thank you, sir. That would mean a lot to me.

CLAGGART: Perhaps to me as well. (*drops his rattan.* BILLY *picks it up and hands it back to him.* CLAGGART *stares at it a moment, then at* BILLY) No. No! Charm me, too, would you! Get away!

BILLY (*surprised and puzzled*): Aye, sir. (*He exits down the hatchway. After a pause in which* CLAGGART *recovers his self-control* SQUEAK *appears*)

CLAGGART (*without turning*): Come here. I thought I told you to put that new seaman Budd on report. Why was it not done?

SQUEAK: I tried, Mister Claggart, sir. I couldn't find noththing out of place. Gear all stowed perfect.

CLAGGART: Then disarrange it. You know the practice. I want him on report.

SQUEAK: Two of his messmates is ones nearly caught me at it before.

CLAGGART: Then be more careful. Now get along and see you make out something. (SQUEAK *scurries off below-decks as* VERE *comes into sight on the quarterdeck*)

VERE: Master-at-Arms. What is that man doing above decks?

CLAGGART: Ship's corporal, sir. A routine report.

VERE: There is nothing in this ship of so routine a nature that I do not concern myself in it. Remember that.

CLAGGART: Aye, aye, sir. With your permission, sir. (*Exit.* VERE *walks along the deck and scans the sails as* SEYMOUR *enters*)

SEYMOUR: Fine evening, sir.

VERE: Yes, a fine evening, Seymour. How is the glass?

SEYMOUR: Falling, I believe, sir. I think we'll toss a little before morning. Well, I suppose I should be in my cabin inspecting the deck logs.

VERE: Stay for a moment, Seymour. In the days and nights to come, you and I will not often have an opportunity to stand easy and talk.

SEYMOUR: Aye, sir. I expect the French will put us to our stations any hour now.

VERE: Are you impressed by omens, Seymour? This seaman we've just buried: I think of him as an omen of some sort, a melancholy prologue to this voyage.

SEYMOUR: Aye, sir. Hard on the sailor, certainly, but that's the service. But we've been lucky in other ways. An accident, now, that's unavoidable.

VERE: It was more than an accident, Seymour.

SEYMOUR: This maintop sailor? How do you mean, sir?

VERE: The man was sent aloft sick, by the Master-at-Arms, contrary to my standing order. Budd, the new seaman, implied as much, and the maintop watch confirmed it. The Master-at-Arms lied to me.

SEYMOUR: What are you going to do, sir? What action can you take? He's a valuable man, one we can hardly do without as things are now.

VERE: I shall do nothing at present, only wait and observe him. No court-martial could do more than strip him of his rank for such misconduct. I will let him have his head until some act puts him squarely counter to the law, then let the law consume him.

SEYMOUR: Why trouble the natural order to no purpose? Shouldn't we let it be?

VERE: Must a man always shrug, let things alone and drift?

Would to God I could take this power of mine and break him now, smash all the laws to powder and be a man again.

SEYMOUR: We must serve the law, sir, or give up the right and privilege of service. It's how we live.

VERE: Live? Oh, you're right. Below this deck are men who at a call skip on the hurling spars against the wind, at Beat-to-quarters run as if they willed it. Yet each of us steps alone within this pattern, this formal movement centered on itself. Men live and die, taken by pattern, born to it, knowing nothing. No man can defy the code we live by and not be broken by it.

SEYMOUR: You are the Captain, sir. You maintain that code.

VERE: Keep an order we cannot understand. That's true. The world demands it: demands that at the back of every peacemaker there be the gun, the gallows and the gaol. I talk of justice, and would turn the law gentle for those who serve here; but a Claggart stands in my shadow, for I need him. So the world goes, wanting not justice, but order . . . to be let alone to hug its own iniquities. Let a man work to windward of that law and he'll be hove down. No hope for him, none. (*Enter* WYATT)

WYATT: Eight o'clock report, sir. Ship inspected and all in order.

SEYMOUR: Very well, carry on. (WYATT *goes off*) By your leave, sir. Good night. (*Exit.* VERE *remains, crosses to the hatch and looks down, then slowly upward at the set of the sails*)

*End of Scene Two*

SCENE THREE

SCENE: *The maindeck several nights later.*

> *Four bells is struck offstage. A sailor climbs wearily down the ratlines, drops to the deck and goes below.* CLAGGART *stands by the larboard rail.*

> *As* BILLY *enters from below decks, he sees the Master-at-Arms.*

BILLY: Hello, sir. (CLAGGART *looks at him without answering, then turns and goes off forward. The* DANSKER *follows* BILLY *up onto the deck*) Well, that's all there is to tell, Dansker. I always lash my hammock just so, and stow my gear same as all the others. They don't get in trouble.

DANSKER: Mister Claggart is down upon you, Billy.

BILLY: Jimmy-Legs? Why he calls me the sweet and pleasant fellow, they tell me.

DANSKER: Does he so, Baby lad? Aye, a sweet voice has Mister Claggart.

BILLY: For me he has. I seldom pass him but there comes a pleasant word.

DANSKER: And that's because he's down upon you.

BILLY: But he's my friend. I know he talks a little strange, but he's my friend.

DANSKER: Nobody's friend is Jimmy-Legs. Yours the least of all, maybe. Lay aloft, Baby. You'll be late to relieve your watch.

BILLY: Aye, Dansker. (*He climbs up the ratlines out of sight. The* DANSKER *watches him go.* CLAGGART *appears, but the* DANSKER *ignores him and goes off aft. As* JENKINS *comes into view climbing down the ratlines,* CLAGGART *gestures off and fades into a shadowy corner of the deck near the quarterdeck ladder.* SQUEAK *enters as* JENKINS *drops to the deck, and intercepts him as he starts down the companionway)*

SQUEAK: It's all right, mate, slack off and stay a bit.

JENKINS: What do you want? I pick my own company.

SQUEAK: So does I, mate, so does I. And if I may make so bold to say it, you'll be smarter to pick your company more careful.

JENKINS: If you got something to say to me, talk up, else I'll get below.

SQUEAK: Don't be hasty, now, mate, don't be in a sweat. It's haste gets good men into trouble. What d'you think of our new hand here, Billy Boy? Mister Claggart's taken with him, too. Fine young fellow, ha?

JENKINS: Talk plain. What d'you mean?

SQUEAK: I overheard him talking just this day. Would maybe surprise you some, what he had to say about yourself and a few other lads.

JENKINS: What?

SQUEAK: Aoh, bit of talk about his messmates. He don't fancy us! Not like his feather boys aboard the merchantman.

JENKINS: You lying cut-throat, try something else! Billy's in my mess; since he come on board he's rare been out of my sight. You're lying, you bloody nark! I know you too well. You'll need to try some other way to get Bill into trouble. Get away, and don't come lying to me no more.

SQUEAK: Aoh, so it's that friendly you are! Well, now, ain't that sweet! You're not smart, Jenkins. Remember, man: I tried to help you out. When you're feeling the cat between your shoulders . . .

JENKINS *(seizing him)*: Damn your lies! Get back to Jimmy-Legs and kiss his butt. And stay out of my way!

(*throws* SQUEAK *down and exits.* SQUEAK *watches him go.* CLAGGART *steps out of the shadows*)

CLAGGART: I heard your little talk. You lack subtlety; but I'm the greater fool to use you in these matters. You're inept.

SQUEAK: Aoh! Why don't you do it yourself, if you don't need me!

CLAGGART: I need nobody, least of all a rum-soaked footpad from the Old Bailey. If you wish to have free rein with your distasteful habits, mind your cockney manners! I stand between you and the flogging whip. Improve your style, or you stand tomorrow forenoon at the gratings!

SQUEAK: I only meant as you could do it better, Mister Claggart, I wouldn't say nothing to . . .

CLAGGART (*cuts him on the arm with his rattan*): Don't touch me!—Keep Budd in petty troubles, that you can do. Unlash his hammock. Keep him on report. In time I'll let you know what plans I have for him. Get aft! (SQUEAK, *eager to get away, scuttles aft as the* DANSKER *enters*) Well, old man. Moon's in and out tonight. There's weather somewhere. (*The* DANSKER *turns down the night lamp over the cabin door and starts off*) Stay and have a pipe.

DANSKER: I have the watch.

CLAGGART: You take your duties as seriously as ever.

DANSKER: Aye. They are all of life for an old seaman like me. (*turns to go*)

CLAGGART: You move away from me as though I were some kind of stalking beast. You avoid me, too.

DANSKER: Your word, John, "too."

CLAGGART: You know what I mean. The hands detest me. You are a hand, older than most, and older in your hatred, I have no doubt. But why, man? You at least should see me as I am, a man who knows how the world's made: made as I am.

DANSKER: How can I know what goes on in your head?

CLAGGART: The enigmatic Dansker. Come, it's dark, we can drop disguises when night serves to hold the disclosing soul apart.

DANSKER: You know who you remind me of . . . maintopman: Billy Budd.

CLAGGART: More enigmas! That sunny, smiling infant with no spleen nor knowledge in his head?

DANSKER: I'll leave you now.

CLAGGART: No, stay a while. This is a night for secrets and disclosures.

DANSKER: You have half the truth and Billy Budd the other. He can't see there's evil in the world, and you won't see the good.

CLAGGART: So. And I take it you come in between.

DANSKER: I keep outside. I am too old to stand between sky and water.

CLAGGART: And yet you hate me, too.

DANSKER: I hate an incomplete man.

CLAGGART: Damn all this talk. Hate me and have done. Let it alone, I say. Whatever else it is, this thing is Man, still!

DANSKER: I'll be off.

CLAGGART: Don't go. The moon's gone under. Let us talk this out. You are a wise man in your senile way.

DANSKER: Then take this for all my wisdom. You recognize the hatred of your shipmates as an honor paid to a soul they cannot understand. Your fine contempt for human love is nothing but regret.

CLAGGART: Stop there. I know the rest by heart. Nothing you say to me but clatters in my belly, watch on watch. Aye: when this arm moves out in gesture of love, it mocks me with a blow. Who lifts this arm? What officer commands this hireling flesh? Somewhere below the farthest marks and deeps, God anchors hearts, and his sea rusts mine hollow. The flukes break in the bottom, and I slack and stand, go in and out forever at God's humor. Look at this sea: for all her easy swell, who knows what bones, ribs and decay are fathomed at her base and move in her motion, so that on the flattest water, the very stricture of the dead can kill that beauty with a dance of death?—Here is a man. He holds, past fathom curves, drowned fleets of human agonies that gesture when the long tide pulls.

DANSKER: Aye, John. But you must know that other men are moved so. Look up some evening at the quarterdeck for another poor thoughtful devil like you, like me, pacing all night between his doubts.

CLAGGART: What, Vere? That fine-drawn manner doesn't deceive me. There's a whited sepulchre, like all soft-spoken charmers of this world.

DANSKER: You don't believe in anything besides yourself, eh John?

CLAGGART: I've said what I have said. I know myself, and look to that. You should try it. Go to your post, old man, and your everlasting duties (CLAGGART *turns away.* BILLY *scrambles into view down the ratlines and calls out excitedly*)

BILLY: Quarterdeck ho!

RATCLIFFE (*coming forward to the forward break of the quarterdeck*): Sound off!

BILLY: Strange sail one mile off the larboard beam!

CLAGGART (*to* DANSKER): A Frenchman! Get to your station.

RATCLIFFE (*on the quarterdeck ladder*): Mister Duncan! Sound Beat-to-quarters! Clear for action!

DUNCAN (*offstage*): Aye aye, sir!

RATCLIFFE: Gardiner! (*Enter* GARDINER)

GARDINER: Sir?

RATCLIFFE: Report to the Captain, strange sail on the larboard beam. Then send Payne to the wheel. (*Exit* GARDINER) Master-at-Arms, send a man to the mast to relay lookout's reports. Inspect battle stations and report to me when they are fully manned.

CLAGGART: Aye aye, sir. (*exit*)

VOICE (*off*): She's a French frigate! Steering east by south! (*Enter* VERE *and* SEYMOUR)

VERE: Prepare to make chase. Have your quartermaster steer small.

RATCLIFFE: Aye aye, sir.

> (*Enter the* DRUMMER *and sound Beat-to-quarters.* *Men run on, to gun stations, rigging, crossing stage and off.*)

SEYMOUR: She's too fast for us, sir. We'll never come up with her.

VERE: We are bound to try, though we were sure to fail. And we may smell powder before this chase is over.

CLAGGART (*re-entering*): Battle stations fully manned, sir!

SEYMOUR: May we try a shot at her now?

VERE: She's drawing south. Yes, commence firing, Mr. Seymour.

SEYMOUR: Larboard battery, fire one!

DUNCAN: Fire! (*Fire one gun.*)

VERE: Fire at will!

SEYMOUR: Fire at will!

> (*Guns fire dissynchronously*)

*End of Act One*

# ACT TWO

SCENE: *The quarterdeck and part of the maindeck a few minutes before 0800. A high wind. On the quarterdeck are* LIEUTENANT WYATT, MIDSHIPMAN REA *and the helmsman,* STOLL.

REA: I'm glad this watch is over. I'm tired.

WYATT: Make your entry in the log before your relief comes up. Bring it out here and I'll sign it.

REA: Aye, sir. What was our last position, do you remember?

WYATT: Thirteen ten west, forty-three forty north.

REA: And an easterly breeze.

WYATT: Aye, make it so. That'll make Ratcliffe happy. Last time he had an east wind, she blew his hat over the side. And put down "Running ground swell."

REA: Aye aye, sir. (*exits*)

WYATT: Helmsman, keep her close-hauled.

STOLL: I can't, sir. Too much cloth in the wind.

WYATT: Well hold her close as you can, and let the next watch reef sail if they like.

STOLL: Aye aye, sir. (*Enter* RATCLIFFE)

WYATT: Morning, Johnny! You're on time!

RATCLIFFE: What's the course?

WYATT: Steady south. Wind's easterly. Glass is dropping.

RATCLIFFE: East wind? Damn it. (*Enter* BYREN, *the relief helmsman*) By the way, you forgot to sign the order book.

WYATT: All right. Thanks.

STOLL: I've been relieved, sir. Byren has the helm.

WYATT: Very well. (*Exit* STOLL) Who's mate of your watch?

RATCLIFFE: The Admiralty midshipman. That lobcock Gardiner, hang him. (*Eight bells*)

WYATT: Where the devil is he? It's eight. (*Enter* REA *and* GARDINER *separately, meeting*)

RATCLIFFE: There he comes. He looks happy. That means trouble for some poor devil. (GARDINER *snatches the log out of* REA's *hands and bounds up to the quarterdeck*)

REA: I've been relieved, sir. Horatio, Lord Gardiner has the watch.

WYATT: Ah, Midshipman Gardiner. The backbone of the British Navy.

RATCLIFFE: The backside, if you ask me.

WYATT: All right, Rea. You can turn in. (REA *exits*)

RATCLIFFE: Pity we lost that Frenchman last night. A little action would season the monotony of these interminable watches.

WYATT: Did you ever hear of a ship-of-the-line running down a frigate, even with the wind? Ah, it's a magnificent morning! Thickening overcast, heavy ground swell, a fresh levanter breeze, and you, Johnny, are the Pride of the Morning!

RATCLIFFE: Mmm. Has the skipper been on deck yet?

WYATT: Not since sunrise. He came up then and paced the deck and stared off east like a sleepwalker. Then went below again without a word.

RATCLIFFE: He thinks too much.

WYATT: Well if you ever make captain, your crew won't have that to complain of, anyway. Am I relieved?

RATCLIFFE: Yes, I relieve you. (*Tosses his cap to* WYATT) Here. Take this below, will you?

WYATT: What? You'll be out of uniform, man. Mister

Gardiner wouldn't approve of your standing watch without a hat, would you, Midshipman Gardiner?

GARDINER: Sir, the Articles state that officers on watch . . .

RATCLIFFE: Well hang it, I lost twelve shillings the last time my hat went over the rail, and this is the only other one I've got. To hell with the Articles.

WYATT: Mind your language! It's downright mutinous. Well, don't expect me to stand your watches if you catch your death of cold. Good morning. (*exit*)

GARDINER: Midshipman Rea, sir, I don't like to say it, but his log entries are impossible.

RATCLIFFE: Then enter yourself, Mister Gardiner. So are you.

GARDINER: Yes sir. But I do think he ought to be told . . .

RATCLIFFE: Go find the Captain and report to him the wind's abeam. Respectfully suggest we ought to take in topsails.

GARDINER: Aye aye, sir. (*goes down stairs*)

RATCLIFFE: And don't forget to tell him I haven't got a hat.

GARDINER: What's that, sir?

RATCLIFFE: Nothing, sir! You got my order. Dump your ballast and shove off!

GARDINER: I thought you spoke to me, sir.

RATCLIFFE: I avoid that whenever possible. Move!

GARDINER: Yes, sir.

RATCLIFFE: Ye gods, what a brat. Nothing off, helmsman. She's well enough thus.

BYREN: Nothing off, sir.

GARDINER (*nearly bumping into* VERE *as he emerges from cabin, followed by* SEYMOUR *and* HALLAM): Atten-tion!

RATCLIFFE: Good morning, sir.

VERE: Morning, Mister Ratcliffe.

GARDINER (*starting after* VERE, *bumps into* HALLAM): Damn it, man, watch what you're doing!

VERE: Midshipman Gardiner.

GARDINER: Sir?

VERE: How long, pray, have you been in this ship, or any ship?

GARDINER: This is my first cruise, sir.

VERE: Your first cruise. A wartime cruise as well. And you are a midshipman. A midshipman, Mister Gardiner, let me tell you, is neither fish, flesh, nor fowl, and certainly no seaman. You're a salt-water hermaphrodite, Mister Gardiner. And unless you have a mind to be generally known as Spit-kit Gardiner, I recommend more tolerance toward the men. Now, is that clear?

GARDINER: Aye aye, sir!

VERE: Very well, you may carry on.

RATCLIFFE: We've a weather helm, sir, and bow seas.

VERE: Take in topsails, if you please, Mister Ratcliffe.

RATCLIFFE: Aye aye, sir. Mister Duncan!

DUNCAN (*enters*): Aye, sir?

RATCLIFFE: Douse your topsails and topgallants. Haul in the weather braces.

DUNCAN: Aye aye, sir. (*exit*) Away aloft! Hands by top-gallant sheets and halyards!

GARDINER: Aloft there! Keep fast the weather sheets till the yards are down, da . . . if you please!

RATCLIFFE: Get aloft yourself, Mister Gardiner, see they do it right, since you're not satisfied.

GARDINER: Sir, the Articles state that . . .

RATCLIFFE: Did you hear me?

GARDINER: Aye aye, sir. (*exits up ratlines*)

DUNCAN (*off*): Haul taut!

VERE: You disapprove of Gardiner, Mister Ratcliffe?

RATCLIFFE: He seems to think he's the only midshipman aboard capable of doing anything properly. He's always looking at you as if your hat weren't squared.

VERE: That is an unfortunate simile under the present circumstances.

RATCLIFFE (*caught*): Oh, I—er— Keep her close to the wind, helmsman. Don't fall away!

DUNCAN (*off*): Let go topgallant bowlines!

VERE: I think Gardiner has had enough correction for one day. Call him down to our level, Mister Ratcliffe.

RATCLIFFE: Aye, sir. Mister Gardiner! You may come off your perch now! (BILLY *descends rigging and starts offstage*) What do you think of our new man Budd, Captain?

SEYMOUR: That boy did a smart piece of work for us last night, sir. He's the nimblest man on the tops I've ever watched. Wyatt wants him for captain of the foretop.

VERE: Very well, let Budd take the post. He certainly deserves it for his actions last night during the chase. I'll speak to him myself.

SEYMOUR: He'll like hearing it from you, sir.

VERE: Hallam, go call Budd, the lad moving forward there. (*Exit* HALLAM. GARDINER *appears, looking sick*) Well done, Gardiner. You may lay below and draw an extra tot of rum. You look s . . . chilly.

GARDINER: Thank you, sir. (*exit*)

SEYMOUR: By the way, sir, Budd has been on the Master-at-Arms' report once or twice for some petty misdemeanor. Nothing serious. (*steps aside with* RATCLIFFE. BILLY *enters, followed by* HALLAM)

BILLY: You sent for me, sir?

VERE: Yes, Budd. Your division officer recommends you for a post of more responsibility. He thinks you can perform duties of a higher station, and so do I, after last night. So I've agreed that you shall have Williams' place on the foretop.

BILLY: But—Williams is captain of the foretop, sir.

VERE: The station calls for a younger man. Lieutenant Wyatt asked for you, and the spirit you showed last night warrants it. That is a real honor for a man so new on board.

BILLY: The Navy's new to me, Captain, but I hardly know anything else but the sea and ships.

VERE: And how do you like us, now that the awesomeness has worn away a bit?

BILLY: The Navy's a bustling world, sir. Bigger than the *Rights of Man,* and I get lost sometimes. But my mates lend me a hand. Why even Jimmy-Legs—beg pardon, sir, the Master-at-Arms, I mean—he's good to me, too.

VERE: The sea and the Navy exact a discipline, but it need not be a harsh one. In some ways I envy the man who dances across the tops and seems to rule the ship and sea below. Up there is a pleach of ropes for you to make a world of. Though winds have their way with tackle of your world, you live at ease against your strength and the round bole of the mast in your back. You are a king up there, while the water curds and frolics at the forefoot. I envy you that stance.

BILLY: You can trust me, Captain.

VERE: I do, boy. Very well, that's all.

BILLY: Aye aye, sir. Thank you, sir, thank you! (*runs off*)

VERE: Hallam, find the Master-at-Arms and bid him report to me.

HALLAM: Aye aye, sir. (*exit.* SEYMOUR *joins* VERE)

VERE: If I had a son, I'd hope for one like Budd.

SEYMOUR: Aye, sir. Fine boy. He's a force for order in this ship, certainly. I hope his charm's contagious.

VERE: One such is enough. Men cannot stand very much perfection. It's a disease that we stamp out at its first rash showing. (*Enter* CLAGGART. SEYMOUR *withdraws*) Master-at-Arms, I want to make a change on the Watch, Quarter and Station Bill. I needn't have troubled you about it until later, but I am especially interested in this change.

CLAGGART: The time of day is indifferent to me, sir.

VERE: Williams, present captain of the foretop, is assigned to the afterguard. I am replacing him with Budd.

CLAGGART: William Budd, sir? You do not mean the so-called Handsome Sailor?

VERE: Aye, William Budd, the new seaman from the *Rights of Man*.

CLAGGART: I know him, sir.

VERE: Do you find anything unusual in this replacement?

CLAGGART: You must be aware, sir, that he is . . .

VERE: Well? That he is what? I know he's an able seaman.

CLAGGART: Nothing, sir. But I wondered if he were entirely trustworthy. He has been aboard such a brief time.

VERE: Long enough to prove himself to me, and to his shipmates.

CLAGGART: Very good, sir.

VERE: He is captain of the foretop. That is all.

CLAGGART: With your permission, sir. Will there not be some dissatisfaction among the foretopmen who have been aboard much longer than Budd?

VERE: Master-at-Arms: I concern myself with these matters. They are none of your function. Until such time as the senior topmen formally object to Budd for incapacity, he is captain of the foretop. Make it so on the Bill. (*exit*)

RATCLIFFE: What are you waiting for, man? Light to dawn? Promotion? You got the order.

CLAGGART: With your permission, sir.

> (*As* CLAGGART *goes off,* RATCLIFFE *spits over the rail*)

*End of Scene One*

SCENE TWO

SCENE: *Forward part of the deck. Night. Eight bells. A
man descends the rigging and goes off.* CLAGGART *enters,
stands by the hatch for a moment, then exits forward.*
BILLY *comes down off watch, drops to the deck and
remains in shadow, leaning over the rail, looking seaward.* JENKINS *stealthily and silently comes up from
below deck.*

BILLY: Jenkins! What you doing topside . . . (JENKINS
*puts his hand over* BILLY'S *mouth*)

JENKINS (*in a whisper*): Stow the noise! (*Releases* BILLY)

BILLY: You're after Mister Claggart, like you said you
would!

JENKINS: Well? What about it? You try and stop me?

BILLY: He knows, Jenkins! I tell you, he knows! He's
ready for you!

JENKINS: Then by God, I'll oblige him! I been waiting up
here every night, waiting for him to come by when it's
dark. Now get away and let me do it!

BILLY: No! I won't let you hang yourself!

JENKINS: I don't give a fiddler's damn what happens to
me! Move out of my way, mate!

BILLY: No! Give me the knife.

JENKINS: The knife's for Claggart. You're a nice boy, Bill,
but I ain't playing with you. You get away below,
quick. This game ain't for boys.

BILLY: Damme, no, Jenkins! You'll hang yourself!

JENKINS: Take your hands off! The moon's under, I can
do it now! Oh, sweet mother of God, leave me go!

BILLY: No!

JENKINS: Yes, by God!

> (JENKINS *strikes* BILLY; *struggle, in which* BILLY *wrests knife from* JENKINS, *and it falls on deck.* BILLY *knocks* JENKINS *down*)

CLAGGART (*offstage*): What's that noise? Stand where you are! (*entering*) You again! Well? Explain this pageant.

BILLY: He . . . I had to hit him, sir. He struck at me.

CLAGGART: Mm. And drew that knife on you, too, no doubt.

BILLY: Yes, sir.

CLAGGART: I have been waiting, forward there, for Jenkins. You intercepted him, I take it.

BILLY: I didn't know you were looking for him, sir.

CLAGGART: You shouldn't meddle, my fine young friend, in matters that don't concern you! I was expecting him. (*Enter* DANSKER) There, help the body up. I do not thank you, boy, for cheating me of the pleasure of his punishment.

WYATT (*offstage*): What's the disturbance there? You, forward on the spar-deck!

CLAGGART: Master-at-Arms reports all in order, sir!

WYATT (*offstage*): Stand where you are.

CLAGGART: The sweet and pleasant fellow saved you, Jenkins. But I reserve you still for my own justice in due time. Say nothing to this officer. (*Enter* WYATT)

WYATT: What's the matter, Master-at-Arms? It's an odd hour for stargazing.

CLAGGART: A slight matter, sir. I found these two men together here on deck, contrary to the Captain's orders. I was sending them below when you called out.

WYATT: Oh, is that all. Carry on, then.

CLAGGART: Aye aye, sir. Now then, get below, both of you. (*Enter* VERE *followed by* HALLAM. *The* DANSKER *goes off*) Attention!

VERE: Wyatt, what's this mean?

**WYATT:** Two men on deck without permission, sir.

**VERE:** Is there no more to this? The story's lame, man. What occurred? (*silence*) Very well, then. Go along, both of you.

**BILLY:** Aye aye, sir. Come along, mate. (*exits with* JEN-KINS)

**VERE:** Your knife, Master-at-Arms?

**CLAGGART:** William Budd's, sir, I believe.

**VERE:** Return it to him. (*exits with* HALLAM *and* WYATT)
    (CLAGGART *raps rail with rattan.* SQUEAK *approaches warily*)

**CLAGGART:** Listen carefully; you may make up for your late mistakes if you do this smartly. Give Budd just time enough to get to sleep. At four bells wake him. Bring him to the lee forechains. You understand?

**SQUEAK:** Mister Claggart, sir . . . we done enough to him. He's a good lad, Mister Claggart. Couldn't it be somebody else? Jenkins, maybe?

**CLAGGART:** So. He's softened your heart too, eh? Do as you're ordered, man, or I'll see your back laid raw with a flogging whip! Remember: I will be watching you. Bring him to the lee forechains. And when you're there . . .

**SQUEAK:** Dansker. Moving forward.

**CLAGGART:** Step back, you fool. Wait for me.
    (*Exit* SQUEAK. *The* DANSKER *enters*)

**DANSKER:** Baby saved you, eh? And you are angry.

**CLAGGART:** Saved me, you say? From what? I've tried to tempt Jenkins to this blow, so as to break his toplofty spirit with his neck; and I am "saved" by that guileless idiot! He'd turn the other cheek to me, in Christian kindness! Well: there's a second pleasure in striking that same face twice. I can destroy him, too, if I choose to do it!

**DANSKER:** Crazy, crazy!

CLAGGART: All right, old man, call it madness then. Whatever its name, it will plunder the sweetness from that
face, or it will kill us both.

DANSKER: You are afraid of him.

CLAGGART: Afraid? Of Budd? What nonsense is that?

DANSKER: He usurps the crew; they turn from hating you
to loving him, and leave you impotent.

CLAGGART: That bastard innocent frighten me! That wit-
less kindness that spills from him has neither force
nor aim. Stand out from between us, or you founder
together, sink in five hundred fathoms with him, if I
want it so!

DANSKER: Aye, then, if you take that tack, let it be both
of us. You expect me to sit by and watch your deliberate
arm seize him and force him under?

CLAGGART: Why not? You have always done that. I
thought your practice was to stay outside. What breeds
the saintly knight errant in you?

DANSKER: I am old, but I have some manhood left.

CLAGGART: What can you do? You've drifted with the tide
too long, old one. You are as involved as I am now.

DANSKER: So you may say. In this ship a man lives as he
can, and finds a way to make life tolerable for himself. I did so. That was a fault. But no longer.

CLAGGART: Stand clear. You haven't courage to cross me.

DANSKER: Eh, I'm not afraid of you; I see your scheme.

CLAGGART: Damn your feeble, ineffectual eyes! (*striking
him; the* DANSKER *falls*) You can see only what I let
you see!

DANSKER: Say what you like. I see your scheme; so will
Captain if need be.

CLAGGART (*pulling him to his feet*): Take a warning for
yourself, old man. And keep away! You are on watch,
eh? Well, go back to sleep again, or I'll report you.
(DANSKER *exits.* CLAGGART *watches him go, then*

*violently breaks his rattan and throws the pieces over side*)

*End of Scene Two*

SCENE THREE

SCENE: *Forward part of the main deck. Four bells.* CLAG-GART *stands with one hand on the rail, waiting. After a short pause, hearing a sound, he fades into shadow.* SQUEAK *enters, bending over and running.*

SQUEAK: Hssssssssssst! (BILLY, *sleepy and rubbing his eyes, enters*)

BILLY: You brought me all the way up here, out of my hammock. Now what do you want?

SQUEAK: I heard you're captain of the foretop, Bill. That right?

BILLY: Aye. What's that to do with you?

SQUEAK: Ah, now you can be more use to your shipmates then ever you was before.

BILLY: What?

SQUEAK: You was impressed, now, weren't you? Well, so was I. We're not the only impressed ones, Billy. There's a gang of us. Could you help . . . at a pinch?

BILLY: What do you mean?

SQUEAK: See here . . . (*holds up two coins*) Here's two gold guineas for you, Bill. Put in with us. Most of the men aboard are only waiting for a word, and they'll follow you. There's more for you where these come from. What'd you say? If you join us, Bill, there's not a man aboard won't come along! Are you with us? The ship'll be ours when we're ready to take it!

BILLY: Damme, I don't know what you're driving at, but you had better go where you belong! (SQUEAK, *surprised, does not move.* BILLY *springs up*) If you don't start, I'll toss you back over the rail! (SQUEAK *decamps.* BILLY *watches him and starts off himself.* DANSKER, *offstage, calls out*)

DANSKER: Hallo, what's the matter? (*enters*) Ah, Beauty, is it you again? Something must have been the matter, for you stammered. (CLAGGART *appears and comes forward*)

CLAGGART: You seem to favor the maindeck, Billy Budd. What brings you topside at this hour, man, against my orders and the Captain's?

BILLY: I . . . found an afterguardsman in our part of the ship here, and I bid him be off where he belongs.

DANSKER: And is that all you did about it, boy?

BILLY: Aye, Dansker, nothing more.

CLAGGART: A strange sort of hour to police the deck. Name the afterguardsman.

BILLY: I . . . can't say, Mister Claggart. I couldn't see him clear enough.

DANSKER: Don't be a fool, speak up, accuse him.

CLAGGART: Well?

BILLY: I can't say, sir.

CLAGGART: You refuse? Then get below, and stay where you belong.

BILLY: Aye aye, sir. Good night, sir. Good night, Dansker. (*exits*)

CLAGGART: I'm glad you saw this mutinous behavior.

DANSKER: Your crazy brain squeezes out false conclusions. He has done nothing except find you out, though he's too innocent to know it.

CLAGGART: I am not hoodwinked by his weak excuse. What else would he be doing at this hour, but fanning rebel tempers like his own?

DANSKER: I stood in the shadows forward when your

pander Squeak slipped by me, running from this place. You set him on, on purpose to trap Billy.

CLAGGART: And I will do that, old man. But you will say nothing about it; see you don't. (*Enter* VERE *followed by* HALLAM)

VERE: Well, Master-at-Arms. You stand long watches.

CLAGGART: Sir. May I take the liberty of reserving my explanation for your private ear. I believe your interest in this matter would incline you to prefer some privacy.

VERE (*to* DANSKER *and* HALLAM): Leave us. Hallam, stand within hail. (DANSKER *and* HALLAM *go off*) Well? What is it you wish to say, Master-at-Arms?

CLAGGART: During my rounds this night, I have seen enough to convince me that one man aboard, at least, is dangerous; especially in a ship which musters some who took a guilty part in the late serious uprisings . . .

VERE: You may spare a reference to that.

CLAGGART: Your pardon, sir. Quite lately I have begun to notice signs of some sort of movement secretly afoot, and prompted by the man in question. I thought myself not warranted, so long as this suspicion was only indistinct, in reporting it. But recently . . .

VERE: Come to the point, man.

CLAGGART: Sir, I deeply feel the cruel responsibility of making a report involving such serious consequences to the sailor mainly concerned. But God forbid, sir, that this ship should suffer the experience of the Nore.

VERE: Never mind that! You say there is one dangerous man. Name him.

CLAGGART: Willam Budd, the . . . captain of the foretop.

VERE: William Budd?

CLAGGART: The same, sir. But for all his youth and appealing manners, a secret, vicious lad.

VERE: How, vicious?

CLAGGART: He insinuates himself into the good will of his

mates so that they will as least say a word for him perhaps even take action with him, should it come to that. With your pardon, sir; you note but his fair face; under that there lies a man-trap.

VERE (*after a pause*): Master-at-Arms, I intend to test your accusation here and now. Hallam! (*Enter* HALLAM)

HALLAM: Aye, sir.

VERE: Find Budd, the foretopman. Manage to tell him out of earshot that he is wanted here. Keep him in talk yourself. Go along.

HALLAM: Aye aye, sir. (*exits*)

VERE (*angry and perturbed*): Do you come to me with such a foggy tale, Master-at-Arms? As to William Budd, cite me an act, or spoken word of his, confirming what you here in general charge against him. Wait; weigh what you speak. Just now, and in this case, there is the yardarm end for false witness.

CLAGGART: I understand, sir. Tonight, when on my rounds, discovering Budd's hammock was unused, I combed the ship, and found him in conclave with several growlers; men, who, like himself, spread unrest and rebellion in the crew. They were collected here, near the lee fore-chains, and when I ordered them below, young Budd and others threatened me, and swore they'd drop me, and some officers they hate, overboard, some misty night. Should you, sir, desire substantial proof, it is not far.

(*Enter* HALLAM, *followed by* BILLY.)

VERE: Hallam, stand apart and see that we are not disturbed. (HALLAM *exits*) And now, Master-at-Arms, tell this man to his face what you told me of him.

CLAGGART (*moving near to* BILLY, *and looking directly at him*): Certainly, sir. I said this man, this William Budd, acting so out of angry resentment against impressment and his officers, against this ship, this Service, and the

King, breeds in the crew a spirit of rebellion against the officers, the mates, and me, urging some outrage like the late revolt. I myself have seen and heard him speak with manifest malingerers and men who growl of mistreatment, harshness, unfair pay and similar complaints. I say this man threatened his officers with murder, and was bent tonight on urging other men to act concertedly in mutiny. I have nothing further to say, sir.

BILLY (*tries to speak, but can make only incoherent sounds. He seems to be in pain from the contortions of his face and the gurgling which is all he can effect for speech*)

VERE: Speak, man, speak! Defend yourself! (*remembering* BILLY's *impediment, goes to him and puts a hand on his shoulder reassuringly*) There is no hurry, boy. Take your time, take your time.

(*After agonized dumb gesturing and stammering, increased by* VERE's *kindness,* BILLY's *arm hits out at* CLAGGART. CLAGGART *staggers, falls, lies still*)

VERE: Stand back, man! It was a lie, then! (BILLY, *shaking, only stares at the body.* VERE *raises the body to a sitting position. Since* CLAGGART *remains inert,* VERE *lowers him again slowly, then rises.* BILLY *tries again to speak, without success; he is crying and badly frightened*) No need to speak now, Billy. Hallam! (*Enter* HALLAM) Tell the Surgeon I wish to see him here at once. And bid Mister Seymour report to my cabin without delay. (*to* BILLY) Retire to the stateroom aft. Remain there till I summon you. (BILLY *exits.* VERE *waits, turning once to stare at* CLAGGART's *body. Enter the* SURGEON) Surgeon, tell me how it is with him. (SURGEON *bends over* CLAGGART *briefly, then looks up in surprise*) Come, we must dispatch. Go now. I shall presently call a drumhead court to try the man who out of God's own instinct dropped him there. Tell the lieutenants that a foretopman has, in an accidental fury, killed this man. Inform the Captain of Marines as well, and charge them to keep the matter to themselves. (SURGEON *exits*) The divine judgment of Ananias! Struck dead by the Angel of God . . . and I must judge the Angel. Can I save him? Have I that choice?

*End of Act Two*

# ACT THREE

SCENE: *Captain* VERE'S *cabin, a quarter of an hour later.*
VERE *and* SEYMOUR.

SEYMOUR: Budd beat a man to death! What had he done?

VERE: Lied again: lied to Budd's face, hoping to kill him
by it. Oh, the boy was tempted to it past endurance.

SEYMOUR: False witness has its penalty, sir. Budd has set
our justice right.

VERE: Aye, too right. This natural, right act, done in an instinct's fever of recognition, was late and fatal.

SEYMOUR: What are you going to do, Captain? Isn't this
last lie of the Master-at-Arms the very act you were
waiting for, so as to let the law destroy him, as you
said? He should have suffered at the yardarm if Billy
hadn't killed him.

VERE: Yes. He should. But by fair process of authority.
Budd has prevented that, and turned the law against
himself.

SEYMOUR: You can't condemn the boy for answering with
his arm for lack of words! The motive was clearly
justified.

VERE: Aye, but was the act? For God's sake try, try to
convince me I am wrong!

SEYMOUR: This Master-at-Arms, you knew him for a liar,
a vicious dog.

VERE: A dog's obeyed in office. Claggart was authority.

189

SEYMOUR: Then authority's an evil!

VERE: It often is. But it commands, and no man is its equal, not Billy, nor you, nor I. It will strike us down, and rightly, if we resist it.

SEYMOUR: Rightly! What power gives evil its authority? We should thank God the man's dead, and the world well rid of that particular devil.

VERE: Our life has ways to hedge its evil in. No one must go above them; even innocents. Laws of one kind or other shape our course from birth to death. These are the laws pronouncing Billy's guilt; Admiralty codes are merely shadows of them.

SEYMOUR: That's tyranny, not law, forcing conformity to wrongs, giving the victory to the devil himself!

VERE: I thought so once. But without this lawful tyranny, what should we have but worse tyranny of anarchy and chaos? So aboard this man-of-war. Oh, if I were a man alone, manhood would declare for Billy.

SEYMOUR: Then do it. Put your strength and your authority behind Budd, and let him go.

VERE: When I think I could have watched him grow in comely wholeness of manhood . . . all lost now. What could have been, quenched in evil, swept out by that undertow.

SEYMOUR: It's more than anyone can have to answer for, Captain; to his peers, or to his God. Let him go free and try on mortal flesh! Will you urge a noose for him; marked like a common felon, and that devil still to have his wish, killing the boy at last?

VERE: Can I do otherwise? I'd give my life to save his, if I could.

SEYMOUR: It's in your hands, Captain. Only you can help him now.

VERE: Billy, Billy. What have we done to you? (*knock*) Yes, come in. (*Enter* HALLAM)

HALLAM: Lieutenants Ratcliffe and Wyatt, sir.

VERE: Let them come in. (*Enter* RATCLIFFE *and* WYATT)

SEYMOUR: You both know why you've been summoned hither?

WYATT: Yes, sir.

RATCLIFFE: Aye, sir, in a general sort of way.

SEYMOUR: Then take your chairs. Ratcliffe. You here, Wyatt. You are appointed members of a court-martial convened under extraordinary circumstances by Captain Vere. I am Senior Member, and I declare this court open. (WYATT, RATCLIFFE, *and* SEYMOUR *sit.* VERE *remains standing, apart*) Sentry, bring the prisoner in. (HALLAM *salutes and exits*) As you know, the Master-at-Arms has been killed by the foretopman, Budd. Whether by accident or by design, and whether the act shall carry the penalty of death or no, you are to decide. There is only one witness, Captain Vere. I shall call upon him to give his deposition as soon as the sentry brings in the prisoner. (*An uneasy silence*)

WYATT: Budd wouldn't kill a minnow without good reason.

RATCLIFFE: What did the . . .

SEYMOUR: I had rather you did not express an opinion until after you have heard the evidence. (*Another awkward silence.* HALLAM *finally enters with* BILLY) Sentry, stand outside. (*Exit* HALLAM) You may sit down.

BILLY: Th-th-thank you, sir.

SEYMOUR: Captain: will you be good enough to give us your account?

VERE (*turning towards them*): I speak not as your Captain, but as witness before this court. The Master-at-Arms early this morning detailed to me an account of mutinous sentiments expressed by Budd, and in particular, spoke of overhearing a specific conversation last night on the mid-watch. He alleged that Budd offered him violence and threatened further violence against the officers.

WYATT: Budd a mutineer! That's absurd, he's the best-liked man . . .

SEYMOUR: Lieutenant Wyatt. Please do not interrupt the witness.

RATCLIFFE: Did the Master-at-Arms specify who the other malcontents were, sir?

VERE: He did not. He said merely that he was in possession of substantial proof of his accusation.

SEYMOUR: With your permission, sir . . . Budd, did you speak with anyone in the Master-at-Arms' hearing last night?

BILLY: I . . . spoke a little . . . with the Dansker, sir.

WYATT: Who is the Dansker?

BILLY: He's just called the Dansker, sir. He's always called so.

RATCLIFFE: I know him. A mainmast sailor.

SEYMOUR: Sentry. (*Enter* HALLAM)

HALLAM: Sir.

SEYMOUR: Do you know a mainmast sailor referred to as "the Dansker"?

HALLAM: Aye, sir.

SEYMOUR: Go on deck and find him. Let him know apart that he is wanted here, and arrange it so that none of the other people notice his withdrawing. See you do it tactfully. I want no curiosity aroused among the men.

HALLAM: Aye aye, sir. (*exits*)

SEYMOUR: Please go on.

VERE: I sent at once for Budd. I ordered the Master-at-Arms to be present at this interview, to make his accusation to Budd's face.

RATCLIFFE: May I ask what was the prisoner's reaction on being confronted by the Master-at-Arms?

VERE: I perceived no sign of uneasiness in his demeanor. I believe he smiled.

RATCLIFFE: And for the Master-at-Arms?

VERE: When I directed him to repeat his accusation, he faced Budd and did so.

WYATT: Did Budd reply?

VERE: He tried to speak, but could not frame his words.

SEYMOUR: And then, sir?

VERE: He answered with blows, and his accuser fell. . . . It was apparent at once that the attack was fatal, but I summoned the Surgeon to verify the fact. That is all. (*turns away*)

SEYMOUR (*to* BILLY): You have heard Captain Vere's account. Is it, or is it not, as he says?

BILLY: Captain Vere tells the truth. It is just as Captain Vere says, but it is not as the Master-at-Arms said. I have eaten the King's bread, and I am true to the King.

VERE: I believe you, boy.

BILLY: God knows . . . I . . . thank you, sir.

SEYMOUR: Was there any malice between you and the Master-at-Arms?

BILLY: I bore no malice against the Master-at-Arms. I'm sorry he is dead. I did not mean to kill him. If I'd found my tongue, I would not have struck him. But he lied foully to my face, and I . . . had to say . . . something . . . and I could only say it . . . with a blow. God help me.

SEYMOUR: One question more—you tell us that what the Master-at-Arms said against you was a lie. Now, why should he have lied with such obvious malice, when you have declared that there was no malice between you? (BILLY *looks appealingly at* VERE) Did you hear my question?

BILLY: I . . . I . . .

VERE: The question you put to him comes naturally enough. But can he rightly answer it? Or anyone else, unless, indeed, it be he who lies within there. (*Knock and enter immediately* HALLAM)

HALLAM: The mainmast man, sir.

SEYMOUR: Send him in. (HALLAM *nods off and the* DANS-KER *enters.* HALLAM *withdraws, closing door*) State your name and station.

DANSKER: I have no name. I'm called the Dansker, that's all I know. Mainmast man.

SEYMOUR: You have been summoned in secrecy to appear as a witness before this court, of which I am Senior Member. I may not at this time disclose to you the nature of the offense being tried. However, the offender is William Budd, foretopman. (*pause*) Do you consent to give this court your testimony, though ignorant of the case at trial, and further, to keep in strictest confidence all that passes here?

DANSKER: Aye.

SEYMOUR (*pushes forward a Bible*): Do you so swear?

DANSKER (*touching the Bible*): I do.

SEYMOUR: Then this is my question. In your opinion, is there malice between Budd and the Master-at-Arms?

DANSKER: Aye.

VERE (*wheeling around*): How!

SEYMOUR: Explain your statement.

DANSKER: How should he not have hated him?

SEYMOUR: Be plain man. We do not deal in riddles here.

DANSKER: Master-at-Arms bore malice towards a grace he could not have. There was no reason for it.

RATCLIFFE. In other words, this malice was one-sided?

DANSKER: Aye.

RATCLIFFE: And you cannot explain how it arose?

DANSKER: Master-at-Arms hated Billy . . .

SEYMOUR: One moment. I notice that you have been using the past tense in your testimony. Why?

DANSKER: I look around and sense finality here.

WYATT: You cannot explain further the cause of Claggart's hate for Budd?

DANSKER: Master-at-Arms made his world in his own image. Pride was his demon, and he kept it strong by others' fear of him. Billy could not imagine such a nature, saw nothing but a lonely man, strange, but a man still, nothing to be feared. So Claggart, lest his world be proven false, planned Billy's death. The final reason is beyond my thinking.

VERE: Aye, that is thoughtfully put. There is a mystery in iniquity. But it seems to me, Seymour, that the point we seek here is hardly material.

SEYMOUR: Aye, sir. Very well, you may go.

DANSKER: One thing more. Since this Master-at-Arms first came on board from God knows where, I have seen his shadow lengthen along the deck, and being under it, I was afraid. Whatever happened here, I am in part to blame—more than this lad. (*to* BILLY) I am an old man, Billy. You—try to—forgive me. (*exits*)

SEYMOUR: Have you any further questions to put to the accused?

RATCLIFFE: No.

WYATT: None.

SEYMOUR: William Budd, if you have anything further to say for yourself, say it now.

BILLY (*after glance at* VERE): I have said all, sir.

SEYMOUR: Sentry. (*Enter* HALLAM) Remove the prisoner to the after compartment. (HALLAM *and* BILLY *exit. A long pause*) Have you anything to say, Ratcliffe?

RATCLIFFE: Yes, sir. Claggart was killed because Budd couldn't speak. In that sense, that he stammers, he's a cripple. You don't hang a man for that, for speaking the only way he could.

WYATT: If you condemn him, it's the same thing as condoning the apparent lie the Master-at-Arms clearly told. I'd have struck him, too. The boy is clearly innocent, struck him in self-defense.

RATCLIFFE: Aye. I'm ready to acquit him now.

SEYMOUR: Good. Then we can reach a verdict at once.

VERE: Hitherto I have been a witness at this trial, no more. And I hesitate to interfere, except that at this clear crisis you ignore one fact we cannot close our eyes to.

SEYMOUR: With your pardon, sir, as Senior Member of this court, I must ask if you speak now as our commanding officer or as a private man.

VERE: As convening authority, Seymour. I summoned this court, and I must review its findings and approve them before passing them on to the Admiralty.

SEYMOUR: Aye, sir, that is your right.

VERE: No right. Which of us here has rights? It is my duty, and I must perform it. Budd has killed a man—his superior officer.

SEYMOUR: We have found a verdict, sir.

VERE: I know that, Seymour. Your verdict sets him free, and so would I wish to do. But are we free to choose as we would do if we were private citizens? The Admiralty has its code. Do you suppose it cares who Budd is? Who you and I are?

SEYMOUR: We don't forget that, sir. But surely Claggart's tales were simply lies. We've established that.

VERE: Aye. But the Nore and Spithead were brute facts, and must not come again. The men were starved out before, but if they should think we are afraid . . .

RATCLIFFE: Captain, how could they? They certainly know Budd is no mutineer.

WYATT: Of course not. Since he came on board, he's done more to keep the crew in hand than any of us.

SEYMOUR: That's true. The men took naturally to him.

VERE: As officers we are concerned to keep this ship effective as a weapon. And the law says what we must do in such a case as this. Come now, you know the facts, and the Mutiny Act's provisions. At sea, in time of war, an impressed man strikes his superior officer, and the blow is fatal. The mere blow alone would hang him, at least according to the Act. Well then, the men on board know that as well as you and I. And we acquit him. They have sense, they know the proper penalty to follow, and yet it does not follow.

SEYMOUR: But they know Budd, sir, and Claggart too, I daresay. Would they not applaud the decision that frees Budd? They would thank us.

WYATT: String him to a yard, and they'll turn round and rescue him, and string us up instead!

RATCLIFFE: Aye, that's a point. It's twice as dangerous to hang the boy as it would be to let him go. If there's a mutinous temper in the crew, condemning Budd would surely set it off.

VERE: That is possible. Whatever step we take, the risk is great; but it is ours. That is what makes us officers. Yet if in fear of what our office demands we shirk our duty, we only play at war, at being men. If by our lawful rigor mutiny comes, there is no blame for us. But if in fear, miscalled a kind of mercy, we pardon Budd against specific order, and then the crew revolts, how culpable and weak our verdict would appear! The men on board know what our case is, how we are haunted by the Spithead risings. Have they forgotten how the panic spread through England? No. Your clemency would be accounted fear, and they would say we flinch from practising a lawful rigor lest new outbreaks be provoked. What shame to us! And what a deadly blow to discipline!

RATCLIFFE: I concede that, sir. But this case is exceptional, and pity, if we are men, is bound to move us, Captain.

VERE: So am I moved. Yet we cannot have warm hearts betraying heads that should be cool. In such a case ashore, an upright judge does not allow the pleading tears of women to touch his nature. Here at sea, the heart, the female in a man, weeps like a woman. She must be ruled out, hard though it be. (*pause*) Still silent? Very well, I see that something in all your downcast faces seems to urge that not alone the heart moves hesitancy. Conscience, perhaps. The private conscience moves you.

WYATT: Aye, that's it, sir. How can we condemn this man and live at peace again within ourselves? We have our standards; ethics, if you like.

VERE: Challenge your scruples! They move as in a dusk. Come, do they import something like this: if we are bound to judge, regardless of palliating circumstances, the death of Claggart as the prisoner's deed, then does that deed appear a capital crime whereof the penalty is mortal? But can we adjudge to summary and shameful death a fellow creature innocent before God, and whom we feel to be so? Does that state the case rightly?

SEYMOUR: That is my feeling, sir.

VERE: You all feel, I am sure, that the boy in effect is innocent; that what he did was from an unhappy stricture of speech that made him speak with blows. And I believe that, too; believe as you do, that he struck his man down, tempted beyond endurance. Acquit him, then, you say, as innocent?

RATCLIFFE: Exactly! Oh I know the Articles prescribe death for what Budd has done, but that . . .

WYATT: Oh, stow the Articles! They don't account for such a case as this. You yourself say Budd is innocent.

VERE: In intent, Wyatt, in intent.

WYATT: Does that count for nothing? His whole attitude, his motive, count for nothing? If his intent . . .

VERE: The intent or non-intent of Budd is nothing to the purpose. In a court more merciful than martial it would extenuate, and shall, at the last Assizes, set him free. But here we have these alternatives only: condemn or let go.

SEYMOUR: But it seems to me we've got to consider the problem as a moral one, sir, despite the fact that we're not moralists. When Claggart told you his lie, the case immediately went beyond the scope of military justice.

VERE: I, too, feel that. But do these gold stripes across our arms attest that our allegiance is to Nature?

RATCLIFFE: To our country, sir.

VERE: Aye, Ratcliffe; to the King. And though the sea, which is inviolate Nature primeval, though it be the element whereon we move and have our being as sailors, is our official duty hence to Nature? No. So little is that true that we resign our freedom when we put this on. And when war is declared, are we, the fighters commissioned to destroy, consulted first?

WYATT: Does that deny us the right to act like men? We're not trying a murderer, a dockside cut-throat!

VERE: The gold we wear shows that we serve the King, the Law. What does it matter that our acts are fatal to our manhood, if we serve as we are forced to serve? What bitter salt leagues move between our code and God's own judgments! We are conscripts, every one, upright in this uniform of flesh. There is no truce to war born in the womb. We fight at command.

WYATT: All I know is that I can't sit by and see Budd hanged!

VERE: I say we fight by order, by command of our superiors. And if our judgments approve the war, it is only coincidence. And so it is with all our acts. So now, would it be so much we ourselves who speak as judges here, as it would be martial law operating through us? For that law, and for its rigor, we are not responsible. Our duty lies in this: that we are servants only.

RATCLIFFE: The Admiralty doesn't want service like that. What good would it do? Who'd profit by Budd's death?

WYATT: You want to make us murderers!

SEYMOUR: Wyatt! Control yourself!

VERE: What is this vessel that you serve in, Wyatt, an ark of peace? Go count her guns; then tell your conscience to lie quiet, if you can.

RATCLIFFE: But that is war. This would be downright killing!

SEYMOUR: It's all war, Ratcliffe; war to the death, for all of us.

VERE: You see that, Seymour? That this war began before our time?

SEYMOUR: And will end long after it.

VERE: Here we have the Mutiny Act for justice. No child can own a closer tie to parent than can that Act to what it stems from: War. This is a wartime cruise and in this ship are Englishmen who fight against their wills, perhaps against their conscience, 'pressed by war into the service of the King. Though we as fellow creatures understand their lot, what does it matter to the officer, or to the enemy? The French will cut down conscripts in the same swath with volunteers, and we will do as much for them. War has no business with anything but surfaces. War's child, the Mutiny Act, is featured like the father.

RATCLIFFE: Couldn't we mitigate the penalty if we convict him?

VERE: No, Ratcliffe. The penalty is prescribed.

RATCLIFFE: I'd like to think it over, Captain. I'm not sure.

VERE: I repeat, then, that while we ponder and you hesitate over anxieties I confess to sharing, the enemy comes nearer. We must act, and quickly. The French close in on us; the crew will find out shortly what has happened. Our consciences are private matters, Ratcliffe. But we are public men, controlling life and death within this world at sea. Tell me whether or not in our positions we dare let our consciences take precedence of the code that makes us officers and calls this case to trial.

RATCLIFFE (*after a pause; quietly*): No, sir.

WYATT: Can you stand Budd's murder on your conscience?

SEYMOUR: Wyatt! Hold your tongue!

WYATT (*jumping up*): I say let him go!

SEYMOUR: Sit down, sir!

VERE: Let him speak.

WYATT: I won't bear a hand to hang a man I know is innocent! My blood's not cold enough. I can't give the kind of judgment you want to force on us! I ask to be excused from sitting upon this court.

SEYMOUR: Do you know what you're saying? Sit down and hold your tongue, man!

VERE: The kind of judgment I ask of you is only this, Wyatt: that you recognize your function in this ship. I believe you know it quite as well as we, yet you rebel. Can't you see that you must first strip off the uniform you wear, and after that your flesh, before you can escape the case at issue here? Decide you must, Wyatt. Oh you may be excused and wash your hands of it, but someone must decide. We are the law; law orders us to act, and shows us how. Do you imagine Seymour, or Ratcliffe here, or I, would not save this boy if we could see a way consistent with our duties? Acquit Budd if you can. God knows I wish I could. If in your mind as well as in your heart, you can say freely that his life is not forfeit to the law we serve, reason with us! Show us how to save him without putting aside our function. Or if you can't do that, teach us to put by our responsibility and not betray ourselves. Can you do this? Speak, man, speak! Show us how! Save him, Wyatt, and you save us all. (WYATT *slowly sits down*) You recognize the logic of the choice I force upon you. But do not think me pitiless in thus demanding sentence on a luckless boy. I feel as you do for him. But even more, I think there is a grace of soul within him that shall forgive the law we bind him with, and pity us, stretched on the cross of choice. (*turns away*)

SEYMOUR: Well, gentlemen. Will you decide. (*Officers write their verdicts on paper before them, and hand them to* SEYMOUR, *who rises, draws his dirk and places it on the table, pointing forward*) He is condemned, sir. Shall we appoint the dawn?

*End of Scene One*

SCENE TWO

SCENE: CAPTAIN VERE'S *cabin, 0400. Ship's bell strikes offstage.* VERE *sitting alone at his desk. Knock at the door.*

VERE: Come in. (*Enter* SEYMOUR) Oh, it's you, Seymour.

SEYMOUR: It's eight bells, Captain.

VERE: What's the hour of sunrise?

SEYMOUR: Four fifty-two, sir.

VERE: Eight bells. And one bell at four-thirty. Odd and even numbers caught between two hands. Budd shall not live to hear the odd made even or wrong made right.—Call all hands to quarters at four-thirty.

SEYMOUR: Aye aye, Captain. (*turns irresolutely*)

VERE: The wind has slackened, I think. How is the glass?

SEYMOUR: It's risen slightly. Sea has flattened out.

VERE: Fair weather after foul . . . it's all nature, nature and law. How exigent are these Mediterranean climates of the heart, and temperate zones of mind!

SEYMOUR: Have you been here all night, sir?

VERE: All night, Seymour . . . All my life moving between dark and dark. It has been a long night, but day will be quick and deadly on the mainyard. D'you think, Seymour, a man can forgive a wrong done of the heart's own election?

SEYMOUR: Most people are decent enough. You can forgive them trespasses.

VERE: No, by God. There's wickedness alive. It's dead now in one man, but it's alive to feel and smell at night. . . . Seymour, go below. Get Budd and bring him here.

SEYMOUR: But Captain . . .

VERE: Do as you're told. Get Budd and bring him here. (SEYMOUR *exits.* VERE *sits motionless for a few moments, then rises and goes to the cabin door*) Sentry.

HALLAM: Yes, sir?

VERE: Who has the deck this watch?

HALLAM: Mister Ratcliffe, Captain.

VERE: Very well. (*pause*) Sentry!

HALLAM: Sir?

VERE: When Mister Seymour has returned, admit him right away.

HALLAM: Aye aye, Captain.

VERE: The wind's still sharp. You must be cold there, Hallam. Go to the leeward side. I'll be responsible.

HALLAM: Thank you, sir. This is the coldest hour now, just before sunrise.

VERE (*closes door, returns slowly to his desk*): The lamp holds steady when the vessel heels. Does the law hang straight in crooked lives? It burns, and shapes nothing but shadows here, plumb in the twisting cabin of the mind. (*Footsteps, voices.* VERE *turns to door. Enter* SEYMOUR, BILLY, *and* HALLAM) Take off the manacles. (HALLAM *frees* BILLY)

SEYMOUR (*to* HALLAM): Outside, man. Bear a hand. (*exits with* HALLAM)

VERE: Sit down. No, it's better that I stand.

BILLY: I was thinking, locked up below there . . . the Captain knows the rights of all this. He'll save me if it's right. Then you sent for me. Is there hope for me, Captain?

VERE: Billy, what hope is there?

BILLY: Tell me why. I only want to understand.

VERE: How young you still are, Billy! Oh I can tell you

this: nothing is lost of anything that happens. I have given you the judgment of the world . . . deadly constraint . . . a length of hemp and a yard-arm. I have done this to you, no one else.

BILLY: I can't get the rights of all that's happened.

VERE: There's not much right, Billy. Only necessity. You and Claggart broke man's compromise with good and evil, and both of you must pay the penalty.

BILLY: Penalty? What for? Would anyone make laws just to be broken by fellows like me?

VERE: Aye, boy. You have learned this late. Most of us find out early and trim to a middle course.

BILLY: Do you mean . . . it's better to be like that?

VERE: Better as this world goes. When a man is born, he takes a guilt upon him, I can't say how or why. And life takes its revenge on those who hurt its pride with innocence.

BILLY: Do you think Claggart knew it would come to this?

VERE: He knew he would kill you, and he died to gain that end. But if you trust me, he'll not win entirely.

BILLY: How could he hate me like that?

VERE: The world we breathe is love and hatred both, but hatred must not win the victory.

BILLY: Claggart is dead. Now I'm to hang. Doesn't that show the law is wrong, when it can't choose between him and me?

VERE: Yes, it's all wrong, all wrong.

BILLY: I don't know, Captain. I never was a hand to wonder about things, but now I think that maybe there's a kind of cruelty in people that's just as much a part of them as kindness, say, or honesty, or m-m-m . . . I can't find words, I guess, Captain.

VERE: There are no words. We are all prisoners of deadly forms that are made to break us to their measure. Nothing has power to overcome them except forgiveness . . . Can you forgive what I have done?

BILLY: I *can* trust you, can't I? *Can* you show me it's all right, my being . . .

VERE (*turns away; a long pause*): It's nearly dawn, lad. In the Spanish villages they're lighting fires.

BILLY: I'm not afraid, sir. (*steps toward* VERE) It's getting light.

VERE: There's no time for either of us left. Go, take the morning. God knows you have the right to it. And when you are on the mainyard, think of me, and pray for those who must make choices. Hallam. (*Enter* HALLAM *in doorway*) Take Budd into your charge. (BILLY *and* HALLAM *go out*) Time has run out.

*End of Scene Two*

SCENE THREE

SCENE: *Main deck aft. Drum-to-formation. Crew forming up.* WYATT, MIDSHIPMEN GARDINER *and* REA.

WYATT: Bear a hand. Form the men up in ranks.

GARDINER: Aye, sir. All right, you! Close ranks! Move up, Stoll. That's better. Talbot, square your hat. Form up straight there, damn it! (*Drum.* MEN *come to attention*)

WYATT: Division commanders report!

VOICE (*off*): Carpenters and gunners, present or accounted for, sir!

VOICE (*off*): Marine Detachment, present or accounted for, sir!

VOICE (*off*): Afterguard, present or accounted for, sir!

GARDINER: Fore, main and mizzentopmen . . . one absentee!

WYATT: All hands will stand by to witness punishment! Stand easy.

VOICES (*off*): Stand easy! (WYATT *walks away from men. Murmur in ranks*)

KINCAID: Where the devil is Billy? He wasn't in his hammock when they piped us up.

O'DANIEL: He'll be getting himself in trouble if he don't fall in.

KINCAID: Who the hell they punishing, and what for?

JENKINS: It's got to be flogging, or they wouldn't have us all up here.

KINCAID: Vere never flogs anybody. And there ain't no gratings up.

DANSKER: They flog men at noon. The early morning's for hanging.

KINCAID: Hanging! (*The word travels back*) Who? What for?

O'DANIEL: The skipper, he don't confide in me no more.

KINCAID: I thought they waited till they got ashore before they hanged a man.

DANSKER: Not in wartime.

JENKINS: He goes up them ratlines, out on the yard, they slips a noose around his neck, and then he jumps and hangs himself.

O'DANIEL: They'd have the devil's work getting O'Daniel to jump.

KINCAID: It's jump, or get pushed.

JENKINS: Where's Claggart? God, you don't suppose it's Claggart! Oh, Judas, let it be that fishblood nark!

KINCAID: Not him. He's too smart, he is.

JENKINS: Where is he, then? He ain't here.

DANSKER: He is here.

KINCAID: Where? I don't see him.

DANSKER: He is here.

KINCAID: Ah . . . you're balmy, old man.

> (*Enter* VERE, SEYMOUR, RATCLIFFE *and the* SURGEON. *Drum sounds Attention*)

WYATT (*to* SEYMOUR): Ship's company present to witness execution, sir.

SEYMOUR: Very well. (*to* VERE) Ship's company present to witness execution, sir.

VERE (*nods*).

SEYMOUR (*to* WYATT): Lieutenant Wyatt, have the prisoner brought forward.

WYATT: Aye aye, sir. (*marches to wing*) Sentries, bring forward the prisoner. (*marches back to his post*)

> (*Enter* BILLY *with two sentries. Astonished murmur through the crew, who momentarily break ranks*)

WYATT: No talking in ranks! (*Continued restless movement and murmurings*) Form up!

GARDINER: You men are at attention!

WYATT (*over subdued muttering*): You hear me? Silence in ranks!

> (*Silence.* SENTRIES *lead* BILLY *to the foot of the ropes.* SEYMOUR *looks at* VERE, *who nods.* SEYMOUR *steps forward and reads*)

SEYMOUR: Proceedings of the court-martial held aboard *H.M.S. Indomitable* on the eighth August, 1798. Convened under the authority of Edward Fairfax Vere, Senior Captain, Royal Navy, and composed of the First Officer, the Sailing Master, and the First Lieutenant of said vessel. In the case of William Budd, foretopman, Royal Navy. While attached and so serving in the aforesaid vessel, he did, on the 8th day of August, 1798, strike and kill his superior officer, one John Claggart, Master-at-Arms, Royal Navy.

> (*Crew breaks out uneasily, astonished, talking excitedly*)

JENKINS: Billy! Did you, boy?
VOICE: Good lad!
VOICE: Serves him proper!
KINCAID: Hi, Billy! Hurrah!

*All together*

WYATT: Quiet! Silence, you men! Form up!

GARDINER: Stand at attention, hang you! Silence in the ranks!

WYATT: Do you hear? (*Excited muttering, low voices*)

SEYMOUR: You will be silent and remain at strict attention until dismissed. (*Silence*) . . . Master-at-Arms, Royal Navy. Therefore, the court sentences the aforementioned William Budd, foretopman, Royal Navy, to die by hanging on the first watch of the day following these proceedings. By authority of his Gracious Majesty George Rex and Alan Napier, Viscount Kelsey, First Sea Lord. Signed, Philip Seymour, Senior Member.

> (*During the last phrases of the reading, the crew, upon hearing the sentence, breaks out again, some stepping forward, shouting; they are in an ugly temper*)

VOICES: No he don't!
Not if I know it!
Hang the jemmies instead I say!
Not Billy, you bloody swineheads!     *All together*
Not him, by Christ!
You ain't hanging Billy, damn your eyes!
Let them dance on a rope's end!

WYATT: Stand back! Sentries, guard your prisoner, if you have to fire!

GARDINER: Stand back, you damned clods! Keep back!

SEYMOUR (*steps forward*): Silence there! You will resume discipline instantly! Be warned. (*waits a silent moment. Men stop in disordered formation*) Stand back into ranks.

GARDINER: Form up again, quick about it now! (*There is a surly movement into irregular lines*)

SEYMOUR (*warily resuming procedure*): Prisoner, have you anything to say? (BILLY *shakes his head*) If you have nothing to say, when the drum roll is sounded, you will proceed to carry out the sentence of this court. (*signals to* WYATT)

WYATT: Sound off!

  (*Drum roll:* BILLY *turns and starts up the ropes*)

VOICES: Get him! Now!

  Bill! Stay where you are, boy, don't do it!

  Wait, Billy! Wait!   *All together*

  Rush the deck, mates! Don't let them do it!

  We're here, Bill, don't you worry!

BILLY (*stops, turns forward, looks at* VERE, *and shouts out loud and clear, without trace of stammer*): God bless Captain Vere!

  (*A second's pause;* VERE *is profoundly shaken;* BILLY *goes quickly up the ropes and out of sight. The crew moves back a step, is silent; officers and men in deep breathless quiet watch him out of sight and are staring overhead as the curtain falls*)

*End of Act Three*

# NOTES ON THE PLAY

It is difficult now, in retrospect, to determine how and why we arrived at a decision to make Melville's novel into a play. We had of course been familiar with the story for some time, and when in 1947 we actually began discussing the dramatic problems entailed in writing a play on the theme Melville gives us, we had only recently been very close to the novel. Perhaps the "Melville Revival" influenced us; it may have been the desire to find a theme and action that was inherently poetic and non-realistic. Above all, one idea or purpose seems clear: that we saw in *Billy Budd* a morality play.

History and the literature of the past serve many functions for the present. Men like to think that they look at the past and its works objectively, with an evaluating eye, yet most of us know that any age seeks from the past justifications and flatteries; looks for ideas in a literature of another time and selects from them those that seem peculiarly pertinent to the seeker, whether the ideas found be actually *there* or not. Writers and critics have a way of reviving the dead with the purpose of forcing them to say certain things we wish they had said, or to reaffirm what they perhaps did say, though too often in accents and in a tone to which we do violence in our translation. But this is no evil, and surely it is a mark of greatness in a writer if his accents and tone are various enough to command the languages of various times and places. For us, as inchoate playwrights, in January of 1947, Melville's story of good, evil, and the way the world takes such absolutes was material enough for two veterans of a war, a depression, and the moving cold front.

Today morality is not popular; perhaps it has never really been so. In our day it is popularly lamented and celebrated in absentia, much modern criticism being devoted to the discovery of morality in the least likely places. Yet to find the stuff of dramatic morality pure is no easy task, since, however hard one may try, Freud will turn up and all one's efforts will post off to the clinic and the analyst's couch to work out there a modern salvation. Thus a critic can say of our play that such a phenomenon as Claggart could never appear in our world with all we know of the psyche and the ego. We doubt that. We are certain that neither a Billy nor a Claggart ever was or could be, and, to undercut a little ground, we add that the same is true of an Oedipus. But all these personae are true as symbol, figuring as they do certain permanent attitudes, qualities, moral images. It is just this figuring forth that Melville's novel so preeminently effects for our time, and if we do indeed lament a lack of standards for this age we can at least see in *Billy Budd* the potentiality of a new vision, a vision that allows a man to think generally about absolutes without feeling he is violating "truth" because he has not polled a sample of his generation to get the "facts." The trouble is, Melville has stated a fact, but it is not the kind of fact men either like or know what to do with.

Perhaps all this has less to do than we think with how our play got written or even started. Once that start was made, however, we found ourselves bound by the novel, and it was only after some experimentation that we realized how little Melville had given us that was theatrical or, perhaps, finished. There was certainly little reason why he should; the drama is surely in the novel, but it is an inner, imagined drama. Our job was to put it on a stage and give flesh to the finely articulated skeleton—

no small task in view of the deceptive nature of the novel. What seems to the casual reader mere padding in *Billy Budd* (the novel) is vital information—about the great mutinies, the Napoleonic Wars, the British Navy, the moral and social climate. And Melville was assuming an audience of some culture (if at this stage he was able to assume an audience at all) which would know about the Rights of Man, the Terror, Rodney, and what manner of man Captain Vere is intended to represent. All this we had to show, to bring to life and to give to the audience in such a way that the information might not arrive as information but as an ambience. We do not say that we have done this, only that it must be done if there is to be a real play. This is a morality play and we do not apologize for its being such.

The version presented here is that of the final Broadway production. The play in this form has passed through several stages. The original version, given by the Experimental Theater in 1949, was in stricter poetic form and was more austere in tone and structure; much of it seemed to us too bald and expository. We have tried to thicken the texture of the play with much added dramatic incident, contrapuntal conflict, and realistic speech. There is, of course, some danger that we have fallen between two stools: what we have done may not entirely please either the average theatregoer or the Melville scholar. But for our part we have done! Our original faith in the novel remains and supports our faith in our own work. We will look far before we find another theme of equal interest or vitality.

Louis O. Coxe
Robert Chapman

# THE GOSPEL WITCH

## A *Poetic Drama*

## LYON PHELPS

FOR MY FATHER AND MOTHER IN CELEBRATION

# Editor's Preface: THE GOSPEL WITCH

*The Gospel Witch* is set in the town of Salem, Massachusetts, during the witchcraft trials that raged until the fury was spent. Although the author, Lyon Phelps, has said that "the play is written in the spirit rather than in the fact of history," by refusing to adhere to historical detail the play captures the ethos of the New England religious mind as it wrestled with the likelihood of demonic powers at work in the town. The contemporary mind, with its sociological, political, and psychological assumptions faces enormous difficulties in penetrating this episode in American history. Yet even today the Salem trials at the end of the seventeenth century have shock and news value. Viewed against the seventeeth-century New England effort to rear an unblemished Zion in the new world, the Salem trials point the truth that judgment belongs to God rather than man. Lyon Phelps has succeeded in delineating the issues in dramatic form and by casting his work in a poetic idiom the play escapes the snare of historical and social realism. *The Gospel Witch* was first produced in an early version by The Poets' Theatre in Cambridge on May 22, 1952, in the court of the Fogg Museum. Lyon Phelps, a graduate of Harvard, was one of the founders of The Poets' Theatre.

# SALEM, MASSACHUSETTS BAY, 1692

That I thy Name may praise, my soule
from prison, oh bring out:
when thou shalt me reward, the just
shall compasse mee about.

# THE SCENES

# THE PERSONS

THE PROLOGUE, *a man from Boston*
ANN PUTNAM
ABIGAIL PARRIS
THOMAS PUTNAM, *Ann's father*
EZEKIEL CHEEVER
GILES COREY
MARTHA, *his wife*
JOHN HATHORNE, *Magistrate from Salem Town*
SAMUEL PARRIS, *minister at Salem Village*
GEORGE LOCKER, *a constable*
PETER BUNT, *a jailor*
MERCY LEWIS, *maidservant at the Putnams'*
A HANGMAN
*Villagers and townsfolk*

# THE PROLOGUE

A MAN FROM BOSTON (*comes before the curtain*)

I was clerk that year for a merchant in Boston named
    Brattle,
a successful trader, whose concern, like his wharf reach-
    ing into the harbor,
reached into community. He watched it all grow, the
    subtle battle
for balance and laughter. He sent us where he could not
    enter—
a prominent man—collecting the kind of story that brought
    us back
to our senses, for we returned after damage enough was
    done.

I'm the son of a judge gone judge myself now, but some-
    how I lack
the passionate reasons I risked that year. I'm rarely alone,
the past seems too clear. The children we taught to think
like adults, when suddenly caught in a late crush of child-
    hood,
went wild for a year. They dredged up the neighborly
    sink
and cess of our grudges; so armed, took what none under-
    stood,
an unnatural holiday. But now, looking back and perhaps
    a bit

too clear in my head, I know I've seen nothing, nothing
  just like it.

(*He turns to go*)

Only twenty were finally trundled off, before
years set houses to rights again. The countryside
  generally
remained unimpressed save by the advance of axes.

(*Exit*)

ANN PUTNAM, ABIGAIL PARRIS, then THOMAS PUTNAM
and EZEKIEL CHEEVER.

*Before the fireplace in the great room of the Putnam
homestead at Salem Farms, two young girls are dressing
a corn cob with tags of cloth. A sense of the lull that
follows high noon fills the room; hard March sunshine
enters from the left.*

ANN: No, Abby, no! Abby, I say no!

ABIGAIL: Why Ann, what's the matter now,
    what have I done now?

ANN:                The lace,
    don't you touch that piece of lace.
    Nobody, except me and my mother
    is fit to touch this bone lace trim.
       *(Takes it against her cheek)*

ABIGAIL: Ann, it's wicked to talk so.

ANN:                   Bosh!
    Trot home to the parsonage. Go home, snivel!
    Your Uncle Parris will say your prayers.
    Abby, you're a baby. And just because
    you live in your uncle minister's house
    you're not smart enough to lecture me.
    Besides, the parsonage is on our land,
    Putnam property. Father says so, often.

ABIGAIL: Ann!

ANN:         Go on, frighten me, if you can.
    Aunt Mary, when she married, wore
    lace on her bodice, this very lace,
    and she was a parson's wife—she lived

where you live now, before Mr. Parris,
on public land, before you were born.
Grandfather gave it to the meeting.

ABIGAIL: Fancy talk Annie! As if you knew
everyone's servants, everyone's secrets.
Before you too were born, remember.

ANN (*dreamy*): Mother says her sister was very
beautiful and ill. Abby, listen,
Aunt Mary died in this very room.
At the parsonage they spied on her,
women like Mrs. Corey—

ABIGAIL: Mrs. Corey?
She never comes down, save on Sunday.

ANN: So you suppose, but she travels—

ABIGAIL (*gasps*): Ann! You mean—

ANN: Never mind. I said,
women *like* Mrs. Corey spied on her,
so she came home to die. Father laid her
so, and she was dressed
in her wedding bodice. Mother lit candles—

ABIGAIL: You never saw.

ANN: My mother said.
Mother never cried until the men
came clodding in and puffed out the candles
to take Aunt Mary away. Then Mother saw
her sister's bone lace trim. This lace.
Some said Aunt Mary was fine and silly,
and Mrs. Corey said so too.

ABIGAIL: O Ann.

ANN: Yes, then Mother cried, they couldn't
stop her. She tore the gentle lace away,
tore it off dead Aunt Mary's cuffs—
she'd show them who was fine and silly!
(*Pause*)
Yesterday she lifted the lace from her dresser
and slipped it to me, and told me.

ABIGAIL:                               Ann,
  you're making it up.
ANN:                    Mother tells me
  everything always. You've got no Mother,
  and Aunty Parris is very dull.
  My mother is beautiful and always sad.
ABIGAIL (*with admiration*):
  Your mother is always telling stories.
  Your mother is pale and always talking.
  O Ann, Mrs. Putnam is wild.
ANN (*furious*):                    Abby,
  don't you say that! Don't you say that
  ever, ever. Mother's lived more troubles,
  even her dreams bear more deaths and hurts
  than your pale pillow returns your tears,
  than you'll hear told of before you're dead!
        (*Grabs* ABIGAIL)
  You little vixen, who said, who said
  My mother's wild?
ABIGAIL:              Ann, you're hurting!
  No one said. I don't know who said.
  Stop it, Ann.
ANN:          A witch told you that.
  Mother's perfect. Who told you? Tell me, Abby,
  or I'll tell Father. Did Tituba tell—
ABIGAIL: Tituba's a black witch and she's in jail.
  Aunty Parris cleans the kitchen pots now,
  you know that, where Tituba witched us—
ANN: Now hush about Tituba, she's confessed.
  Did Mrs. Corey tell you in church?
ABIGAIL (*sulky, frightened*):          Mrs. Corey,
  she never speaks to any of us. She
  sails past us on her husband's arm
  as if children were irreverent.
ANN (*savagely breaking the doll she is making*):
  Mrs. Corey, Mrs. Corey, Mrs. Corey,

she told you Mother was wild. She tried
to whisper to me too, last night.
She hates my lovely mother.—Even when Father
spoke of her pride in church, Mother sighed,
went to her room and fastened the door,
and Mother cried.

      Now Mrs. Corey tries
to suffocate me with my pillow, and I
asleep and all alone. I know it's she.

ABIGAIL: She's very prayerful. D'you think—?
People have said
your father was very fond of her once.

ANN: Yes, yes, the old witch. I'll teach her to be wise.
Abby, give me those pins!

ABIGAIL:        Ann, you mustn't.
We mustn't continue what Tituba taught us.

ANN (*shrieks*): Give me those pins!

  (*Quiet and strange*)

         Abby, look at the puppet,
that's Mrs. Corey. She called Mother
horrible names—she tried to choke me
with feathers and tears—she knows I'll tell.
This doll is Mrs. Corey, Abby; now,
hand me the lancet pins.

ABIGAIL:       Ann, be careful,
Uncle Parris says that's devils' play.
He'll prize you out of the pews and pray at you.
No, Ann, don't.

ANN (*stern*):    Give me your hand—
soft baby fingers. Now, grasp the pin.
Press it, Abby, press it in,
right into Mrs. Corey, Abby. There.
There.

  (*She laughs. Enter at the back* THOMAS PUTNAM,
  ANN's *father, and* EZEKIEL CHEEVER, *a deacon of
  the Meeting*)

ABIGAIL: No, Ann, don't, O! Help, help!
　　(*She sobs*)
PUTNAM: Children! Ann, what are you doing?
　　(ANN *drops* ABIGAIL's *hand, and falls sitting to the*
　　*floor, weeping too, and choking*)
Answer your father, Ann. What are you doing
with cobs and cloth in front of the fire?
Answer me, Ann.
CHEEVER: 　　　　　　She's pale as milkweed,
arched as a crone at ancient prayers.
Be careful, Thomas.
PUTNAM: 　　　　　Ann—
　　(ANN *is kneeling, hands and lace clenched over her*
　　*face, tense and silent throughout the next scene.*
　　ABIGAIL *is still crying*)
Abigail Parris, what's this about?
Ezekiel, we have come timely.
ABIGAIL (*hysterical*):
Mr. Putnam, we meant no harm.
PUTNAM: 　　　　　　　Abigail,
Your eyes are swimming with
more than tears. What do you mean, no harm?
CHEEVER: I know the girl, Tom. Let me talk to her.
ABIGAIL: Indeed we meant no harm, Mr. Cheever,
we were only playing.
CHEEVER: 　　　　　Playing at what, Abby?
What happened?
ABIGAIL: 　　　　We scratched some dry cobs
in the rick behind the kitchen, sir—
Ann said we could dress some babies; she
had tags of canvas and a stretch of cream lace,
a trim—
PUTNAM: Mother's lace? Ann—
　　(*Ann shudders*)
ABIGAIL: 　　　　　　　　It's
hurting her, sir.

PUTNAM:  So it seems.

CHEEVER: A puppet! Abigail, the cob's a puppet.

PUTNAM (*quickly*): Ann has a doll of her own upstairs,
she doesn't need—

CHEEVER (*sharp*):  This is serious.
Abigail, take that wretched thing and chuck it
into the fire—

PUTNAM:  Wait! Mightn't it
have a name?—

CHEEVER:  A name—
(ABIGAIL *starts to speak, but checks herself*)
  Confound it, Tom,
hoodoo should be nameless in New England!
Get rid of that doll, and the other, too.
Abby, you march out to Mary in back
and she will walk you home to Uncle Parris.
Hustle along, child!
(ABIGAIL *on her way out whispers in* ANN's *ear*)

ABIGAIL:  Annie, sorry about your old lace.
(ANN *shudders again*)

CHEEVER: Run along, Abby.
(*Exit* ABIGAIL)
  Now, Thomas.

PUTNAM:  Daughter!
Ann! What is the trouble, child, speak
to your father.

CHEEVER:  Do not touch her, Tom,
the girl's haunted—

PUTNAM:  Afflicted.

CHEEVER:  We cannot tell
with what. This seizure grips her often, Tom?

PUTNAM: Alas, Ezekiel, recently, yes. Most frequently.

CHEEVER: I beg you, Thomas, do not touch her.
You care for her health—

PUTNAM:  Yes—

CHEEVER:  Leave her then

for the moment to the Doctor
whose practice is most precious, Tom.

PUTNAM: But—

CHEEVER: Doubt is not your metier. Remember
we are here for a purpose makes us
each a witness. God's timing may
seem hazardous where most provident, but
like his sanity, it's beyond us, perfect.
We have arrived punctually.

PUTNAM: You've not been
fathered by Bibles, born among schoolmasters
and bookliness for nothing. Thank you, 'Zekiel,
I'll draw her back softly.

CHEEVER: Recall her with habits
she may recognize. Draw the lace gently
out of her fingers—the stuff almost appears
to strangle her. Then perhaps she will speak
what glares out of the corner that makes
a cat of her.

PUTNAM: Ann child,
here's Mr. Cheever from the meeting with me.
He's sent by the ministers' court to ask you
a most important question.

CHEEVER: She won't understand.
Talk homely.

PUTNAM: I know my daughter, Ezekiel.
She's a clever lass for her mother and I
hide nothing in this house. Listen, Ann,
who's there with you now?
        (*Pause*)
                        Come, give me the lace.
Look up. Father will hold it for you, safe.
        (*He tries gently to remove the trim*)

ANN: No! Never. You may choke me,
pinch me to death. You shan't steal
my pretty lace. You're a cruel lady!

CHEEVER: There is one there.

PUTNAM:                              A woman. The lace,
Ann thinks an amulet.

CHEEVER: Essential it may be.
Leave it with her.

PUTNAM:              Ann?
Here, Ann, take father's hand.
Who's there with you?
Who torments you?

ANN: Father, Father, a ghost, a most devout ghost!

CHEEVER: No, child, a ghost it cannot be.
Is it the spectral
shape, the form of one you know?

ANN: Hold me!

PUTNAM:        Ann, is it
Mrs. Corey?
Some have it in the village
she's about.

CHEEVER: Thomas!

PUTNAM:                    Look carefully, who
does she *say* she is?
Ann, it's most
important we know who is there.
Has Mrs. Corey returned?

ANN (*hoarsely*): Witch. Witch.

CHEEVER: Speak up, child, do not be afraid.
Your father and I are sent to talk with
Mrs. Corey this afternoon. She'll not
dare hurt you. First, now you must tell us
what clothes she wears—

ANN:                        There. O.
Please, ma'm, do not hurt me. Father,
she's slipping away. O, she says,
she won't hurt me more this afternoon.
She says she's to hurry quick back home
to wait for you. She'll fly! She'll fly!

CHEEVER: The clothes, child, the clothes! Tell
what she is wearing.

PUTNAM:                      Be careful, Cheever!

ANN: O she's fading, but she is returning.
She's leaving because I shouldn't see
her clothes, but she's coming back
tonight to pay me out—

> (*Suddenly she claps her hand over her mouth,
> struggling not to speak*)

                              Uhh—kk—kk—not—tell!

Kk—the—wife—of Giles.

PUTNAM:                      Martha. Martha Corey—

CHEEVER: Child, how is she dressed?

PUTNAM:                      Quick, Ann—

CHEEVER: We must know. We must prove—

ANN (*serene*): O Father, I am blind now. I cannot see.

> (ANN *slumps to the floor*)

CHEEVER: How very irritating.

> (PUTNAM *kneels beside his daughter, passing his
> hands through the air before he lifts her*)

PUTNAM:                      In the name of mercy,
satan-witch, withdraw! Release my child!

CHEEVER (*quiet*): What proof, what proof?

PUTNAM (*turns at the stairwell,* ANN *in his arms*):
Proof, Mr. Cheever?

**CURTAIN**

**SCENE TWO**

GILES COREY, MARTHA COREY, then THOMAS PUTNAM
and EZEKIEL CHEEVER.

*The great room of the Corey farm is empty at rise. The
furniture is similar to that of the Putnams' although the*

*arrangement is plain. Nothing is extra, nothing is
furnished—the functional room of a prosperous farm-
house. It is still early afternoon. Through a door comes
the sound of boards and barrels kicked and shifted,
roughly.*

GILES (*off*): Tarnation take him! the meechy little lizard.
I'll have the tan off that flibberty boy
for hiding my saddle. Why, darnblast it,
he's the gizzard of a trifle, where's my
saddle? the flea—
    (MARTHA *enters, down to the stair landing*)
MARTHA:          He's not such a mite, Giles.
GILES (*off*): Bladder of a mouse, where's my saddle?
The truant—
MARTHA:        Do stop skittering the
barrels about—you'll only have to tidy up.
They're dry and the hoops will slip.
Fortunately for him, John's lightfoot it
off to town to see the fun. It's
his afternoon.
    (*Silence. Long pause. Enter* GILES)
GILES:        Martha, he's where?
Not with my saddle!
MARTHA:        So you've
misplaced the saddle. John walked.
GILES:            Who walked him?
Who let the rapscallion traipse today?
I'll bleach his hide when I catch the sneak.
MARTHA: Don't rile so easy, Giles. John needs
his skin as much as you need yours
and more. God knows, he eats
enough to fill it up to you,
high, wide and handsome. Gi, you rile
too easy—you just reduce yourself.
GILES: I'm sorry, sweetheart—

MARTHA: I said he'd ride
no horse of ours to the village today.
He's young, barely an age to hire,
no age to understand—but those
who run to stare remain to hiss,
talk gossip into scandal. Then
the course is obvious in these matters.
(GILES, *at the window, half turns, affectionately*)
GILES (*softly*): Yere, chick, chick, chick. Yere, chick!
MARTHA: Mock me, old Split Foot, if you wish,
just remember when the maples turn,
each of us is challenged, each invaded
by the very one we make example
of. Peepers and the scandal mongers
retreat in accusation. They who hoof it
to watch, catch the disease; and to cure
their own fleshed up security, they judge
the outbreak worst where it's most easily seen.
No, I didn't let the boy go, Gi,
but he went.
GILES: While I shuck out
pocketsfull of pine trees
to hire a hand to water my cattle,
he scampers.—What are you talking about?
MARTHA (*ironic*): Witchcraft, Giles, witchcraft.
GILES: Careful, Martha.
You're always a shade too easy and quickly
up with the words. Always I'm just
beginning to understand you, when
off you move into a new
calm tantrum of language. Martha,
they'll have you for it, too.
MARTHA: Who, Giles?
GILES (*hesitates*): Well—
MARTHA: Lift me the hamper, Giles.
(*She sorts the clothes*)

GILES: You take that boy—I'll whip him proper
for skitting—
MARTHA:          There's enough of whipping, Giles.
GILES: Never you mind, you're my wife, yes,
and the best I've had, but—
MARTHA:                    —second and best.
Why, thank you, Gi.
GILES:               You may be my wife
but Martha, I won't be off my point.
Listen to me! Take that pesky boy,
scuttling down to the meeting house
as if it were a holiday.
He doesn't even set to ask me, Sir,
may I hike the saddle? He swipes it—
MARTHA: Not while I'm mistress in your house.
John's a kind lad but he's no master here.
And that's my point, Giles. John didn't
steal your saddle. No one did.
Johnny hasn't got the saddle.
GILES:                    Then who—?
MARTHA: (My sanguine husband!) Love me, Giles,
but don't you trouble to learn me.—It's
sleepy in you. A good thing too,
we'd only garner crab apples if you did
instead of hauling the best hay south
of Fairmaid Hill. I'll tell you where
your saddle is, I hid it. The pummel's
under the ticking. It's upstairs.
GILES: You what—? Damnit, I know you said.
What right have you? Whatever for?
MARTHA: Only the right of one who cares.
I hoped you'd ask: I know you won't
walk into the village with a bunged up foot,
weak and sore, in that condition.
So I hid the saddle.
GILES (*laughs suddenly*): So you hid the saddle.

Well now, my Martha, you're an ornery wife,
praise be, and it's spirit, starch and sauce
and none of this lady, lady kittle-kattle,
and I thank my judgment for the day
I brought you home, for we've made more pegs
for the oxbow than plugs for the cider barrel—

MARTHA: Why Giles—

GILES:                    A spiel for the credit side
of the ledger, dear heart. You might say
we've kept it pretty well in the black.

MARTHA: Goodness, Old Nick's full of surprises
now the sap's risen. Give me a hand
with the bed sheets, Split Foot.

GILES:                    No, you don't!
No indoors work for a man in March. Now,
what made you think I'd traipse to town
on an afternoon like this? There's seeding,
and mash to be turned, a deal too much
to shilly-shally off like a reckless lad.
A week of clear days—

MARTHA:                    The scrawny lilac
by the pump is budding before the others,
first again. You'd think the drip
would drown the roots or throttle the neck
in a choker of ice. Spring will be sweet, sweet—
the bobolink sang this morning.—Giles,
I'm not getting a thing done. Now you
get out of here!

GILES:                    The ground is soft
up in the orchard already. All right, all right!
        (*Turning, as she shoos him out he wrenches his
        lame foot with a howl of pain*)

MARTHA: O Giles, your foot again!

GILES:                    The dadblasted cart
backed on my ankle yesterday.

MARTHA:                    Sit here, Gi.

Let me loosen the thongs.

GILES: Leave it, leave it,
the blood'll be back in a minute.

MARTHA: Here,
I'll fetch you a beaker of cider.

GILES: That's
more like help.

(MARTHA *goes out back for the cider*)
O Martha, I forgot to warn you,
when I was out on the fence in the east field
Henry came by for a chat—

MARTHA (*off*): Henry?

GILES: Yes, can you have forgotten Henry Crosby,
your beloved son-in-law, Henry?

MARTHA (*returns*): Well.
What's Henry doing down from Salem
mid-week? Why didn't he come up to the house?
Is he too uppity to talk to your wife?

GILES: Now Martha. He was just in overnight,
to trade with Ingersoll at the tavern.
When I told him William and Sarah
were coming with the children in from Beverly
he said that he and Sue would join us.

MARTHA: That's like him. He won't see this house,
no, nor the land around us teeter
even so slightly towards the more attentive.

GILES: What have you got against Henry, Martha?
(*She hands him the cider, and kneels to unlace his boots*)

MARTHA: Nothing, Gi, nothing at all.
It's what he holds against me I can't help.
You remember when Henry's father died,
old John Crosby that was born out of London?

GILES: Why not? He could tip a whole barrel.

MARTHA: Well, Henry's mother acted bewitched,
almost out of her mind—that was all right.

But Henry with her, they draped the house,
and themselves and all the furniture,
with black and more black, yards of the stuff
everywhere and on everything.

GILES:                              What's wrong with that?
Mourning's proper.

MARTHA:              But Henry with her,
the bees—

GILES (*laughs*): The bees?

MARTHA:                      Yes, she got the idea,
goodness knows where, from Henry perhaps,
that all their bees like little rascals,
would leave their boxes and never come back,
unless they informed them by draping the hives
with big black bows, that their master was dead.

GILES (*roars with laughter*):
Small wonder Henry says you mock him
with peccadillos!

MARTHA:              Why it's a fool thing
poor Sarah Good who wanders so,
might entertain.

            (*She pulls off his boots*)
                  There. Is the pain gone?
            (*He kisses her forehead, stands up, picking up his
            boots*)

GILES: Gone like the bees. Well, you never
can tell. Henry's sensible enough.
Martha, we've dawdled sufficient for today.

MARTHA: Just right. Giles, I'm so very glad
you didn't pack off like a drover on holiday
to the village to gossip. Let those in the village
drive their own sheep.

GILES:                      To gossip?
Gossip, is it? That's what you call
gossip, and three set witches already
jailed for torturing up mere girls!

MARTHA: Girls, mere girls. Yes, the children
   are much to be reckoned with, poor bored
   and frightened little kept-in creatures.
   Winter's dull for freckled wenches,
   young for marriage, a hot man in the bed.
   Call him the Devil—O yes, it's dull—
   a stool by the fire, the few winter chores done,
   nothing to speak of save what is read
   out of the good Book, nothing to think of
   save, Am I? Am I, one of the Chosen?—
   the men in the fields, or off in the woods.
   It's bleak for them, but it's not for us
   to condone the chitchat that could be fatal.
   Indeed, Giles, there's some for whom I fear
   a hanging's the only pleasure.

GILES:                          Martha, there's
   one thing even you can't guess. You
   don't imagine what's charged the meeting—

MARTHA: We go to church—

GILES:             —but weekdays, Martha, weekdays!

MARTHA: You manage to tell me. What concerns us
   happens on Sundays. That's my pleasure.

GILES: For God's sake, Martha, pay some attention!
   A terror beyond us is driving the cattle.
   Why yesterday, I went to fetch the ox, well,
   out of the woods about noon; I went
   to raise him, for he lay down in the yard;
   he could not rise to be yoked, but dragged
   his hinder parts as if he'd been hip-shot.
   Men say—

MARTHA:       But after he did rise.

GILES:                          True. But you,
   you never leave the farm except
   to church, and there you pray—

MARTHA:                          —as well I may.

GILES: I do not doubt it. But that's all you do,
  you never linger after to banter with neighbors—
MARTHA: I don't have to, I know what's going on.
  It's all in the sermon, I listen to the sermon.
  My husband, his family, my home and the fields,
  these are my village.
GILES:                    Martha, you're a good wife.
  You're out-to-elbow with your own thoughts,
  sometimes bristly with hymns I can't follow,
  but good I don't doubt. You've taught me
  much, yes, and a year ago took me to my
  first sacrament.
                    They make me a member
  at this late date, and I'm glad. But this
  you can't teach me. You don't know
  what rake-hell's rising in Mr. Parris' parish.
  You don't guess how far devils may press us.
MARTHA: The girls cry out.
GILES:                    But d'you know why?
  And on whom they do so? And how? You do not.
  One child, afflicted by the devil of Tituba,
  cried out what clothes the Carib negro wore
  at the very moment, how she did up her hair.
  She caught it so precisely, the ghost of the slave
  hot to escape Nancy's godly eyes
  fled screaming in a wolf skin. Lickerty-split
  the men crossed the road to the parsonage kitchen—
  the seizure took hold in Ingersoll's tavern—
  cowering in the woodshed the old witch stood
  dressed as the girl described. Next day
  at the court they are holding in meeting—
  they've got John Hathorne and Nicholas Noyes,
  (the Reverend Noyes), and Corwin down
  from Salem Town—even the wolf skin
  Tituba confessed to—

MARTHA:                          God, how can we grasp
    sanity unless
    the great insanity we worship shake us
    until our fear is all!
                          Heathen Tituba
    torn from the Barbados, her familiar forest
    of tropics, of snakes, of yellow birds,
    and shipped, a slave, to our foreign forest
    which Mr. Parris would people with anglified
    witches where we have natural wonders
    to haunt us, real Indians to hunt us;
    Parris enslaved her, pitiful priestess.
    She must have had carriage in her own clime,
    but here, a heathen, they cry out against her,
    the godly children she was bought to nurse!
    Tituba did badly to fear, not God,
    but foreign girls. So she confessed—
GILES:                                      —yes—
MARTHA:—the hoodoo she knew. What has the devil
    to do with Tituba? Must we accept
    that too?
GILES:          Accept?
MARTHA:                    In order to reject, Giles,
    now I will confess I never saw
    Tituba dressed other than in canvas
    bound round her waist, her hair held so.
    How should the girl not know?
GILES:                                      Tituba's in prison.
MARTHA: O Giles, why can't you understand?
GILES: You're talking blather, dangerous blather.
    I must protect—at least one in the family
    must follow what the court is after.
MARTHA: Giles, I won't argue. What hurts the girls
    could be far more than winter, but
    whatever it is, it's in themselves,
    and me, and—

GILES: Martha! Can you say that!
In you—?

MARTHA: In all of us.

GILES: No. O, no!

(*Pause*)

Can you have heard what the women say now?
That the girls are crying out again, against
one who seems most devout.

MARTHA: Seems, Giles?
Do you believe it?

GILES: Believe what, wife?
(*Looks at her, puzzled*)
In witches? Martha, what have you heard?
They haven't named the new witch yet,
but Mrs. Putnam says she's heard one
choking her daughter.

MARTHA (*quiet*): May there be mercy,
where mercy appears to be least needed.

GILES: Martha, Henry says Tom Putnam
was very fond of you in school,
often carried your books, or something.
Martha, what are all of them up to?

MARTHA: Please Giles, leave me alone, the house
this time of day is the waitingest job,
my job, Giles, and your house. Surely
we've whittled so much of the afternoon
it's time you fetched and drenched the horses.

GILES (*loud*): I know how and when to use my horses!
Clean the house! Pray! You're no more safe
than those you pray for, if you pray for them.
Small thanks you'll get. Where's my saddle?

MARTHA: I told you, Giles, upstairs. I can only do
what I can do—wisdom's a limited virtue.
Until supper, Giles.

(MARTHA *starts off, but turns softly in the door-way*)

GILES (*going upstairs*): Who would tell her
what they're saying, unless I do.

> (GILES *goes out upstairs and returns bearing the
> saddle, grumbling*)

For everything you do there's one to stop you.

> (*He sneaks out*)

MARTHA: Some men have a perfect demon for
seeking out their particular accusers.

> (MARTHA *pauses in the doorway, deep in thought.
> She walks slowly over to the corner where there
> is a cedar chest, looking at it as if it would burn
> her to touch the lid. When she opens it, which
> she does quickly, she begins to sing*)

MARTHA (*sings*):

> Once was a girl whose only sin
> Was this, she lived alone.
> She sought no man to take her in,
> To build her a house of stone.
>
> She kept a cat, and in a cage
> Two yellow singing birds.
> Her love rode off to the Indian wars,
> She took to raising herbs.
>
> They said, Her man will not come back
> From forests he now lives in.
> He's stained his cheeks with chestnut juice
> For the love of an Indian.

> (MARTHA *lifts from the chest a colored jacket, a
> piece of ribbon and a comb. In front of the mirror
> she readjusts her wear, so it seems exotic, but is
> mainly the same*)

> She ran bright ribbons through her hair,
> Each day a different color.
> Neighbors said, She does not care,
> Surely she has a lover.

They watched her door, but no man came,
And no man went away.
Each noon she turned as pale as moons,
Each night she turned more gay.

As she failed she sang a song
To make their grey eyes change,
I am a girl has done small wrong
Though I am strange.

In crystal balls I do not gaze,
The Tarot I don't deal in,
I tell my lies with a buttercup,
Or a toss of an apple peeling.

They said that she had lost her head
Because she died alone,
No mortal husband in her bed.
They built her house of stone.

(MARTHA *takes the wash upstairs, leaving the stage
empty. A loud knock at the door. Enter first*
PUTNAM *and then* CHEEVER *after a second knock*)

CHEEVER: No one's home, the house is empty.

PUTNAM: She's here, she's nowhere else.
I've always wondered how she would keep
a house.

CHEEVER:  We should have waited
until she answered the door. It's not
in keeping with our business, Thomas,
to enter uninvited.

PUTNAM:            It wasn't my choice
to come here uninvited—or invited.
Mrs. Corey may be a member of
the Covenant in excellent standing, but
the Devil's agents are craftily chosen
and chosen for life, and dark is hid under
the light, remember that, Ezekiel.

CHEEVER: But we're sent by the meeting to one of our own,
to question first; to accuse, perhaps not at all.
PUTNAM: My daughter is being driven from her senses!
Waver a jot now, and we shall all be divided
by hypocrites.
There were gangling years
when I was not unfond of Martha, she
had a way could charm goldfinches off
branches they sat on, or chatter a catbird
out of his nest and into the bushes.
Since then, 'Zekiel, I've sometimes wondered
where such uncanny magic came from.
CHEEVER: She was always honest. Tom, it's not right
to speak of a woman in her own castle
when she's not at home. At least let's
conduct ourselves in the fashion of dignity.
(MARTHA *enters above on the landing of the stair*)
PUTNAM: Giles Corey passed us across the fields,
galloping to town through Governor's Plain,
after his boy who is already there.
Corey didn't see us, but believe me, Ezekiel,
there's more than innocence in this room.
You saw him ride away as if possessed.
(MARTHA *comes down*)
MARTHA: Why good afternoon, gentlemen. Tom. Mr.
Cheever.
I'm sorry I wasn't down to answer the door
when you came in. I can hardly say
you weren't expected, but not so early.
Tom, it's good to see you in my home
on no matter what errand after so many years.
Mr. Cheever, take a chair.
CHEEVER (*sits*): Thank you, Martha.
PUTNAM: Ezekiel! So, Mrs. Corey, you are at home.
MARTHA: Tom, don't look so shocked. I never

leave the house when there's work about.

PUTNAM: As if no other woman ever worked.
    My wife's an invalid—

MARTHA:                Tom. I know.

CHEEVER: Martha, we're here on a most serious errand—

MARTHA: I know what you are sent for, Ezekiel,
    you come to talk about being a witch.
       (*Pause*)

CHEEVER: God help you!

MARTHA:              —But I am none.
    I can't help people talking to me.

PUTNAM: There's far more than talk abroad, madam, as
    you
    just now have mysteriously indicated.

MARTHA: Talk, Thomas, talk. Don't madam me,
    we've been neighbors and friends for years,
    in school, in church, in this rocky land.
    Despise proximity, bury connections,
    then we shall truly be taken by what
    we can never prove. Tom, can you face that?

PUTNAM: The cries of persecuted children, Mrs. Corey,
    cannot be disguised by frivolous talk
    of gossip.

MARTHA:     So I *am* named.

PUTNAM:               You knew!

MARTHA: I didn't *know*.

CHEEVER:             Even old friends
    come as God's proctors when deviltry seizes.
    Listen to him, Martha.

MARTHA:             Who has called out on me?

PUTNAM (*turns away*): Ezekiel, please, will you—

CHEEVER:                Martha, I fear
    we won't have time for delicacy now.
    Tom's daughter, Ann, and Abigail Parris
    and now the others complain of your witchcraft
    in no haphazard terms, but saliently.

That's why we come directly to you,
an occasion you don't seem unprepared for.
MARTHA: How have I done them hurt, I would know?
PUTNAM: Don't you pretend to be wronged. You know
far better than we, how you visit them,
by night to suffocate, even by daylight
to drive them crazy or to the Devil.
MARTHA: Do I so? And yet my house is clean.
Your daughter sees me whenever she wishes,
but does she tell you what clothes I wear?
Answer me that.
        (*The men turn away*)
                    Are you really surprised?
Does she tell you what clothes I wear?
CHEEVER: Forfend! Who expected vision of both!
        (PUTNAM *draws* CHEEVER *aside*)
PUTNAM: I tell you, Cheever, here's more than appearance,
the woman has infernal divination.
God make us sly! Remember my daughter
cried, 'Now I am blind, I cannot see.'
What further proof—?
CHEEVER:                Confront her, Thomas,
confront her with what has happened. Satan
is not wiser than God.
PUTNAM: You'll not speak first?
CHEEVER:                    It was not my daughter.
MARTHA: You must speak lower, gentlemen.
My ears are only human ears.
It seems I cannot even keep out
whisper and secrets under my own roof.
Does Ann Putnam tell what clothes I have on?
PUTNAM: No, she doesn't, God protect her from you.
You can best tell why—you blinded her
before she could tell. She fell, helpless, down.
I carried her up to her bed myself,
where she lay like a child enchanted and mute,

but stilled because you promised to leave her
for three pathetic hours. How might she say
what clothes you wear—or that you're dressed
a shade too oddly here and now?
> (*Pause*)

MARTHA:                                        Well.
> (*Softly*)
Giles, though he didn't know it, was right.
Ezekiel, this is preposterous. Thomas,
I see, is naturally over-wrought
about his child, as well he may be—
discipline should be kept well at home
and not thrown out of it, like slops.
It's disgraceful to slander the innocent so.

CHEEVER: The disgrace, Martha Corey, is to your church
and to your God.

MARTHA (*incredulous*): But I go to my church,
and I praise my God, my God and yours.

PUTNAM: Blasphemy!

CHEEVER:                      In the weird battle
many come and go disguised.

MARTHA: Put away the trumpets, Mr. Cheever!
It begins to look as if you'd succumbed
to this neighborly madness. You're a sound man.

CHEEVER: Madness it is—

PUTNAM:                              —to gamble with infernal engines!
Leave her to them. Why, I think she believes—

MARTHA: Yes, indeed, Tom Putnam, I
do not *know* your westering witches!

PUTNAM: You know more than several: Sarah Osborne,
Tituba and Sarah Good, all accused,
rightfully examined and properly jailed.

MARTHA: Mrs. Good is an idle, cheeky woman,
I know, a door-to-doorway tramp.
You do well to question her health,
or at this late date, her sanity. Surely

she spreads nothing more infernal
than careless ways, and the rotten smell
of the rotten tobacco she puffs in your face.
She never goes to church, sad woman,
nor to the doctor. I go to both,
doctor for my children, church for my peace.
Praise of God is my only holiday!
PUTNAM: Outward, outward, it's all outward.
MARTHA: O, Tom!
        Look here, you don't know what you're about!
Do you presume to turn over souls for lice
as you'd leaf a cabbage, or gouge a potato?
An excellent farmer like you knows better
than to let his stock trample down fences.
You are no soul doctor! Just you trammel
divine responsibility and you'll quickly see
what can happen. Then you'll get devils;
I tell you what fraction of God you know
will forsake far more than the earth you walk.
You'll have more invalids than wives and children!
CHEEVER: O my God, Martha.
PUTNAM:         You still need proof, Mr. Cheever?
CHEEVER: We're not delegated to examine this woman.
Martha Corey, you should know
that as a matter of course a warrant will be
issued for your arrest. You will be
accompanied under small guard to the ordinary
of Deacon Ingersoll. Until that time
you may be sure we shall fast and pray.
I bid you do the same.
PUTNAM:         If she can.
No witch stays put until she be hanged.
    (*Exit* PUTNAM)
MARTHA: Ezekiel, how do we justify our anger?
CHEEVER: That's each for himself to tell. Martha,
if you are no witch you should have been

a minister—both deal in stern prerogative.
These days will tell. May whatever fraction
of God you pray to, aid.

MARTHA:                          I know my innocence.
So shall the magistrate's eyes be cleared
by innocence.

CHEEVER:              Good afternoon, madam.
　　　(*Exit*)


CURTAIN



SCENE THREE


MARTHA COREY and GILES COREY.


*The same, some hours after sunset. The square of the
window, although night has fallen, makes a lighter rec-
tangle of blue that appears to float, like a match lit in a
dark place, on the blue-blackness which fills the room.*
MARTHA COREY's *profile, as she sits immobile looking out
across silent fields, is outlined along one edge of the sash.
A shadow crosses the panes, and* GILES *enters with a
lantern.*


GILES (*calls*): Martha! Martha! You there, Martha?
My God, they've got her already.
They wouldn't dare—they can't have arrived
ahead of me. O Martha.

MARTHA:                          I'm here, Giles.

GILES: Confound it, Martha, what a turn you gave me!
What are you sitting there in the dark for?
Sweetheart, are you all right?

MARTHA:                          Of course.

GILES: Then why are you sitting there in the dark,

hands in your lap, still as an owl?
Martha, are you praying?

MARTHA:                    You might say that.
Giles, stand by me here for a moment,
I've something to tell you. Come on, it's all right!
I won't hex you.

GILES:                    You're not what they say, but
Martha, you do say the goldarndest things.
You're not an easy woman.

MARTHA:                    It's no easy land.
Look, Giles, how the land flows back from our windows.
There at the fields' edge, the blue-black forest;
what d'you think's out there, cloven hoofs, witches?
or feathers and Indians? Which is strange,
which is familiar? We fear familiars,
English witches instead of true terror
lurking in the strange woods. That's it!
That's what we fear—and we're pushing it back.
I push, and the circle of home grows larger;
you clear the timber, and the fields bleed,
push up rocks to detain the plough;
and we pick up the rocks, and build us fences
to mark the property and keep the cattle.
And every year the land's circumference
ripples back from the rocks they landed
on at Plymouth. The circles, Giles,
will never stop where God drops the rocks
at the edge of an old world we once knew.
But the fear!
                    Why must we always
*know* what we fear, fill the natural spaces
between us with ghosts? There's too much
space between human beings.
When something's real to fear why do we
look for witches between good neighbors?

GILES: Martha, they asked me in the village today,

Does your wife believe in witches?

MARTHA: Did they, Giles?
Look out of your window. I love this land.
But often and often since I came to you,
washing the dishes, weeding the vegetables,
churning the cream in the butter firkin,
knitting jerseys for my man, thank God,
and thank God he's a man, sweeping, scrubbing,
shining windows—often and often
I look up: there's the always edge of the clearing.
I look up, and I am foreign again.
I love this land, but like my mother,
I'm suddenly foreign against the forest,
this endless America, this sea of dry land
(no ships save axes), this new-found pattern
of highroads that don't exist for us yet.
I'll not live to see, but the children will.
Giles, it must be a terrible God
who shook out America, a terrible God.
And when I pray, it's just as if
He didn't know Himself—that gigantic!
But I am greater for having prayed.

> (GILES *has left her side and is stumbling around
> the room in the dark. She reaches for his hand, not
> finding it, turns*)

Giles, where are you?

GILES: Looking for candles,
damn it!

MARTHA: Giles, don't leave me!

GILES: Martha,
what's going on here—if a man can't come
home to a well-lit house at the day's end,
what's he worked up to? Tarnation take it,
he may just as well go straight to bed.

MARTHA (*rises*): Sorry, old Split Foot.

> (*She lights the room*)

                                                  Of course, you're hungry.
Supper's warming at the fire,
your kind of meal: parsley stew
from yesterday's beef, hot corn pudding,
and cider for chilblains.

GILES:                                 Sweetheart—
        (*He sees her*)
Great guns, Martha, you look so young!
What've you strung through your hair?

MARTHA: O this, I forgot.
        (*She strips the ribbon from her hair, and runs to
        the chest*)

GILES:                                 Forgot what? What're you
all rigged up in these flamigigs for—
to greet your old man? This is a new tack.
Martha, you're not—

MARTHA (*smoothes the dress over her belly*):
                                                  No. No.
        (MARTHA *lays the ribbon in the chest, goes to the
        fireplace for* GILES' *supper. He sits at the table,
        following her movements with his eyes, fascinated,
        as she sets his meal in front of him*)
                                 Giles, they were here.

GILES: Who?

MARTHA:    Tom Putnam and Ezekiel Cheever.

GILES:                                                  So that's
where they were. Putnam and Cheever, eh?

MARTHA: You should have been here, Giles,
you should have been with me.

GILES: The fancy clothes for gentlemen,
your looking so young, the gentle talk—
Tom Putnam was here—

MARTHA:                          Giles! Don't say that!
Don't even think it!

GILES:                          Your wedding jacket.

MARTHA: It's not, it was Mother's. Don't look at me

like that, with eyes like coppers
in the fire.
            You've always wondered—
you've always wanted to know what passed
once between Tom Putnam and me.
And I'd have told you long ago
but you'd have made it something like
an indigestible clot in your head
because you wouldn't have understood.
Neither did Tom, except for one
fantastic May. He carried my slates.
But you, I love; you're a part of me,
unsolvable, insoluble part of me.
You, you don't need to understand.

GILES: I try, but how can I, Martha, how can I?
You say each thing a thousand times
in a thousand different ways. Which
of these would you have me catch on to?

MARTHA: Whichever you wish, which is what you do,
and what you should do.

GILES:                     Sometimes I'm sure
you're hiding something—what is it, Martha?

MARTHA: Nothing. Now listen, I'll tell you. The day
was clear as an Indian's eye, and bright
where the giant birch showers the mill race
with yellow snow. I was splashing my feet
crazily in white and yellow water,
and Tom had followed me half-way home.
I started talking to him, the way
I've just been talking to you now, Giles,
at least that's where our talk today
all came from, above the turbulent mill race.
But then it was wild and delirious,
and I scared him royal. Yes,
Tom Putnam loved me. We were young.
We were sixteen, and that's old enough,

but he loved above the shoulders, the fire
just never came on. It never burned.
Love can start early in here you know,
but I scared him, I didn't mean to, but
I scared him nevertheless. You don't scare.
I always looked from the sea inland,
and Tom was always scanning the sea
for ships, familiar with men from England.
Tom listened, alas, he always listened
and went away, sad, to familiar things
as if I were someone he'd love to love,
and couldn't hold. Well, oddly enough
when he wed Ann Carr in the parsonage,
frail Ann Carr with her English ways,
I knew that was right—he got a woman
who really can scare, and with familiar things.
Look at the daughter—

GILES:                    Martha, you know
perhaps Tom Putnam is using that girl—

MARTHA: For what? No, Gi, Tom's not using her.
The daughter, with the mother's brains, is using
him.
        Giles, let's forget the Putnams,
at least until the warrant arrives?

GILES: Warrant? What warrant? They came here to serve
a warrant on you, in my own house
when I was away? A warrant for what?

MARTHA: You've been to town, Giles. You should know
as well as I. Suppose you tell me.

GILES: Not my wife on my property!

MARTHA: Don't get rackerty, Gi, there's nothing
to doubt—I've been through that today.
They wish to examine, and my innocence
will show the magistrates well enough.
A day in the meadow together, or pruning
the apple orchard will set us both right.

They merely resent that I will not join
the twit and skulduggery. Let's forget it
for now, old Split Foot—
    (*She comes up to him*)
GILES:                 Martha, stop it!
You don't believe witches. All right, you don't.
They said as much at Ingersoll's.
But give the devil his due. Pet names
or no pet names, it's a dangerous thing
to fool around with a name like that.
I said I'd make you realize
hanging's afoot, and we'll start right here.
No more old-deviling me for love.
You can have what you want without that—
MARTHA: Who said I don't believe in witches?
I believe in my God; witches and wizards
have nothing to do with it. Giles, who said
I don't believe in witches?
GILES:                 Martha, I said.
They asked me in town today, and I said.
If you're so innocent what does it matter?
MARTHA (*turns away*): O Giles, what do you do this for?
Why d'you talk to those people about me?
GILES: Sweetheart, I didn't sign. No deposition
will get my name unless I know
whose peas are being split, and what
the words are up to—
MARTHA:             What've you done?
Giles, what happened in the tavern?
GILES: The Putnams have got the town in conniptions,
and the others with them, and with some reason.
The girls are driven to terrible things,
jumping and leaping and flapping like birds
driven before an invisible thunderhead.
They do nothing to stop them, they can't. Betty Parris,
tried to leap into the fire shouting,

'The Book, *she's* after me to sign!'
The ministers sat around with long, pale faces,
writing it down. They asked me why you
never visit the village with the others,
except to church. Then Henry asked me
to tell them, Did you believe in witches?

MARTHA: He's gone that far—

GILES:                 Henry would help.
I'm sure he means well—he thought you did.
But I knew you did not, and so I said so.
But I signed nothing.

MARTHA:            Thank God for that!
    (*She looks around as if for something to do with
    her hands*)
The sand is down. O Gi, it's getting late.
Henry means as well as a disowned child
means well when his father has cut him off.
You haven't touched your food. The spoon
won't even want washing. Not the stew, not the sauce.
What's wrong? Aren't you hungry?

GILES (*rises*):            Not tonight.
Come up to bed.

MARTHA:       Are you sure?

GILES:              Sure.
Don't worry, dear, any more tonight.
Now come.

MARTHA:     Giles, pray with me first—
we must draw together in this, as in all,
we must stand together.

GILES (*on the stairs*):
Sweetheart, to speak plain
as you often do, I cannot pray
with you. I haven't got the words
you use—we'll fall to arguing
about mere words. You put me off.
Now come to bed.

MARTHA: In church on Sunday,
then I'll speak innocence in my prayer.

GILES: Sweetheart, you're not going to church
this Sunday, or next, or any day
until they get this thing cleared up.
You told me not to go, and now,
after today, town's no place for you.

MARTHA: I shall go none-the-less before they return
to take me by warrant. I'll sit in my pew,
like any innocent woman. They'll see.

GILES: Now, come.

MARTHA: You'll not pray with me
tonight?

GILES: No, not tonight. It's time for bed.

MARTHA: All right, Giles, be impatient!
I'll come up when I'm good and ready.

GILES (*laughs*): Then it's Tom Putnam, is it?

MARTHA: No Gi,
it's you.

CURTAIN

SCENE FOUR

The MAN FROM BOSTON, MAGISTRATE HAWTHORNE,
EZEKIEL CHEEVER, REV. SAMUEL PARRIS, THOMAS PUTNAM,
ABIGAIL PARRIS, ANN PUTNAM and the girls, GILES COREY,
then MARTHA COREY with CONSTABLE LOCKER, and the
Villagers.

*The Examination of* MARTHA COREY *takes place in the
Salem Village Meeting House, from the pulpit and platform and from the forward pews. The building is white,
inside and out, the windows square, the panes of glass*

*also square. The pulpit is square and white—it is a clean place. The villagers enter severally, gossiping, the jury of girls with them, quiet and orderly. In some cases, an older woman leads one of these to the forward pew where the girls sit together, and returns to her own place with reassurances and back glances of compassion. The men and women do not sit together. While this is taking place, at the front, the man from Boston, posing as a villager in his cups, half accosts a few of the men as they enter, in a jocund manner from which each tries to extricate himself. One tries uneasily to quiet him.*

MAN FROM BOSTON: Now, sir, I ask you,
  what constitutes a crime?
  Well, speak up. What, eh?
  Look at it historically.
  Forty years ago, eavesdropping,
  meddling, neglecting
  work, taking tobacco,
  scolding, all on record;
  naughty speeches, hmm?
  Profane dancing, a kiss,
  making love without consent
  of friends, carelessness
  about fire, uncharitableness
  to a poor man in distress;
  bad grinding at mill,
  wearing great boots, ha!
  Wearing broad bone lace and
  ribbons—all of us, guilty!
VILLAGER: Please, my good man—
VILLAGER: Such frivolity!
MAN FROM BOSTON:
      (*The man appears to recognize each. They behave as if this were impertinence from a stranger*)
  And twenty years ago,

abusing your mother-
in-law, wicked speeches
against sons-in-law;
confessing yourself
a Quaker, speaking
out in meeting,
all on record; cruelty
to animals, drinking
tobacco, that is, chewing,
all of us, guilty!
Kicking one another
in the street,
leaving children alone
in the house,
pulling hair, pushing
your wife in public,
selling dear, all on record—

VILLAGER: Be quiet!

VILLAGER:            Mind
your own business.

VILLAGER: Hush—

MAN FROM BOSTON: And recently,
what constitutes a crime?
The ninth commandment,
digging up the grave of,
say, Sagamore of Agawam,
on record, on record;
and going naked
into the meeting house,
playing cards and
rebellious speeches
to parents, reporting
a scandalous lie,
reproaching the minister,
selling strong water
by small measure, all

on record, all of us,
guilty, and
dissenting from the rest of the jury, yes,
on record, all of us, guilty, but not so
guilty. Not so guilty.

(*Magistrate* JOHN HATHORNE *has entered above
with the ministers and* EZEKIEL CHEEVER. *The Reverend* PARRIS, *who will act as scribe, takes his place
at the table and prepares his pen and paper. The*
MAN FROM BOSTON *breaks into roars of laughter*)

HATHORNE: Ezekiel, who is that man?

CHEEVER: I'm sure I don't know, John.
He's never been with us before.

HATHORNE: I believe the man is drunk.

CHEEVER: Deacon Ingersoll would sell no spirits
at this hour, not on a day of fast.

HATHORNE: He must carry them privately.
Will someone give the strange
gentleman leave to go? We
are here on no merry matter.

(*Some move to eject the man, but he acts first*)

MAN FROM BOSTON: Magistrate John Hathorne, I'm much
obliged
at your hospitality; excuse me, pressing
matters require I go directly.
(*Exit*)

HATHORNE: How very odd. Thomas, the children are here?

PUTNAM: Ann is here, and the others, John.

HATHORNE: You have my particular sympathy.
We are all disturbed.

PUTNAM:                    Thank you, John Hathorne.

HATHORNE: Is Dr. Parris ready?

PARRIS:                    My paper is prepared,
the pens sharpened. But, your Honor, may I
protest a final time I be permitted
to share the questioning with you

here at this wretched woman's trial—

HATHORNE: Sir, here's no trial, here's examination—

PARRIS: But the accused is in my parish, sir.

HATHORNE: Dr. Parris, this has been fairly settled.
You claimed the propriety yourself
of keeping a permanent record here;
the record is still your faithful office.
Ezekiel.

CHEEVER: Quiet. Quiet in the meeting house!

HATHORNE: Dr. Parris, the charges if you please, sir.

> (PARRIS *passes a paper to* HATHORNE. *Enter* GILES
> COREY *alone at the back*)

(*reads*) 'There being complaint made before us by
Thomas Putnam and Hugh Keney, yeoman both of
Salem Village, against Martha Corey of Salem Farms,
for suspicion of witchcraft, and thereby done much hurt
unto the bodies of Ann, the wife of Thomas, and Ann
the daughter of said Thomas, also Abigail Parris, one
of the family of Dr. Parris, we hereby open the examination of the said Martha Corey who has been ap-
prehended on suspicion of being a witch.'
Bring Mrs. Corey—Constable, bring in the accused.

> (MARTHA COREY *is brought in by Constable* GEORGE
> LOCKER, *her wrists bound behind her back with
> cord. There is a ripple, like a sigh, from the girls
> which draws all eyes*)

The minister will open the examination with prayer.

PARRIS (*rises, and steps forward, looking into the congregation*):
Almighty God, Governor of heaven,
and in no small part, with no disloyalty
to those in corporeal office, mayor
of this village, discover Your hand
invisible guide of our lamentable necessity.
I ask You first, O Lord, for myself as scribe
in the examination You ordain for this woman,

that my mortal hand be served not by
weakness but by divine compunction.
And further, that these holy children,
servants of Your peace and citizens
of Your earthly kingdom, may come to peace.
There are places where they used to enjoy
much of Your presence; although You do not visit
persons for the sake of places, yet visit
places for the sake of Your citizens.
You have confided the Devil visits
even these places, the best persons here.
No place I know of has got such a spell
as will always keep the Devil out.
The meeting house wherein we assemble to Your good
is continually filled with holy citizens;
but if our eyes were so refined as the Servant
of the Prophet had his eyes of old,
we should now see a throng of devils in
this very place. The Apostle has
intimated Angels come among us;
likewise we see devils rendezvousing here.

    (*Re-enter the* MAN FROM BOSTON, *behind the*
    *crowd, quietly, in his own character*)

There, a devil rocks one asleep, but not today.
There, a devil makes another to be thinking,
he scarce knows what himself, but not today.
As Satan was hissed out of Paradise, we cannot
shut him out of our private devotions,
until gloriously we return at length
to High Places of the air. Until that time
grant we may prepare Your city in our fields.
Stem the dark tide on our imperfect island.
You above all know the names the Enemy chooses;
grant we may share that wisdom, as out of the mouths
of babes we execute the examination of this woman.
Amen. Even so, Lord Jesus, come quickly!

HATHORNE: So be it.

    (*Pause*)

LOCKER:        Your Honor,
this is the body of Martha Corey,
according to warrant.

HATHORNE:        Thank you, Constable.
You've completed your search?

GILES:        He has, indeed,
the bungling poker!

HATHORNE:        That will do, Mr. Corey.
George?

LOCKER:        We've made diligent search for
images and such like, but found none.

HATHORNE:        George,
release her hands. Martha, Martha Corey,
you are now in the hands of authority.
Boundaries between farms may become obscure
as friends and neighbors grow old. The lines
in eternal plans are exact, without age.
Don't presume on familiarity, Mrs. Corey;
we are on God's business.

        Tell me now,
why you hurt these persons?

MARTHA:        I do not.

HATHORNE:        Who does?

MARTHA: Pray, Mr. Hathorne, give me leave to pray.

HATHORNE: Mrs. Corey, we didn't send for you
to go to prayer—but tell me why
you hurt these?

    (*He points to the girls*)

MARTHA:        I'm an innocent person.
I never had to do with witchcraft
since I was born. I'm a gospel woman.

    (*Outcries among the girls*)

ANN: Gospel Witch! That's she! For shame.

ABIGAIL: Gospel Witch! Gospel Witch! Shame, O shame.

HATHORNE: Don't you see these complain of you?

MARTHA (*stoutly*): The Lord
open the eyes of the magistrates and ministers!
The Lord show his power to discover the guilty!

HATHORNE: Tell us who hurts these children.

MARTHA: I do not know.

HATHORNE: If you be guilty of this fact, d'you think
you can hide it?

MARTHA: The Lord knows.

HATHORNE: Well, tell us
what you know of this matter.

MARTHA: Why, sir,
I'm a gospel woman, and do you think
I can have to do with sorcery too?
    (*Outcry among the girls*)

HATHORNE: How could you tell then, what this child
    (*Girls fall silent whenever the reference is directly
    to them*)
was bid to observe what clothes you wore,
when certain members of this meeting came
to speak with you?

MARTHA: I did not *know*. I—

CHEEVER: I bid you, Martha, don't begin with a lie.

PUTNAM: Your Honor, if I may have your permission
I'll speak to this point.

HATHORNE: Mr. Putnam, you have
my permission.

PUTNAM: Cheever and I hardly crossed
the stoop of Martha Corey's kitchen,
coming directly from my afflicted daughter,
when this woman, our greetings barely made,
met us with words I'd like to ignore.
"I know what you're come for," and she smiled,
"to talk to me about my recent witchcraft."
And shortly after, John, for indeed we were very
much surprised, she added, "Then did the girl

describe the clothes that I have on"?
All this, before the urgent purpose
of our visit was revealed to her.

HATHORNE: Revealed?

PUTNAM: We had not told her.

MARTHA (*quoting* ANN):
"Now I am blind, I cannot see."

HATHORNE: Who told you that?

MARTHA: Thomas said the child said.

CHEEVER: You speak falsely!

HATHORNE: Dr. Parris read
from the deposition.

PARRIS (*reads*): ". . . whereupon Mrs. Corey asked us
again with very great eagerness, but does Ann Putnam
tell you what clothes I have on?" . . . uh . . . "and
we told her, No, she did not, for Ann told us you
came and blinded her . . . Mrs. Corey made but
little answer to this but seemed to smile at it as if
she had showed us a pretty trick."
It is signed by Putnam and Mr. Cheever.

HATHORNE: So. Why did you ask if the child told
what clothes you wore?

MARTHA: My husband told me
the other children told.

HATHORNE: Who told you
about the clothes? Why did you ask
that question?

MARTHA: Because I heard the children
told what clothes the others wore.

HATHORNE: Giles Corey,
did you tell your wife?—this woman?

COREY (*angry*): I didn't tell her anything
about *her* clothes, seen or unseen.

HATHORNE (*pauses to look at* COREY, *then to* MARTHA)
Did you not say your husband told you so?

(MARTHA *looks down for the first time*)

    (*Pause. Then, outcry*)

CHILDREN: She's lying. She's afraid. She will not **answer!**

HATHORNE (*loudly, for the first time*):

Who hurts these children? Now look upon them.

Aren't you appalled they're visited so dreadfully?

MARTHA: I cannot help it—I can't help their disorder.

    (*Pause*)

HATHORNE: Did you not say you would tell the truth

why you asked that question? How you came

to that knowledge?

MARTHA:             I did but ask Putnam.

HATHORNE: You dare thus to lie in all this assembly?

You're now before authority. I expect the truth.

You promised it. Madam, speak now,

and tell who told you about the clothes.

MARTHA: Nobody. Nobody told me my clothes

would come into question in my absence.

HATHORNE: Then how did you come to know the children

would be examined what clothes you wore?

MARTHA: Because then I would know the child to be

wiser than any person if she knew what

another wore if that other was not with her,

especially if that other, as I did,

wore clothing she had never seen.

HATHORNE: Give an answer! You said your husband

told you—

MARTHA:     He later admitted the children

had said it was I afflicted them, but

then it was too late.

HATHORNE:          But madam,

how did you know why Cheever and Putnam

visited you at home? Answer me truly,

will you say how you came to know why they came?

MARTHA: I had heard speech that the children said

one known devout, a member of meeting,
no rambler this time like poor Sarah Good,
but an honest woman was torturing them.
I thought that men from the church would come
to examine if another member was rumored—

HATHORNE: But how did you know it?

MARTHA:            I believed they would come.

HATHORNE: Did you not say you would tell the truth?
Who told you what they came for?

MARTHA (*pauses*): Nobody.

HATHORNE:           How did you know?

MARTHA:            I did think so.

HATHORNE: But you said you knew so.

ANN:           Look! Look!
A man, a tall dark man whispers
in Mrs. Corey's ear!

HATHORNE:       A man?

ABIGAIL:          A tall dark man.

ANN: He's telling her how to be out of it.

HATHORNE: What did he say to you?

MARTHA:           We mustn't believe
all these distracted children say.

HATHORNE: Can't you tell us what that man whispered?

MARTHA: I saw nobody.

HATHORNE:        But didn't you hear?

MARTHA:           No.

(*Cries from the girls*)

HATHORNE: If you expect mercy of God,
you must look for mercy, madam,
in God's way, by confession.

MARTHA:         Pray you, sir,
give me leave to go to prayer.

GIRLS: No. No, never! She can't.

HATHORNE (*sternly*):        D'you think
to find mercy by aggravating your sins?

MARTHA:          A true thing.

HATHORNE: Then look for mercy, Mrs. Corey,
  in God's way.
MARTHA:          So I do, by prayer.
HATHORNE: Confession precedes prayer, madam.
  Give glory to God, and confess.
MARTHA:                    But I
  cannot confess.
HATHORNE:     Cannot?
MARTHA:              I am innocent.
HATHORNE: Don't you see how these afflicted
  children charge you. Look at them. Pity them.
MARTHA: We must not believe distracted persons.
HATHORNE: What d'you employ to hurt them?
MARTHA:                              Nothing.
  I employ nothing.
HATHORNE:       Haven't you said
  our eyes were blinded, you would open them?
MARTHA (*ironic*): Yes, to accuse the innocent.
HATHORNE:                            Read
  the evidence of Henry Crosby—will all
  here present bear in mind that
  Mr. Crosby is this woman's son-in-law.
MARTHA (*soft*): By Giles' first wife.
PARRIS:                    Your Honor, Henry
  is unable to appear today due to
  an indisposition of his wife,
  and the distance from Salem Town. Have I
  permission to read from his evidence?
HATHORNE: Please, Parris, please.
PARRIS (*reads*): "On March the nineteenth, I, Henry
  Crosby, being a relative of Martha Corey, and my
  father Giles Corey refusing, accompanied my father's
  wife to the home of Thomas Putnam upon the advice
  of the magistrates . . ."
HATHORNE: The pith, Parris, the pith.
PARRIS:                    Yes, your Honor.

". . . upon the entrance of Mrs. Corey, Ann Putnam experienced the most terrifying convulsions and foul tortures, crying out that Mrs. Corey was unmistakably responsible for her affliction. Ann fell to the floor declaring her torturer had, roasting on the spit, turning before the fire, the unplucked body of a great bird, resembling an owl—"

HATHORNE: To the point, Parris.

PARRIS: ". . . upon returning to the ordinary of Deacon Ingersoll, where my father's wife was being detained pending examination, this woman told me—in the presence of others, and with a cultivated simplicity of speech—that the girl could not stand up before her—"

HATHORNE: Why can't the girl stand up before you?

MARTHA: I don't know.

HATHORNE: What did you *mean* by that?

MARTHA: I saw them fall down.

HATHORNE: It seems to be an insulting speech, if they couldn't stand before you.

MARTHA: They cannot stand before others.

HATHORNE: But you said they can't stand before you. Tell me what turned upon the spit by you?

MARTHA: You believe the children who are distracted. I saw no spit.

HATHORNE: Here are more than two accuse you of witchcraft. What do you say?

MARTHA: I am innocent.

PARRIS: Your Honor, Crosby concludes by quoting his mother—

MARTHA: Henry's my stepdaughter's husband.

PARRIS: —quoting she said, the Devil can't stand up before her.

HATHORNE: D'you dare
accuse the girl of—
MARTHA: I didn't mean it so—
I didn't say—
VOICES (*interrupting*): She did! She did! She said—
MARTHA: What can I do? Many rise up against me.
HATHORNE: Madam, confess.
MARTHA: Why so I would, if I were guilty.
HATHORNE (*gently*): Martha, you're a gospel woman,
will you lie?
ANN: Gospel Witch!
ABIGAIL: Next Sunday's
a sacrament day, but the Gospel Witch
shall not come here to hurt us.
MARTHA: No.
I shall not.
(*Pause*)
HATHORNE: You charge these children with distraction.
It's a note of distraction when persons vary
in a minute, but these girls fix on you.
This is hardly the manner of
distraction.
MARTHA: Obsession, your Honor, may
extend the heart of a man, or break it;
obsession may be supremely sick,
or supremely sane. It is not sensible.
But distraction, sir, like a wagon unhorsed
on a curve, may plunge obsessively towards
any object away, often the lowest,
and that most directly. It's always misled.
HATHORNE: There's truth in that, madam, feelingly spoken.
It remains to be fixed whose proof will stick
and whose will vary, these children who sit
so rigidly now, or you who stand
so stoutly.
Distraction is

a serious charge. You have the chance
to prove it. I'm here to examine.
    (*He looks at the girls who do not move*)
                Now.
Follow me with care to answer exactly
in a manner that will be understood.
Why did you say the eyes of the magistrate
and the minister's eyes were blinded? We came
to be terror to evil. You say you'd open
our eyes, we're blind—

MARTHA:               —if you say I'm a witch.

HATHORNE: You said you'd show us.

MARTHA:              I didn't mean demonstrate.
I thought you would see.

HATHORNE (*sly*):       Why, show us now.

MARTHA: Mr. Hathorne, if I may have leave to pray—
    (*Outcries and protests*)

GIRLS: Gospel Witch! She'll strike us. Witch, Gospel Witch!

HATHORNE: Mrs. Corey, with what did you strike the maid
    at Mr. Parris'?

MARTHA:        I never struck in my life.

HATHORNE: There are two that saw you strike her with
    an iron rod.

GIRLS:       Yes. Yes.

MARTHA:         I'd no hand in it.

HATHORNE: D'you believe these children are bewitched?

MARTHA: They may be, for aught I know—I'd no hand in
    it.

HATHORNE: You say you're no witch. Maybe you mean
    you never covenanted with the Devil.
    Did you never deal with any familiar?

MARTHA: No. I never.

HATHORNE: What bird was that the children spoke of?

ANN: Say what bird, what yellow bird?

ABIGAIL: A yellow bird.

MARTHA:            I know no bird.

ABIGAIL: She lies! See, Mrs. Corey lies!
Last Sunday in the meeting Mrs. Corey sat
high on the beam there, between her fingers
she suckled a yellow bird.

MARTHA:                    I know no bird, child.
Where I sat I always sit.
Neighbors, God knows, allow me that.

ANN: It was her shape.

ABIGAIL:                    Witch!

GIRLS:                    Gospel Witch!

HATHORNE: It may be you've engaged you will not
confess, but God knows.

MARTHA:                    So He does.

HATHORNE: Why were you unwilling your husband
should come here to the former session?

MARTHA: But he came, for all.

HATHORNE:                    Didn't you take
his saddle off?

(*Pause.* MARTHA *looks steadily at* GILES)

MARTHA:          I didn't know
what it was really for.

HATHORNE:                    You didn't
know what the saddle was used for?

MARTHA:                    I
didn't know it would be to my benefit
to remove his saddle.

(GILES *starts forward*)

VOICE (*cries out*):     She wouldn't have us
help to find more witches out!

GILES: We'll all be damned if you find out more.

(*He storms out, exit*)

HATHORNE: And did you say you would open our eyes?
Madam, why don't you?

MARTHA (*laughs*):          I never thought of a witch.

HATHORNE: Is it a laughing matter to see
afflicted persons!

MARTHA: Ye are all against me,
and I cannot help it.

HATHORNE: Don't you believe
there are any witches in Essex county?

MARTHA: I don't know there is any.

HATHORNE: Don't you know
that Tituba confessed?

MARTHA: I didn't hear her,
and in these matters I cannot learn
dividing voice from person by gossip.

HATHORNE (*to the others*):
She'll own nothing without several witnesses,
and yet deny for all.

> (MARTHA *bites her lip. The girls who have been
> following her fanatically in real fear of what she
> might say, have unconsciously begun to imitate
> her gestures. They cry out*)

VOICES: Look, look.
She bites her lip!

MARTHA: What harm's in that?

VOICES: The girls are in pain. She's drawing blood!

PARRIS: I believe it's apparent she's practicing witchcraft
in the congregation. There's no need of images.

HATHORNE: Martha Corey, what d'you say
to all these things that are apparent?

MARTHA: If you will all go hang me, sir,
how can I help it?

HATHORNE: Hang you? Who speaks
of hanging, Martha?

Were you to serve
the Devil ten years? Tell how many.

> (MARTHA *laughs*)

ANN: The yellow bird is with her again.

ABIGAIL: On her hand!

HATHORNE: What d'you say to this?

> (MARTHA *clasps her hands. The girls do likewise*)

ANN (*hysterical*): She cracks my fingers. She breaks my
   hands.

PUTNAM: Forfend!

ABIGAIL: Stop her, stop her. She's
   breaking my hands.

HATHORNE: Constable, fasten her wrists.
   (LOCKER *does so. The girls subside*)
   Why did you say you'd show us?
   (*Pause*)
                                    What book
   would you have these children write in?

MARTHA: What book? Where should I keep a book?
   I showed them none, have none, brought none.

HATHORNE: What book did you show to Abigail Parris?

MARTHA: None. If the Devil appears in my shape—

VOICE: Don't listen! My neighbor, Jonathan Parker,
   some years ago once called this woman
   a witch. A witch!

HATHORNE: Record the evidence.
   Madam, who *is* your God?

MARTHA: The God that made me.

HATHORNE: What is his name?

MARTHA: Jehovah.

HATHORNE: D'you know
   another name?

MARTHA: God Almighty.

HATHORNE: Does *he* tell you—
   that you pray to—that *he* is God Almighty?

MARTHA: Who do I worship but the God that made me?

HATHORNE: How many gods are there?

MARTHA: One.

HATHORNE: How many persons?

MARTHA: Three.

HATHORNE: Can't you say,
   so there is one God in three blessed persons?
   (*Silence*)

Mrs. Corey, don't you see
these children and women are rational and sober
as their neighbors when your hands are fastened?
Release her wrists!

> (LOCKER *releases* MARTHA's *arms. She stands*
> *quietly.* ANN *cries out, and* MARTHA *clasps her*
> *hands. The girls become hysterical*)

PUTNAM: She bites her lip!

> (*Uproar*)

HATHORNE: The law and the church demand you tell
why you hurt these children, or who does?

MARTHA: I can't tell you who does this thing,
or why. I only know I've no hand in it.

HATHORNE: Why did you say if you were a witch
you should have no pardon?

MARTHA:                          Because I am
a gospel woman.

HATHORNE:          Constable,
remove the prisoner.

> (MARTHA *is taken out. The noise subsides*)

PARRIS:                          Need we see more?

> (*General shaking of heads*)

HATHORNE: As a result of this examination,
and with charges of persons present,
we commit Martha Corey, wife
of Giles Corey of Salem Farms
to the jail in Salem Village as
*per mittimus* to be given.

PARRIS:                          So be it.

> (*General exit*)

Where d'you suppose Giles Corey went
in such a hurry?

HATHORNE:          Why? Did he leave?

PARRIS: As if the Devil were chasing him—
or calling him—

HATHORNE:  Well. Well.
(*Exit magistrate and ministers*)
MAN FROM BOSTON (*detains a villager, confidingly*):
Don't mistake me, I think the woman dangerous
but at the beginning Hathorne might have
given her leave to pray, friend,
don't you think? She needs it now.
VILLAGER: Who knows, when the storm spills,
whether the birds fly up or down.
One prays at the core of it, but to whom?

CURTAIN

SCENE FIVE

ANN PUTNAM, THOMAS PUTNAM, and MAIDSERVANT.

ANN PUTNAM's *bedroom. It is late afternoon, just before
sunset, the first week of September. As the scene progresses the room grows dark, until at the end the only
light is that of* ANN's *candle.* ANN *lies in bed, apparently
asleep, but subconsciously awake. Her father sits beside
her talking to the maidservant, who has just entered the
room with a cup of milk.*

PUTNAM: It's no use, Mercy. Ann won't touch it.
Can't you remember even the sight
of milk chokes her up? The last time her mother
brought a cup of it in to her
Ann took it and poured it across the floor.
She turned to the wall and wouldn't eat.
Ann hasn't allowed milk nearer than poison
for the past five months—

MERCY:                              But, sir, I thought—
PUTNAM: Thought nothing. What's got into you, Mercy?
MERCY: Milk's fattening, sir, and certain she needs
   a handsome pound or two around her thighs.
   I warmed a cup—
PUTNAM:                    Mercy, are you mad, miss?
   She'll have a seizure. I never thought milk
   an ill thing before—exhaustion's really
   what has kept Ann in bed since April
   when she's not with you and the girls in court.
MERCY: The trials haven't exhausted me, sir.
   I've not lost weight, wouldn't you say sir?
PUTNAM: No more nonsense! It's time you behaved.
   You take that stuff back to your mistress, Mercy,
   down in the kitchen, like a good girl.
MERCY: Hush, sir, you'll wake up Ann, poor baby.
   God knows she barely gets enough sleep
   with all of you after her—besides, Mrs. Putnam
   isn't in the kitchen; she never is.
   What d'you hire me for?
PUTNAM:                         What's that mean?
   Get back to your work where you belong!
MERCY: You shouldn't talk to me like that, sir.
   You'll wake your little daughter. Take my advice,
   send Ann back to Tituba—
PUTNAM:                         Tituba, Mercy?
   Tituba's in prison! She can't play nurse
   to children from prison.
MERCY:                      You got her confession.
   I don't see why poor Tituba should stay
   in prison any more. We've nothing to do now;
   she kept us happy all winter long
   around her fire with stories and games,
   besides—
PUTNAM: Besides, what?
MERCY:                    Tituba's got medicines,

a powder she puts in raw chicken's blood.
Tituba was never dreary,
I knew they'd stop us going to her.
Why d'you suppose Ann won't drink milk?—
she doesn't tell you everything, you know.

PUTNAM: Never mind the milk, Mercy. Ann needs rest.

MERCY: Ann fears milk from the Coreys cattle.
—But this is warm, from a nurse that's given
suck to a male child, with drops of blood
from a knick in a he-cat's ear—

PUTNAM: That's enough.

MERCY: I found the receipt in Mr. Burrough's book,
and when I told Ann, she said, Please, please.

PUTNAM: Ann needs none of your potions, Mercy Lewis.
Ann needs rest. And no more of these taxing
trips in and out of court in Salem.

MERCY: O no, sir,
we love the trials. Ann loves the trials.
She looks much better when she comes home.
Especially the last one—Mrs. Corey's.
She'll laugh no more when old man Jacobs
and his seamy like call us witch-bitches,
and tell us what we need is a man.
I don't want to leave you and Ann,
please Mr. Putnam—

PUTNAM: Quiet down, Mercy.
No one's talking of sending you off.
Get to the kitchen and start our supper.
You've said quite enough about your elders.

MERCY: Please, Mr. Putnam, I mean no harm.
You never pay me much attention,
and I like to talk with you so much.

PUTNAM: Go along, Mercy, the chores are waiting.

MERCY: Yes, sir. Thank you.

(*Exit* MERCY)

PUTNAM: Dear Lord, when,

when will this thing come to an end?
Martha, Martha, you had such a way
of laying shadows with vigorous talk.

ANN (*pretends to wake*):
Father.

PUTNAM (*starts*): Thoughts are wandering again.

ANN: Father? Father, where have you been?
    (*She reaches out her hand*)

PUTNAM: Here all along, child. I've been nowhere.

ANN: I dreamt you left me. Please hold my hand.

PUTNAM: A foolish dream.

ANN:                   Who were you talking with?
I dreamt you talked with Mrs. Corey.
Does she trouble you too?

PUTNAM:               My silly little Ann.
Don't you worry about me.
                    You're quieter, dear.

ANN: The witches come and go, as if
three times an hour when angels pass
the rooftree, devils to chide them follow
after, soon after, to curse the beauty
and torture me.

PUTNAM:          Think only angels, dear.
Mercy will soon be up with your supper.

ANN: Father, d'you think Mercy is beautiful?
Will I be as beautiful as Mercy is?

PUTNAM: Mercy's nineteen—you're beautiful now.

ANN (*looks as if out the window and screams*):
Father, light my candle. Hurry!

PUTNAM: Dearest, it's hardly dark out yet.
You can't rest well with light in your eyes.

ANN: Light that candle!
    (*He obeys*)
                Don't let it flicker,
ever, ever. When you aren't looking
Mrs. Corey's shape will come hurt me.

Father, we must have more flames, one
for each witch; she's coming for certain
to snuff one out, and her husband too.
I know they will. More light, father;
I cannot sleep, and you say I must.
 (PUTNAM *fetches two more candlesticks, but does
 not light them*)
Father?
PUTNAM: Try not to speak, dear. Sleep.
ANN: Father, do you remember the man
people said Giles Corey murdered?
Mother mentioned him—
PUTNAM: Joseph—was that his name?
He worked for Corey when I was a boy,
and died at home some time after.
Joseph. Joe Goodell. That's years ago.
ANN: No. He didn't die.
PUTNAM: Finally Martha
took him home—Goodell was often
in feeble health. She told his family
he was hardly fit to work.
Later Corey was tried for it;
Giles was always in one suit or another,
the kind of man people talk about.
Though some had said Goodell died
from beating, Corey was quickly acquitted.
Yes, I remember some such story—
ANN: Father, Goodell didn't die.
He was murdered!
PUTNAM: Ann, what're you
trying to say? Forget these things
you hear.
ANN: I didn't hear, I saw.
PUTNAM: Before
you were born? Ann, what d'you mean?
 (ANN *screams*)

PUTNAM: What's the matter?

> (ANN *sighs, rises stiffly from the hips until she is sitting bolt upright in bed*)

ANN: Don't be afraid.
Here's one to tell me a story I must
repeat to you, and you must listen.

PUTNAM: Who, Ann. Who?

ANN: Strange man, what's
the sheet at your neck, bound over your shoulder?
Yes, I will. Repeat after you. My parents
must not be allowed to forget.

> (*Mechanically*)

Giles Corey—
My former master murdered me—
because the Devil told Mr. Corey—
he should not hang for that—so he—
Yes, yes!
Now God has hardened Corey's heart—
so he will not follow the Court's advice—
and die an easy death.

Yes, Yes! Go on, sir!

> (*Pause*)

PUTNAM: Ann! Ann! Speak!

> (ANN *sighs again, shudders*)

ANN: —I will come again!—

> (*She falls back on the pillows*)

PUTNAM: You'll be remembered. Ann, are you well?

ANN: I feel much better. Now I shall sleep.
Father, you see I must have these candles.
You see, I can't tell the difference between
Mr. Corey and Goodell in the dark.
One is bad and one is good.
I must tell the difference, mustn't I?—
in the light *and* in the dark?

> (MERCY *enters with soup*)

MERCY: Here's your supper, poor little dear.

ANN: Mercy, I'm not hungry tonight.
   Give soup to Father. I'm half-asleep.
     (ANN *turns to the wall*)
PUTNAM: Remember, Mercy, and don't forget it,
   we must keep this candle burning.

**CURTAIN**


**SCENE SIX**


JAILOR, GILES COREY, and JOHN HATHORNE.

*A cell in the Jail at Ipswich, early that evening. A late ray of sunshine penetrates the tiny barred window which meets the ground by the river outside, and on the inside is five feet up from the jail floor. At one side a portion of the jail corridor outside the cell can be seen. A key turns in the lock, the door squeals, and* PETER BUNT *the jailor enters, followed by* GILES COREY, *from the corridor.* GILES *stops in the door frame, lifts his arms over his head and places the flat of his palms up against the stone lintel.*

JAILOR: Yes, sir. Back home, home again.
   Home's the place that always smells
   the same, and by God, here we are.
GILES: Dear Lord, these stones are cold, and the sun
   baking the walls outside like tarts
   all day. This is where the night chill springs.
JAILOR: Can't hurt you here, go ahead. Talk!
   Open your mouth, old man, you've stood
   tight as a clam in the witness stand,
   and silent as steeples for three solid days.
GILES: Warm, they've not been warm since father

went down with the men to the sundrenched quarry
and crowed them out, and carted them here,
and piled them up for peace and order.

JAILOR: It isn't healthy—perhaps the place
that always smells the same is home;
here it's like bilge, like sloshing bilge,
where the river flows past at window level.

GILES: Cold, O God! to their granite marrow.

JAILOR: Hoho, so now he's going to chatter,
going to spatter the air in here
with words for a Christian jail he thinks
too good for a Puritan court of law—

GILES: If I were the strongest man in Essex,
or ten years younger, how many stones
like these could I hold on my chest, breathe,
and not cry out, Guilty! or, Not Guilty!
to satisfy a passel of fools.

> (*He drops his hands*)

I could not warm them, all these stones.
They'd still be cold.

JAILOR:         He's opened his mouth
to chat with the air as if the air
were private as mother's milk, and filled
with vigorous phantoms to answer back.
Ho, there! You, there!

> (*He stabs the air with his keys*)

        See, sir, nothing.

GILES: She's a woman, I've had much need of—
if I could see her now. The fools—
dear heart, I've done much harm to you—
O the fools—to you and to myself.

JAILOR: So who's a fool?

GILES:         Yes, man, you're right.
The trapped fool scolds the fool who's free.
Jailor, your salt smacks of the sea,
you still speak oceans on dry land.

JAILOR: That's it, sir, talk away all,
  chatter it all out, you'll feel much better.
  They always do. Makes me think of my dogs,
  mascots they were, names of Scat and Scamper,
  right on ship board, until one day
  Scat got crushed when a gun broke loose.
  We buried him in Davy Jones
  with flag and high whistle, all the honors.
  When his carcass slid into the sea
  Scamper jumped after, she couldn't wait—
  we never thought of that—two bull terriers.
  They left a pup who shipped to ripe old doggage.

  But Scat was the one. While Scamper howled,
  he used to stare from his corner cabin
  when the waves went wild, as if the spray
  were full of devils; until old Scamper,
  she got him to bark too. It pleased the men.
    (*Pause. Moonlight through the bars*)
  Don't take it hard, sir. Look at this window;
  bars mean nothing. Hey Scat, hey Scamper!
  come sick the devils out of the window;
  come shoo the witches, r'arf, r'arf r'arf—
      (GILES *leaps at him, and grabs him around the
      neck*)
GILES: Witch? Who's a witch, you goddamn wretch!
  She's no more witch than the Governor's wife.
  I'll teach you to name them. Now—who's wizard?
JAILOR: O, not you, sir. I'll not name one.
      (GILES *shakes him again*)
GILES: Now—who's a witch?
JAILOR:                        Sure, not the lady—
      (GILES *drops him*)
  whoever she is—
GILES:            My wife, Peter.
JAILOR:                        Yes, sir.

GILES: They've cooped her in Salem where I can't see her.
JAILOR: No, sir.
GILES:     What d'you mean, no sir?
JAILOR:                              Yes, sir.
    Please, sir, your wife's a very brave lady.
GILES: Who told you that?
JAILOR:                    There's some that whisper
    she stands like a tree before the norther.
    Between you and me, sir, I never saw witches
    that didn't turn into something worse
    than bitches, or something less, when all's said.
    There's things far worse, and in foreign ports
    I've seen weird work I can't even describe.
GILES: Peter, I haven't laid eyes on my wife
    since the day I walked out when they had her there
    before the ravens—the world went scarlet—
    I was afraid I would, as she watched me,
    say something further would do her no good.
    I had to think, I had to think.
    My muscles walked me out, may God forgive me.
JAILOR: She will, sir.
        (JAILOR *trots over to the grill, and looks out on
        tiptoe*)
GILES:        Perhaps, Peter, perhaps.
JAILOR: You're in the same kettle; she will.
                Now look at that
    the bloomies still out, white in moonlight;
    she plants them for pity, a last look, she says,
    to save their souls. She lives here by
    the river where the pirates passed
    to the gibbet last year. Hospitable creature.
        (*He laughs*)
    Why praise be, guess who's up to the door!
    Magistrate Hathorne, all on a black horse.
    An honor, an honor! Excuse me, sir.

(PETER *runs to the door of the cell. It clangs behind him*)

GILES: Keep him out of here, Peter. There's nothing but teeth and silence for him in here.

(*Giles goes to the grill, and stands looking out. He will not turn completely around until* HATHORNE *leaves*)

HATHORNE (*calling, off*):

Peter, Peter Bunt! Where is that clown!

(*Peter stands in the corridor until* HATHORNE *joins him*)

JAILOR: Yes sir, your Honor. Down here, your Honor.

HATHORNE (*off*): Mr. Bunt, where's the Corey cell?

JAILOR: Who sir?

(HATHORNE, *lantern in hand, appears in the corridor*)

HATHORNE: Who sir! Why sir, the man from Salem Farms accused of witchcraft.

JAILOR: Ah, the silent man who mumbles nothing. What's he down here for?

HATHORNE: If it's your business, you can't have witch and wizard in one jail. Well, Mr. Bunt, how's your wife's catarrh?

JAILOR: Fancy you remembering, sir. Mrs. Bunt's went on to greater riches a year ago. It's most unusual your coming here, sir.

HATHORNE: I'm sorry to hear it. Giles Corey is not a usual man. You must watch with care.

JAILOR: He won't try to leave, sir. He likes it here. This morning changing the water I left the door wide open. He won't go near it. And this afternoon coming back from court he walked like a lamb to the fold, and no word.

HATHORNE: Extraordinary. But you never can tell. Which is his?

JAILOR: It will do no good, sir,
  talking to him.

HATHORNE: That's for me to judge.

JAILOR: Well then, here sir.

> (PETER *unlocks the cell door.* HATHORNE *enters
> alone*)

HATHORNE: Thank you, Mr. Bunt.
  It's blacker than Gehenna, yet
  all's filled with racing spheres—

JAILOR: Why sir, the moon's still in your eyes.
  The dark often dazzles gentlemen here
  who enter from brighter out-of-doors.

HATHORNE: That will do, Bunt; close the door.
  Ah, there you are, by the window of course.
  Good evening, Mr. Corey.
  No civil answer? Come, sir, come,
  you can make it easier for us both.
  You must've seen conference in the offing
  between us for the last three days.
  In point of fact, I was quite sure
  that's what, with taciturnity,
  you bargained for.
            No answers, none?
  No private confession you wish to make?
  You've always acted strongly as a man of pride,
  and cleared yourself in court if need be—
  and need there has been—when gossips talked.
  Still not a word?
            You'll not reply?
  This is not flattering, sir, not wise,
  not kind, and believe me, Corey, kindness
  today is only on my side to play with.
  Well sir, I've brought you news—

> (GILES *turns, and regards him*)

  but first, as a man of acumen
  in business matters, you've always been

successful in the material world.
Give more thought and preparation
for some success in the world after this.
Don't stare at me in stupid silence!
I'll make you—
                    we'll make you respond—
if you divide the community, we'll
make you respond to heavier pressures
than I can bring to bear. You were
brought three times before my court,
before the magistrates and ministers;
and three times you refused to plead
to honest charges that are tearing
your family, and all the towns
apart, and each in the eyes of God.
Today was your last before the court—
        (GILES *laughs*)
Mock me, and you'll get serious laughter!
You know where they say your mirth comes from.
I have often wondered the last three days
whether you know that without a plea
there can be no trial—but law applies
even here in this newest of worlds.
One way remains before the full
extent of law must push to extremes
which even you can't possibly visage.
        (GILES *turns back to the window*)
Giles, confession in the realm of the spirit
is not of specifics the world demands,
and that confession is made to oneself.
What I demand is not from your citadel,
not what drives you that generates there;
I only want your return to community,
or a symbol of it for the congregations,
and I want it in writing. You can guess
the Corey defection carries singular weight

in Essex and even as far as Boston.
I cannot afford—well, put it this way,
a plain confession can do you no harm—
it could relieve less understood pressures
within yourself—as friend to friend,
it could help me. In my duty, of course.
Sir, d'you hear me?
>            (GILES *laughs again*)
>                        This is impossible!
I'll have you down on your back for this.
You never were sharp in spiritual matters,
a toady to a clever wife.

GILES:                    Perhaps.

HATHORNE: Don't you dare ignore me!
>                        Look at it
this way, ignorance is no respecter—
you're losing to the future, Corey.
Your property, the land you own,
granted your father years ago,
and turned by you to a fruitful farm,
will be lost to you and to your heirs,
or go to those two of them who dared
to testify to Martha's witchcraft.
>            (GILES *whirls on him and he steps back*)
A witch is subject to attainder,
if he be convicted. Listen with care!
You can confess, and clear your name,
and convey your land to heirs forever.
It's too late to save that terrible woman,
your wife. She refuses every way,
and her sentence is passed—

GILES:                    Martha!
Martha, I did this to you.

HATHORNE:                Giles,
there's time, still time to confess to me.
You often quarrelled with your wife—

yes, that's what they say—but quarrel with me
and there's no way left, and nothing left.
If you confess, no matter what
the present status of your wife,
you may save her soul.

GILES (*roars*):          Her soul!
       (*He clutches the bars of the window to restrain
       himself*)
You devil in vestments. Dear God, don't
let me add murder to the wrong I've done her!

HATHORNE (*backing*): Bunt, Mr. Bunt! Get in here im-
     mediately.
     Help!
       (*The jailor steps through the door where he has
       been listening*)

GILES:     Hathorne, you've nothing to fear of me.
       (*Giles turns back to the window. Bunt remains in
       the door*)

HATHORNE: All right, Giles Corey, you'll not confess,
not yet. But the law requires
a terrible justice—the danger now
to community and neighborhood
which you've provoked requires the full
application of law, prison hard and strong,
*peine forte et dure*—

JAILOR:                I've heard of that
in London, in London. It's horrible.

HATHORNE (*backing to the door*):
As befits those men who refuse to plead
by the common law of the land, the accused
will be placed between two boards and piled
with weights until he plead or die.
Mr. Corey, will you confess—

GILES:                Get out!
       (HATHORNE *turns on his heel and walks from the
       cell into the corridor*)

HATHORNE: And by the way, Peter Bunt, although
  it may not seem mandatory to you
  I wouldn't forget to lock for the night.
     (*Exit*)
JAILOR: O, sir!
GILES:         Leave off, good Peter. It's done.
JAILOR: He's left his lantern.
GILES:              It is done.
  We'll make his lantern throw light for us.
  Get me a pen, some ink, and a table.
  Crosby will never go in where Martha
  planted her garden and lived with me.
  I've letters to write. One you will take
  to a friend of mine, old Thomas Wade,
  Justice of the Peace in Essex—
JAILOR: Sir, he can't help you—he can't possibly
  get you out of here—
GILES:           Never mind, Peter,
  Not in the sense you imagine he can't.
  He can deed me still. He must bring
  several witnesses, I'll pay him well.
  Hop to, Peter lad, we've serious work
  before night climbs up the river again.

CURTAIN


SCENE SEVEN

The MAN FROM BOSTON, GEORGE LOCKER, MARTHA
COREY, REV. SAMUEL PARRIS, and EZEKIEL CHEEVER.

MARTHA COREY'S *cell in the Salem Town Jail is still bare
although she has made it her home for the past five
months. She sits by the barred window embroidering*

*and from time to time looking out. At one side is the passageway leading to the other cells and to the prison entrance. The* MAN FROM BOSTON *enters this passageway followed, somewhat reluctantly, by* GEORGE LOCKER, *the constable.*

MAN FROM BOSTON: Which cell holds the convicted lady?
LOCKER: They're all occupied—eight will be hanged.
MAN FROM BOSTON: Well, I see they keep the hive right
    busy.
    Which is the housewife from Salem Farms?
LOCKER: Martha Corey, you mean? She's lived right here
    for nigh on five months. What d'you want
    with Martha Corey? As my name is
    George Locker, she's peaceable and quiet—
    except when the Reverend Parris comes.
    He's coming shortly for the last time.
MAN FROM BOSTON: She's behind this door then.
                    Tell me, George,
    had you heard some graves can never be filled?
    In winter the ground sinks, and in the spring
    the gravel's unsafe for an honest man—
    the Devil comes up to catch his foot.
LOCKER: You don't say so, sir?
MAN FROM BOSTON:             I do. And do you know,
    two widows once that lived together,
    hating each other's footsteps, at it were,
    would clip off fingernails over the fire
    and burn them up quickly so the one couldn't find
    body scraps to spell a hex on the other?
LOCKER: You don't believe a fingernail could
    destroy a woman's immortal soul,
    now do you, sir?
MAN FROM BOSTON: Well, George, I don't know—
    On the other hand, you never can tell
    who will say what to you next. It's well

to know the stories before another does.
Now you tell me, George, how's Martha Corey
behaved in jail.

LOCKER:                    I can't let you
see her, sir. She's near her end.
She's been a lady always—it's a
kind of more-than-she-might-have-been air
she has. She's never complained, save once
she said she longed for a sister or for
a daughter—a woman to chat a bit with.
She came with a quick tongue, she leaves with gentle
farewells from the shabby community here.
If she's a witch (I've no doubt she may be),
then more's the pity for witches like her.

MAN FROM BOSTON: What would mean the most before she
mounts the cart, tomorrow, George?

LOCKER: That's easy. News of her husband, if I
read you right, sir. That's impossible.
No one's to see her, no one at all.

MAN FROM BOSTON: I've got that news. May I speak to
her, George?

LOCKER: No one at all.
                    Didn't I see you
first at the trials, behaving oddly?

MAN FROM BOSTON: Listen George, I've a job to do,
charity call it, for a few in Boston
who know that compassion to function must be
anonymous where there's no precedent for it—

LOCKER: D'you have credentials?

MAN FROM BOSTON:                    I have a letter
        (*Shows it*)
from my employer, you understand,
I only show it when I must.
        (LOCKER *whistles*)
Fifteen minutes with her, George?

LOCKER: Fifteen minutes it is, Lynn Moody.
I've heard there were clerks for the merchant
in Boston who's spreading the humorous papers.
Thomas Brattle's a man for the facts.
It's good to get people laughing again,
even if—

MOODY:     Laughter's come too late
today. But not too late for tomorrow.
          (*Voices in the corridor*)

LOCKER: Walk to the end of the corridor, Mr. Moody,
and stand in the shadows until I call.
It's the minister come to pray over the laa
          (*The man goes down the corridor. Enter* DR. PARRIS
          *with* EZEKIEL CHEEVER *behind*)

PARRIS: Well, George, I wondered where I'd find you.
They said you were down here. Anything wrong?

LOCKER: Nary a thing sir, couldn't be quieter.

CHEEVER: 'Afternoon, George.

LOCKER:                    Sad business, Mr. Cheever.

PARRIS: Well, open the door!

LOCKER:                    Right away, Mr. Parris.
          (PARRIS *and* CHEEVER *enter* MARTHA'S *cell. She
          looks up and returns to her sewing*)

MARTHA: Good afternoon, Ezekiel.

CHEEVER:                    'Afternoon, Martha.

MARTHA: I'm sorry you had to come here too.

CHEEVER: It's been no pleasure, Martha Corey.

PARRIS: You'll excuse me, Cheever. Mrs. Corey,
have you no greeting for your minister?

MARTHA: You're not my minister, Mr. Parris,
not any longer, by your own choice.
I've only One.

PARRIS (*to* CHEEVER): No change here, sir.
Perhaps, Mrs. Corey, you'll be pleased to know
I'm here for a dreadful purpose today.

MARTHA: There's nothing more you can do, Mr. Parris.

CHEEVER: Martha, be careful. There is one thing—
passed by the elders—

PARRIS:                    That will do, Cheever.
Mrs. Corey, you'll not confess
to the fatal acts the holy court
and the hand of God discover in you?

MARTHA: Your God and Mine have no communion.
I'm innocent but not of what you think;
and guilty, yes guilty, but not of your charges.

CHEEVER: Go on, Martha—

MARTHA:                    He couldn't grasp it.

PARRIS: Will this satisfy witness, Mr. Cheever?
A final chance, madam, you'll pray with me?
God is merciful to the last.

MARTHA:                    Mr. Parris,
I would I could pray with one here today;
I've sore need of company in that office.
Your chance to maintain the church as one
is past, and I'm one you cannot keep
in your set kind of community.
If you can tell me honestly
you really come to pray with me
and all that means, why, yes—

CHEEVER: Martha, we haven't! Parris, I'll wait
for you outside, if I must wait.
This agony's useless—you know just what
you're going to do because you've done it.
Why bargain for peace when you've raised the noose?
She'd die with more love if you never told her.
God keep you, Martha, pray for us all
if you find we're wrong—
            (CHEEVER *leaves quickly*)

PARRIS (*watches him go*):   Mrs. Corey,
there's no room in decision for men of weak will,
don't you agree?

*(She looks away)*

            Now, Mrs. Corey
the Devil's a taskmaster stern as he is
only because God wills it so.
You remain adamant as that sanguine man,
your former husband. Will you pray for him?

MARTHA: My former husband?

PARRIS:                      In the eyes of God.
Your church has excommunicated you.

MARTHA: My neighbors?

PARRIS:                   Your church pronounces
excommunication.

MARTHA: I'll not pray with you, sir,
indeed I'll not pray with you. You
and your mantis-ilk copy the insect rather
than the insect you. You teach my once neighbors
the frigid gesture and not the holy act.
You knew this before you came poaching today,
but sheep won't follow a slaughter ram always.
I didn't think you could reach me again,
but this does me much hurt, Mr. Parris.
My grandfather knew the town of London
like the palm of his hand. New England he grew
to know like the palm of the other hand.
He loved both dearly; when he knotted
both hands as one gesture, face into face,
in him the old and new came together.
He always turned his applause to praise
because he knew what and Whom to praise—
a posture great to be taught to children,
for such I was, a girl in his eyes
until I was married at thirty-two.
                      When he died
he was felling a monstrous mother oak
and it struck him down in this Essex County.
He smiled.

Unless you have something
you long to share with me today—
God help me, I fear I've not seen it—
leave me now to prepare what I must.
You've lost the subtler kindnesses;
loving God you lose a love of life,
loving life I lose a lack of God.
I see by your face you can't understand.
Please leave me, sir, my time for anger
is overpast.

PARRIS: She will not be moved.

(*He leaves the jail.* MARTHA *buries her head in her hands*)

MARTHA: (*calls*): George! Constable George Locker!

(LOCKER *returns in the doorway followed by* MR. MOODY, *the man from Boston*)

They call you Constable Locker, George.
I still know George. A favor for a friend.

LOCKER: Be careful, Martha, they're bare out of earshot.
If that man ever meets the good Lord
there's going to be an argument—

MARTHA: George,
little Dorcas Good,
Sarah's tiny daughter in the cell
across the way, how old is she?

LOCKER: She can't be more than six, Martha.

MARTHA: They call her witch? Was she examined?

LOCKER: They call her witch.

MARTHA: Alas, once I spoke cruelly
of poor old Mrs. Good. I thought I was free
to judge her harshly. She's hair on her brains,
two eyes to turn away from accusers,
two ears to hear birds sing more sweet
than men, their praise of a day on earth,
a heart that can beat faster still as I have.

Bring the child to me here for an hour,
good George?
LOCKER:        Madam, do not ask,
the jail is watched; children prattle.
God knows she'll whisper to no one strange
though she whimpers now when she's moved about
from cell to cell.
MARTHA:        Then take her these,
Children love apples to eat in dark places;
she, I think, has none to fancy her.
LOCKER: I can and I will.
MARTHA:         D'you remember the woman
who left these at the jail last week?
These that hung heavy yesterday
were blossoms when they brought me here
last May. Giles loved those trees.
That was his daughter, sweet Sarah Cleeves
come down from Beverly. Take her this cloth
of flowers I've worked tomorrow—?
LOCKER (*beckons* MR. MOODY):
I cannot, madam.
But here's a man will do that for you,
and whatever else there's left to do.
MARTHA: What man?
LOCKER:        A man from Boston, madam.
     (*Exit* LOCKER)
MOODY: Martha Corey, how do you do?
Here's meeting I've long looked forward to
with pleasure and admiration. I bring
news from one you love.
     (MARTHA *puts her hands to her hair*)
MARTHA:        What news?
MOODY: It's only a letter—
     (*She brightens. He responds quickly, to save her
     feelings*)

                              I must tell you
    it may be his last—
            (*He offers the letter. She smoothes her skirts with
            her hands*)
MARTHA:                       Why sir, *that's* the only news!


      CURTAIN



SCENE EIGHT


    LYNN MOODY (the man from Boston), PETER BUNT, GILES
    COREY.


    *The corridor before* GILES COREY's *cell in the Ipswich
    Jail. A grilled window shows faintly at one side through
    which comes the low sound of rain on the river. It is
    late at night the evening of the same day, and* PETER
    BUNT, *the jailor, is half-asleep, half-drunk on a stool
    before the grating, his hand around a jug on the floor
    beside him.* LYNN MOODY, *the man from Boston, finds
    him so.*


MOODY: Well, fancy that, asleep! Here's
    an alert devil.
            (*Shakes him*)
                    Which witch have you there?
JAILOR (*wakes*): Help! Forfend! What?
                              Oh, it's you.
            (*Laughter*)
MOODY: What witch today, hmm?
JAILOR:                       No witch—not yet.
    A silent partner, a true farmer,
    my friend. He never splits his teeth,
    lowers from uppers, they'll use them yet

to grind with at the devil's mill
before he utters another mortal word.

MOODY: Calm down, Peter, a parable's for Sunday.
This jail stinks of no human smell.
They've got the hell they deserve, now wouldn't
you say? This corridor's the worst.
Who's *your* witch?

JAILOR: Shut up, you fool.
The man can hear you. It wasn't twenty
minutes ago he groaned again.
Every twenty minutes. Once in the navy
I heard a ship's hull grind on coral
all of a night long before dawn freed her
to sink. He moans like that.
Every twenty minutes.

MOODY: You coward.

JAILOR: Damn it, sir! Why'd you think
I got a bottle right under Hathorne's
blessed nose? May he—!

MOODY: Swear
in here and you'll be damned—

JAILOR: I'll be
damned if I don't swear here—at least
in my log.

MOODY: Well, Peter, beware
of consigning authority to a strata
that's even far too hot for you.

JAILOR: Yes, and damn virtue too, damn
everything but courage—

MOODY: Peter, my friend,
you're blue, blue drunk. Tell me,
who's your witch friend?

JAILOR: Blast it, sir!
(*He drags the man away from the cell door, across
the corridor*)
Have some of your precious righteous respect!

Come up over here by the window, sir,
if only for air!

                As sure as the Ipswich
backwaters here—

MOODY:             My God, I can hear
the wet rain ticking the wetter river!

JAILOR: —that man's no witch, but he's dying, sir,
and tomorrow they're hanging his wife for trying
to save herself by a prayer in court
to God knows whom. I'm stupid about
such legal matters, but God help me,
I know that man's no wizard there.
He's dying by plan—d'you hear me?—plan.
He'll carry more weight to the promised land
(if there be any) than any man ever
has from this country.

    (*Drinks and offers*)

                    Try some, sir,
if you're bound to stop by even a minute.

MOODY: No.
*Peine forte et dure,* for refusing to plead,
to be pressed to death with rocks.

JAILOR:                    That's it.

MOODY: Giles Corey, yeoman of Salem Farms.

JAILOR: You know him, sir?

MOODY:                No. Not really.
I've heard the charge.

JAILOR:             Three times your authorities
dragged him into court. Three times
they demanded he plead two words or one,
simply Guilty, or, Not Guilty, sir,
so they could try him. He doesn't scare.

MOODY: I know. He doesn't scare.

JAILOR: Corey never parted his lips.
The cold stones piled now on his chest
cry out for mercy. Corey's made

of harder stock. Three awful times
they solemnly read, now what d'you say—?

MOODY: *Peine forte et dure.*

JAILOR: They piled
the weights, him stretched upon the floor,
until he'd say the words. Three times
an hour since then, a moan. No more.
He planned it.

MOODY: Planned it, Peter?

JAILOR: You're a questing gentleman, sir.
I've seen you
prowl through here before. Didn't you
engage to take his letter to his wife?

MOODY: Yes.

JAILOR: Did she receive it?

MOODY: In her hand.

JAILOR: I see it in your face, you want to know.
That farmer's not a conversational type,
he's no confider. I've watched and guessed.
He'll carry it off.

MOODY: What?

JAILOR: Ask why the bottle? Ha!
No man can coward me, without
he'll stop through my explanation, or get
pinned to the wall until I'm finished.
I've laid my share of wives, sir, you
may as well know; and each one, she
cleaned me out. But when a man
*in extremis* prays to God
first through his wife, asks her forgiveness
first, you may be sure
his mind's made up. And I, I heard
Giles Corey pray.

MOODY: To Martha Corey?

JAILOR: O Lord, there followed such a scene, sir.
You wouldn't believe. Before they brought

the weights, he said, "I'll prove to you
forever she's no witch." His son-in-law
one Henry Crosby, a poppy-faced,
punctilious little man, came in here
and made the mistake of trying to justify
the testimony he'd given against Mrs. Corey,
trying to tell him his wife was justly
condemned. Giles Corey's rage alone
almost carried him into the yard outside.
He had the Crosby man thrown out,
out of the jail! He called again
for a Justice of the Peace, and got him.
Old Justice Wade drew up his will
right here, and left the Ipswich jail,
murmuring, half-dazed, "That's one no one
will ever break—I've never seen the like!"

MOODY: No one will break! What did it say?

JAILOR: This will surprise you. Nothing more
than, "I, Giles Corey, lying under
great trouble and affliction, knowing
not how soon I may depart this life—"
he left everything, lands, meadows, housing,
cattle, money, apparel, movables,
immovables, everything freely and quietly,
without challenge, forever, to—

MOODY: To whom? To Crosby?

JAILOR:                                        Never! To another
son-in-law who refused to come to court
to testify against his step-mother.
From that hour Giles Corey has said
no word though some have come to see him.

MOODY: Not one word!

JAILOR: And, as I said, at intervals
a moan. O sir, this twenty minutes
is near to an end. I bid you, drink,
if you will stay!

MOODY: No thank you, friend.

JAILOR: It would have been simpler if I had placed them,
but they brought men down from Boston to do it.
Listen to the game they set for me,
if you won't join me. Perhaps you have
Latin titles for this one. Do you see
these twins?—bowls like brothers.
Why, yesterday, three times a day
they let me put three morsels of bread,
dry as pumice, one for each time
the man refused to plead. And I
required to sit and push them to him!
Today, again the game, with water.
Tomorrow—

MOODY: I pity you, poor man.

JAILOR: —nothing.
Pity the man in there!

MOODY: He's well beyond
the devils he leaves the rest of us with.
    (*At the outside window*)
See how the moon and the rain make paths
to the window across your tea-colored river.

JAILOR: The river's awash, high tide from the marshes.
An hour until dawn—

MOODY: One hour to Salem.
Peter, I must go.

JAILOR: Do, sir. Go!
A moment ago a puff of breeze
like a squall off the prow of a ship in bright weather
mixed with it the call of a catbird, mocking,
and the scent of Mary Peabody's roses
around the front steps of the jail.
It got down this foul alley and made me think
of the smell of an old French whore. That was
twenty minutes ago—he groaned.

MOODY: Not much longer, Peter.

JAILOR: Thank you.
   I don't know why you're here, but go.
   Go, before—who are you, sir?
MOODY: A clerk, Peter, just a merchant's eyes,
   gathering facts for letters he writes
   to men of influence, and some of wit.
   Call me recording angel for
   the merchant Brattle who is suing libel
   against a girl's parents because she accused
   him of a similar—
GILES (*cries out*): Pile on more rocks!

**BLACKOUT**

**SCENE NINE**

ANN PUTNAM, THOMAS PUTNAM, EZEKIEL CHEEVER, and
MERCY LEWIS.

ANN PUTNAM's *bedroom.* ANN *is in bed. The room is
pitch dark. It is two hours before dawn of the same day.*

ANN: Pile on more rocks! Pile more rocks on him!
   I shall die first! O bid them hurry, help!
   I cannot breathe with all these heavy stones.
   Light, father, light!
       (*Enter* PUTNAM *in his nightshirt with a lighted
       candle. He has been under great strain and shows
       it*)
PUTNAM: I'm with you, child.
   You shall not die, Ann, *you* shall not.
   That snail of justice, Magistrate Hathorne,
   on a turtle's back is climbing Gallow's

Hill. Child, you'll get your peace
before another sunset. It's almost morning.
Why, rest another hour, Ann,
and when the tide ebbs, this dark room
will whiten before the familiar sun
reaches the sash again. We'll get your peace
before another day is down.

ANN: I'm quieter, Father.

PUTNAM:                    Sleep an hour,
if you can. I left your mother
sleeping profoundly at last, thank the Lord,
as if at the heart of the storm no pulse
shook her—

ANN:          Father, I need you here.

PUTNAM: Yes, dear. I know. I know. She sleeps—
I disentangled the poor, thin arms
your mother threw around me, as she reached
back from something nameless.
Cold, she was cold, in the bed where we lay
together so many years; warmth fled from me
through our stricken embrace, and she slept.

ANN: Father, don't leave me.

PUTNAM:                    Father will sit with you.
Horrors shall not afflict us much longer.
May I put out the light?

ANN:                    The light? O no, Father,
never quench the light! It's a tiny flame
to ask for—they shan't put out our candles.
I can't sleep; and I must sleep. You say I must.
More light, Father, we must have four now—
A candle for me, two for them,
the Corey witches; the extra one's yours,
for you will need one too, won't you?
So when they snuff their own forever
ours will still burn. Fetch another.

       (PUTNAM *brings another candlestick*)

PUTNAM: There, Ann child, the candles are ready.
　Sleep, go to sleep. I—
ANN (*drifting off to sleep*): If Corey witches come—
　you'll match them—won't you? There, I'll try—
　to sleep—
PUTNAM:　　Do, child, do. Father will sit
　close with his book.
　　　(*Her eyes are closed*)
　　　(*from memory*) "Notwithstanding,
　I have a few things against thee,
　because thou sufferest that woman Jezebel,
　which calleth herself a prophetess, to teach
　and seduce my servants—"
　　　　　　　　My God, how cold,
　how cold my little wife's arms.
　　　　　　　　　　Martha—
　after all these years, how could you live
　with that bungler, that devilish rustic—
ANN (*screams*): Father, the candles! More light, I must
　have
　light and more light. Hold my hand!
PUTNAM:　　　　　　　　Dear God,
　what've I said? The name of her, even the name—
　　　(*He lights three more candles*)
　—of the Father, and of the Son and of the
　Holy Ghost, forfend!
　　　(ANN *sighs, and sits up again in the bed*)
ANN: He's back, and I must listen.
　Why Father, you're shaking. Don't be afraid.
PUTNAM: Who, Ann, who?
ANN:　　　　　　Ssh. I must listen.
　Why yes, Mr. Goodell, I hear you clearly,
　but you strain my eyes.
　　　　　　　—Blow out the Corey candles.
　　　(*Blows*)
　So. So. O strange man, what's your news?

Your hair's so black, and so very wet. You say
grave things are not for a girl to know? Yes.
    (*Mechanically*)
—Giles Corey murdered me by pressing my chest—
yes—in with his feet. Yes, go on, sir!
—So it is done to Mister Corey
as it was done to me these years ago!—
    (ANN *shudders and sighs*)

PUTNAM: She does this to herself—can that be it?

ANN:—Don't forget me; I shall not come again—
    (*She falls back on the pillows*)

PUTNAM: Forget? Forget? How can I ever forget?

ANN: Father, they were so heavy. Now, I sleep.
    (*A knock. Enter* CHEEVER)

CHEEVER: Thomas!

PUTNAM:         Quietly, 'Zekiel, Ann's fallen asleep
after many months of startings, wakings,
driven dreams and bedevilled images.
Perhaps her angels passed this way
trafficking elsewhere—if angels they be.
She's been pressed by the Devil's coven
as if old Corey's rocks had fallen
and fossilized her own green soul.
Somehow the grain has coarsened.
What brings you out so late? So early.

CHEEVER: Those terrible rocks have crushed already
one who kept his will unbroken.
That should be enough to satisfy—

PUTNAM: Giles cut at last. Ann lived
his end right here—she lived him down.
To satisfy? Who speaks of that?—
of satisfaction speaks of heaven,
of heaven on earth, a dream of having
acted rightly. Alas, poor Ann—
    (ANN *whimpers, then calls out in her sleep.* PUT-
    NAM *turns sharply*)

ANN: Father! Father, damn them, Father!

PUTNAM (*breaks*): More invalids than wives and maids—
>    (*He runs to the door and calls down*)
> Mercy! Mercy! Get you up here!
> One of her kind for one of her kindness.

ANN: Here's Mrs. Corey—strike her, Father!
> Kill the witch. She's got the doll
> I made of her, she'll beat me with
> the witchling that I made of her.

PUTNAM: Silence, child! Ah Cheever, what
> twists my daughter? We are led
> into valleys of pitch. There's nothing
> man or girl can do for peace now.
>    (*To* ANN)
> Mercy's coming.
>    (*Enter* MERCY LEWIS, *disheveled with sleep*)
>                Sit with that child.
> Do anything, take her hand,
> just keep her quiet. It's something too late
> for heavenly peace, but we can have some
> human silence. Blow out the candles.

MERCY: Mr. Putnam, you said Ann needs—

PUTNAM: Do it, miss. Snuff them all out.
> This pitiful colony of lamps are not
> lights enough to justice it for us.
> Ann's got to rest.
>    (MERCY *squats by the bed and snuffs the candles
>    fearfully.* ANN *whimpers.* PUTNAM *draws* CHEEVER
>    *aside*)
>                Bring the lantern
> away, Ezekiel. Tomorrow's hanging
> questions me, sir, although it may
> release another.
>    (*Points to his daughter*)
>                Her God exacts the all.

CHEEVER: Yes, my poor Tom, but not so easily.

A crowd's already around Gallows Hill
with murmurings of "His courage!" and,
"The will deeds to the innocent heirs
the wife's good name—"

PUTNAM:                  His devil's catching!
He calls my every thought to witness;
each misgiving argues a neighbor.
I must think. I must think!

CHEEVER: One wrote out on Ipswich Jail,
"A Plethora of Witches Will Not Suffice
the Appetite for Naming More!" Another
rumbled it out in a lion's voice,
and melted safely into the uneasy crowd.

PUTNAM (*weeps*): Who are we hanging? Things un-
hinge—
it's much too late—

CHEEVER:                Courage, Tom,
is *the* most appalling virtue. Martha
will bravely weather. She'll work it out.

PUTNAM: What of us, Ezekiel, what of us?

> (PUTNAM *grips* CHEEVER'S *arm. Pause. Again the*
> *sound of rain*)

Your overcoat is soaking wet.

CHEEVER: I thought this chaos a public test.
I was mistaken, it's a personal trial.
For Martha, it's late. Tom, we must abide.
We've built a gallows where the heart cracks—

PUTNAM: What can I do?

CHEEVER (*angered*):          Think what you feel—
how may I tell you what to *do*?—

> (PUTNAM *pauses*)

Come to the fire, Tom. Perhaps
the heavy rain will clear by daybreak.

FADEOUT

SCENE TEN

PARRIS, HATHORNE, LYNN MOODY, THE GIRLS, TOWNSMEN, VILLAGERS and MARTHA COREY.

*Gallows Hill, Salem, at mid-September dawn. It is very dark along the ground although the sun just touches the tops of the elms and maples. The crowd, which enters below, remains shapes in a heavy obscurity. The ladder mounts to a platform under a great oak. Singing of the hymn begins in half-distance and rises to crescendo as the townsmen and villagers group beneath the gibbet.*

CROWD (*sings*):

> On my right hand I looked, and saw,
>    but no man would me know,
> all refuge failed me, for my soul
>    none any care did show.
>
> Then to thee Lord, I cried and said,
>    my hope thou art alone;
> and in the land of living ones
>    thou art my portion.
>
> Because I am brought very low,
>    attend unto my cry.
> From my pursuers save thou me,
>    which stronger be than I.
>
> That I thy Name may praise, my soul
>    from prison, Oh, bring out;
> when thou shalt me reward, the just
>    shall compass me about.

PARRIS: Lead us not into temptation,
for Thine is the power and the glory
for ever and ever. Amen.
CROWD: Amen.
HATHORNE: Officer, are you prepared?
HANGMAN: Everything
is ready, your Honor.
HATHORNE: Dr. Parris,
you've spoken with the condemned?
PARRIS: Everything
tongue can say has been said. She does not
listen. Witch Corey still protests
innocence, deplores her accusers, and will not
pray with her former pastor. Leave her
to the gallows and to God!
The church can do no more, sir, after
excommunication.
VOICE: It's come to that!
VOICES: Excommunication!
VOICE: Aye, and will come to more, much more.
HATHORNE: Hangman!
HANGMAN: Sir.
HATHORNE: Let Martha Corey,
condemned for being a witch in Essex,
mount the ladder.

> (*The crowd is silent as* MARTHA, *brought forward
> by* LOCKER, *mounts the ladder to the platform, just
> struck with sunshine. As she steps into the lights
> the girls cry out*)

GIRLS: Witch! Witch! Gospel Witch!
Gospel Witch!
MOODY: Speak, madam, if you can!
MARTHA: Magistrate Hathorne, give me leave to pray.

> (*A random election takes place in the crowd*)

PARRIS: Don't allow it!

VOICE: Can a guilty woman pray?

GIRLS: No, never. Gospel Witch! A witch can't pray.

MOODY: Sentence has been passed. Here's no pardon.
Grant her a citizen's last right.

VOICES: Speak! Pray! Allow the woman to pray.

HATHORNE: Silence. Citizens, this woman's no longer
in human hands.
(*Pause*)
The holy law
of Massachusetts Bay, stronger than witches,
made against devils, recognizes
this woman's right to—pray, if she can!—
before her sentence is executed.
(*Pause*)

MARTHA (*looking into the faces of the people below her*):
Almighty Father, maker of Heaven and High Places,
and gardener of the earth below me now,
ordainer even of the fatal tree these men
have builded from your woods, remember me!

For I would have these know,
as my beloved parents knew who freely came
into the barbarous forest for their peace
what in this recent business I have learned.

Ours is a learning land which yields when we
give, so I do yield to you that these may give.
And I would have these see that innocence
cries out for itself alone. I will tell

my innocence no longer in public places.
Sire, as a farmer numbers his mornings
by the infant height of grain he planted,
in the first beard, or later by the heavy heads

of maize, tossing staunchly in an August wind,
or finally by the depth of footprints

margining his fields after first frost,
so I come upon the pattern of dawn today,

but like an awesome joke, near the end of it.
My neighbors know that I was never free
of their community.
   (*Here, birds begin to wake the catbird, the yellow
   warbler*)
When the green passing at the twilight roads away
comes to a darkness tonight, may these remember
   morning.
While memory is mine, Sire, I pray today
for my good husband Giles, lately a farmer,

lately living a holy citizen among these others.
His grave was stoned, monumented at his very passing,
prison strong and hard they caused his death by rocks,
pressed upon the body singly to make the body speak.

My husband did not weigh the gravity
of what was meant until, words spent, they acted.
Giles spoke with them until he saw me taken,
then stopped his mouth for all. I thank you, Sire,

he cannot greet me here with eyes of flesh.
Now, I would be reminded Giles failed me
that he might to the great community prove
his final worth. O Sire, my husband

was not an introspective man as many Elect must be.
He entered late and by another gate. Grant
my failure also here today a second test,
courage is not the knack of avoiding failure.

I find that courage, Father, is my endurance
to give my failure further final hearing
before invisible eyes.
                    To end I pray for neighbors,

for these and for myself, your holy, fallible citizens,
that we come into our eternal franchise,
to witness failure upon a moment, so durably
we may succeed, and green over the pregnant land.
My God, I praise you for your blessed birds,
that I have heard singing on this occasion.
  (*The drum rattle*)

  CURTAIN

Unto Jehovah with my voice,
  I did unto him cry:
unto Jehovah with my voice,
  my sute for Grace made I.
2. I did poure out before his face
  my meditation:
before his face I did declare
  the trouble me upon.
3. O'rewhelm'd in mee when was my spirit,
  then thou didst know my way:
I'the way I walkt, a snare for mee
  they privily did lay.
4. On my right hand I lookt, & saw,
  but no man would me know,
all refuge faild mee: for my soule
  none any care did show.
5. Then to thee Lord, I cryde & sayd,
  my hope thou art *alone:*
& in the land of living ones
  thou art my portion.
6. Because I am brought very low,
  attend unto my cry:
From my pursuers save thou mee,
  which stronger bee than I.
7. That I thy Name may praise, my soule
  from prison, oh bring out:
when thou shalt me reward, the just
  shall compasse mee about.

*The Bay Psalm Book*

# PRODUCTION NOTE TO THE PLAY

*The Gospel Witch* is designed so that emphasis may most meaningfully be placed on stage lighting rather than on representational completeness in the details of scenery. The play is written in the spirit rather than in the fact of history.

For the original Poets' Theatre production in 1952, overture and between-the-scenes "music" was composed on a tape of carefully edited birdcalls re-recorded from records taken in New England fields by the Audubon Society. A background of country sounds, distant crows cawing, bitterns pumping and splashing, advanced the tone. Calls of birds, like the voices that speak from the documents of those who preceded us, do not vary as down the years we revise the face and temper of the land.

Early American furniture, which is by line and by materials of construction close to some of the most worthy contemporary furniture, was used.

In the costumes and flavor of manner it is well to differentiate clearly between the towns of Boston, Salem, the Village of Salem, and the isolated homesteads of Salem Farms, bearing in mind the prosperity of the Putnams and the Coreys with the greater accent on utility in the Corey homestead. The portraits of the period are an excellent guide.

Ann Putnam should be played between the ages of thirteen and fifteen. Abigail is slightly younger; Mercy is older, about nineteen.

Scene Ten may suggestively be staged as following Scene Nine without a break; when the light fades on the men around Ann Putnam's bed, the group holds in silhouette at one side to form the edge of the crowd that collects below the gallows.

The complete text of the hymn as sung in Puritan Meetings is printed on page 315. A director may find more or fewer stanzas useful to open Scene Ten.

L. P.